The Adrienne Kennedy Reader

ALSO BY ADRIENNE KENNEDY

Deadly Triplets: A Theatre Mystery Journal

People Who Led to My Plays

Sleep Deprivation Chamber: A Theatre Piece
(with Adam P. Kennedy)

The Adrienne Kennedy Reader

ADRIENNE KENNEDY

Introduction by Werner Sollors

University of Minnesota Press
Minneapolis — London

The University of Minnesota Press gratefully acknowledges the generous assistance provided for the publication of this book by the Helen and Joseph Lewis Philanthropic Fund of the Jewish Community Federation of Cleveland and by the Peter B. Lewis Family Philanthropic Fund of the Jewish Community Federation of Cleveland.

Published by the University of Minnesota Press
111 Third Avenue South, Suite 290
Minneapolis, MN 55401-2520
http://www.upress.umn.edu

Library of Congress Cataloging-in-Publication Data

Kennedy, Adrienne.
    [Selections. 2001]
    The Adrienne Kennedy reader / Adrienne Kennedy ; introduction by Werner Sollors.
        p.   cm.
    ISBN 0-8166-3602-8 (acid-free paper) — ISBN 0-8166-3603-6 (pbk.: acid-free paper)
    1. African Americans—Drama.   2. Racially mixed people—Drama.
I. Title.
PS3561.E4252 A6 2001
812'.54—dc21   2001001666

Printed in the United States of America on acid-free paper

The University of Minnesota is an equal-opportunity educator and employer.

11 10 09 08 07 06 05 04 03 02 01   10 9 8 7 6 5 4 3 2 1

Contents

Introduction

Werner Sollors

ADRIENNE KENNEDY'S WORK, presented in its first substantial collection here, has affinities to the work of Sam Shepard, Amiri Baraka,
Ntozake Shange, Arthur Miller, Edward Albee, and Wole Soyinka. Simultaneously, it echoes the entire dramatic tradition, from Greek tragedy
to the theatre of the absurd, from Euripides to Shakespeare, and from
Chekhov to Tennessee Williams. Inspired by the themes of Hollywood
movies and by cinematic techniques, Kennedy's highly acclaimed and
frequently staged works have been praised as surrealistic dream plays,
hauntingly fragmentary and nonlinear lyrical dramas, high points in
the development of the American one-act play, and dramatic harbingers
of feminist themes in contemporary Black women's writing. Kennedy's
dramatic work has an unmistakable style, characterized by fragmentation,
ritualistic repetition and variation, and radical experimentation with
character and plot. And while it comes to life most fully in theatrical
production, it is also indebted to the literary form of lyrical drama that
invites reading and rereading.

All of Kennedy's works confront social and psychological terrors,
past and present. Her drama is autobiographically inspired, shaped by
her experience and generational vantage point, and packed with allusions
to American popular culture. Kennedy's most important works explore
the tragic condition of daughter, mother, father, sibling, and lover in
the painful web of American race and kin relations in which violence
can erupt at any point.

Born Adrienne Hawkins in Pittsburgh in 1931, the playwright spent
her childhood and youth in Cleveland, with frequent visits to Montezuma, Georgia, where most of her relatives, black and white, were living.

It was there, she remembers, at a place she could reach only by Jim Crow car from Ohio, that her neighbor Sarah Clara gave Kennedy the inspiration for the names of two protagonists. There, too, a procession of Black churchgoers gave her a feeling of aesthetic intensity, which resurfaced later when she viewed Giotto's frescoes. Fairy tales, complicated stories about racial ancestry, and the lore of a mythical England as the ultimate country of origin and the home of Jane Eyre further enriched the stigma of the South, which she later called a "strange mesh of dark kinship between the races."

In Cleveland, movies inspired the author-to-be. She immersed herself deeply into the world of the Hollywood magazine *Modern Screen* and musical entertainment, and she admired such luminaries as Bette Davis, Paul Robeson, Lena Horne, and Orson Welles. After graduating from Ohio State University and marrying Joseph Kennedy, she moved to New York and began to write. In the big city she was also drawn to modern art and the theatre (especially Arthur Miller and Tennessee Williams, but also Chekhov and Lorca). During a prolonged stay in Europe and Africa, she broke into print with the experimental short story "Because of the King of France," published under a pen name in the African journal *Black Orpheus* and reprinted for the first time in this volume.

After reading works by African writers Chinua Achebe and Wole Soyinka and studying masks in Ghana, Kennedy turned toward playwriting and created, in the course of the 1960s and 1970s, an impressive group of experimental plays. The *Dictionary of Literary Biography* proclaims, "Working outside the familiar realistic style, she ventures into uncharted territory of the theater as well as the mind." The playwright became a force in modern drama circles, winning awards and collaborating on literary projects. From 1962 to 1965 she was a member of the playwriting unit of the Actors Studio. In 1967, while in London, she collaborated on the dramatization of John Lennon's book *In His Own Write*. She was awarded three Obie awards by the *Village Voice*, two Rockefeller grants, and a Guggenheim fellowship, and has taught drama and playwriting at several universities, including New York University, the University of California at Berkeley, and Harvard University. She has also received the Third Manhattan Borough President's Award for Excellence, a Lila Wallace Reader's Digest Fund Writers' Award, an Academy Award in Literature from the American Academy of Arts and Letters, and the Pierre LeComte duNouy Foundation Award. Adrienne Kennedy is one of only five playwrights to be included in the third edition of the *Norton*

Anthology of American Literature. During the 1995–96 season at the Signature Company in New York she was the subject of a dramatic retrospective that provided an occasion for renewed critical attention.

Funnyhouse of a Negro (1964), coproduced by Edward Albee, won Kennedy her first Obie award. The drama presents four aspects of a self ("Sarah"): Patrice Lumumba, the first president of the Congo after its independence from Belgium who was assassinated in 1961 (at a time when Kennedy was staying in Ghana), is associated with an African patrimony and the figure of a father. Christ is both the childhood savior and a sinister entity; he is also linked with the image of marriage, especially Mary's in Giotto's fresco. Queen Victoria was inspired by the statue in front of Buckingham Palace, which comes to life threateningly as a white figure of domination and terror. Finally, the Duchess of Hapsburg is the sister of the Belgian King Leopold II, Charlotte Maria Amelia, better known as the beautiful romantic wife of Maximilian, the ill-fated Hapsburgian Emperor of Mexico. Charlotte turned insane when the Mexican enterprise failed and her husband was executed upon Benito Juarez's victory. Her part was played by Bette Davis in William Dieterle's lavish film *Juarez* (1939), a movie that impressed Kennedy deeply.

These four "selves" embody contradictions such as black and white, male and female, and colonialism and independence, yet they are also strangely identical. They speak and repeat the same lines, at times in unison, Greek-chorus fashion. The masks, with their "great dark eyes that seem gouged out of the head" furthermore evoke Oedipus; and the dominant issue is the "recognition of myself," or, paradoxically, the "recognition against myself." In such a context the queen's famous question from *Snow White,* "Who is the fairest of them all?," reveals its troubling cultural connotations.

Though the title evokes the image of an amusement park, the play has serious overtones: it explores a split heritage and the central self's suicidal refusal to accept part of that heritage—or to recognize herself in that part. Repetitions and variations of long passages create a rhythm of twelve "movements" that extends beyond characters, plot, or any sense of a stable setting. In the repetitions, strong images, such as those of a dreamlike Africa or the mother's loss of hair, become haunting. Kennedy also develops an elaborate bird imagery with religious, racial, mythical, familial, and existential associations, without settling on any one meaning. Inspired by Psalm 55:6, the Holy Ghost in Giotto's fresco, an African bird mask, Poe's "Raven," and the spiritual "Sometimes I

Feel Like a Motherless Child," the bird image also alludes to the Afro-American tradition of the "Flying African" that Toni Morrison explored in her novel *Song of Solomon*. In particular, the owl, as a bird of wisdom associated with the motherless Greek goddess Pallas Athena (whose African origins have been obscured), keeps a fairly constant presence in Kennedy's work.

In *The Owl Answers* (1965), the presentation of changing sets and characters continues and intensifies. In Clara Passmore—whose last name may allude to the theme of racial "passing"—illegitimacy, racially mixed identity, conflicts between mother and father, and cultural tensions between England and America converge. Characteristically, the set is a collage of Old and New World places, all of which strangely coexist: "*The scene is a New York subway car is the Tower of London is a Harlem hotel room is St. Peter's.*" The characters have alternating identities, and the figures of Shakespeare, Chaucer, and William the Conqueror form the Greek chorus of an English literary tradition that challenges Clara's claim to an English ancestry. The first word of the play, which this English chorus addresses to Clara, is "Bastard." The complex family relations, reminiscent of Langston Hughes's play *Mulatto* (1935)—written from a son's perspective—are represented through Clara's changing identities as white man's "blood" daughter, black cook's daughter, black reverend's foster daughter, Virgin Mary, and owl.

Clara refers to England as the place of "our ancestors," yet this ancestry denies her a place as descendant. A female equivalent of "everyman," She does not bear the name of her White Father (Mattheson) that would establish an ancestral entitlement. It is as if half her parentage did not count in the strange racial genealogy that Clara confronts. Now that her father "died today or was it yesterday" (an allusion, perhaps, to the beginning of Albert Camus's novel *The Stranger*), she is not even permitted to attend his funeral. St. Paul's universalist promise of a Christianity without ethnic boundaries seems forgotten in St. Paul's Chapel, where the funeral is held. England, the home of the Brontës, does not welcome the avid *Jane Eyre* reader. Clara repeatedly speaks the loaded sentence, "I was the only Negro there." Refused acceptance in the white father's world that is so clearly a part of her, Clara denies her relationship to her father and tries to create, and then fend off with a knife, new alternative father (and God) figures for herself on the New York subway. The mother's way to St. Paul's Chapel is through suicide, a path Clara does not follow. Instead, she turns into an owl. Kennedy's next plays continue the investigation of animal imagery, as parts of magical transformations and as a counterstatement to racism. The American Academy of Arts and Letters stated that, with Kennedy's "unique theatrical voice," "Her visions of the black world include the white, as if to remind us that race relations are double. Her use of myth and characters played by more than one actor anticipated much in modern theater." It also anticipated much in her future works.

In *A Rat's Mass* (1966), the siblings who are the main characters are surrealistically and literally represented as half animal and half human, reminiscent of a Max Ernst collage. Two "pale Negro children" are also half rats: "*BROTHER RAT has a rat's head, a human body, a tail. SISTER RAT has a rat's belly, a human head, a tail.*" A mass, complete with transubstantiation, and a religious procession provide the setting for Kennedy's strategy of ritualistic repetition, subtly revealed as the children play hide-and-seek in an attic. Rosemary, the ostentatious Christian, has worms in her hair, Medusa-fashion, and represents the lure of evil, perhaps as a perverted Pied Piper of Hamlin for Brother Rat and Sister Rat. The non-rat Rosemary is arrogant about her background and, though loved by the siblings, turns out to be an accomplice of fascist killers who act out a nightmarish Anne Frank scenario for the half-rat brother and sister in hiding.

A Lesson in Dead Language (1966) presents another character who is both human and animal by identifying the Teacher also as a White Dog. The setting is a Latin class that turns into an absurd ritual of instruction, vaguely reminiscent of Eugène Ionesco's play *The Lesson.* Using the format of a lesson, Kennedy has her characters recite lines in unison, and has them repeated by different speakers (in one instance the Pupil repeats the White Dog's prophetic line: "Calpurnia dreamed a pinnacle was tumbling down"). Caesar's death and the end of childhood (or the beginning of woman's sexual maturity and her initiation into adult culture) are metaphorically related through the shared omen of the blood that accompanies both events. Hence Calpurnia's dream (which was to warn Caesar of the Ides of March) is recited by the Pupils, who have started to menstruate. The play obviously alludes to Shakespeare's *Julius Caesar,* perhaps to the film version by Joseph Mankiewicz (1953) in which Greer Garson played Caesar's wife, who dreams of a lioness whelping in the streets, graves opening up, and clouds drizzling blood upon the Capitol.

Sun (1968) was written in memory of Malcolm X and is dedicated to Kennedy's father. This doubling of father and Black political martyr-hero continues the pattern of the identification of the Black father and the world of Patrice Lumumba and Paul Robeson. The theme of the play, the violent death of Black leaders who struggle for the liberation of their people, is presented in an unusual lyrical form. Man is the only character and speaker in the circular pageant, whose pace is marked by cosmic and human orbits. One sequence sets the stages of embryo, birth, and early youth against the background of an orange sun spinning, slowly being replaced by a yellow sun and a black sun.

An Evening with Dead Essex (1972), produced at the American Place Theatre in 1973 and at the Yale Repertory Theatre a year later, is based on the political theme of violence. The play is set in a film studio in which the actors (Kennedy's stage directions suggest that the actors' real names be used on stage) confront the news story of the death of Mark Essex, who was killed by more than a hundred bullets on the rooftop of a New Orleans motel in 1972. Image projections, news headlines, political speeches, Vietnam War facts, and scenes of Dead Essex's religious childhood and his life as a sailor are juxtaposed with Nixon's birthday, the Stars and Stripes, and such songs as "Jesus Loves Me," "My Country 'Tis of Thee," and "When I've Done the Best I Can."

A Movie Star Has to Star in Black and White (1976), which looks at Hollywood stardom, diverges from Kennedy's other plays because it is divided into three scenes instead of one act. The piece opens with the Columbia Pictures Lady; there is film music, and the actors are made up to look exactly like Bette Davis, Paul Henreid, Jean Peters, Marlon Brando, Montgomery Clift, and Shelley Winters. "Supporting roles are played by the mother, the father, the husband." Each scene is simultaneously set in a film and in a "real" place. The characters who have the names of movie stars and are made up to look just like them are positioned in key moments of the respective film. Yet the lines they speak do not come from the movies; instead they echo, and occasionally quote from, Kennedy's earlier plays. There is, for example, a passage about the writing of *A Lesson in Dead Language,* and a character named Clara who, on five occasions, reads from "her" play *The Owl Answers.* In other words, Kennedy lets the movie stars speak her own lines. No character emerges that is fully exempt from this Kennedy projection, except perhaps the male stars who are silent. The stage directions specify that if Montgomery Clift, Paul Henreid, and Marlon Brando *"did speak they would speak lines from their actual movies."* There is also a correspondence between film and drama. Irving Rapper's *Now, Voyager* (1942), for example, is a movie Kennedy associated with her own ocean voyage to Europe and Africa, a voyage that resulted in her first published writing.

In the film, which takes its title from a line in Walt Whitman's poem "Now Finalé to the Shore," the mental patient Charlotte Vale (Bette Davis) undertakes an ocean voyage on the recommendation of her psychiatrist, Dr. Jaquith (Claude Rains), in order to escape her domineering mother (Gladys Cooper), who never wanted her to be born. Charlotte meets the unhappily married Jeremiah Durrance (Paul Henreid) on board, and their short-lived romance begins her emancipation and her cure. Love and voyaging seem connected to the victory over a family trauma. Kennedy wrote, "If I were an actress I would want to play roles like Bette Davis." Instead of creating characters like Bette Davis, Kennedy makes Bette Davis into her own character.

Kennedy's plays of the 1960s and 1970s are the condensed expression of a theatrical mind that has integrated diverse autobiographical, political, and aesthetic elements into an effective modern form. Read together, these plays constitute a full-fledged modern attempt at rewriting Greek family tragedy, complicated by the American difficulties with interracial kinship. It is no coincidence that Kennedy, in the tradition of such works as Countée Cullen's *Medea* (1934) and Wole Soyinka's *Bacchae* (1973), has also written a contemporary adaptation of Euripides, her *Electra and Orestes* (1980), which is included in this volume.

With the self-reflexive style of *Movie Star,* Adrienne Kennedy's dramatic work had come full circle. The play projected a new phase of creative work. In the late 1980s and the 1990s, Kennedy produced even more unique contemporary dramas. In 1987 she published *People Who Led to My Plays,* which the novelist Ishmael Reed calls a "new form of black autobiography." That memoir in the experimental form of quick glimpses also sheds much light on Kennedy's personal drama, since Kennedy drew on it for her play *June and Jean in Concert* (1995), included here, for which she received an Obie in 1996. June and Jean are twins who play the piano, sing, and write, in Kennedy's autobiographic voice, about a magical and haunting past that includes "Dead Aunt Ella," Mother, Father, and other characters. June's death in 1943 is the central traumatic event that the play confronts ritualistically; in the second half of the drama June's ghost appears and ultimately becomes visible to Jean. Kennedy continued autobiographic prose experimentation with *Deadly Triplets: A Theatre Mystery and Journal* (1990).

The playwright's dramatic cycle *The Alexander Plays* (1992)—including *She Talks to Beethoven, Ohio State Murders, The Film Club,* and *Dramatic Circle*—extends the more overtly political side of her work, while presenting her familiar division of a lyrical persona into antithetical selves, a Nkrumah and a Beethoven, a Thomas Hardy and a Frantz Fanon. The lyrical monologue *The Film Club* specifically continues Kennedy's exploration of the power of popular culture (movies in particular, and Bette Davis especially). In all four plays the central character is the authorial projection Suzanne Alexander, and the settings are Cleveland, Ohio State, Ghana, London, New York—the places familiar from Kennedy's autobiography and drama. Suzanne Alexander also suggests the self-reflexivity that Kennedy's work has reached, as Suzanne offers an incomplete answer to questions about her work.

In 1991, while Kennedy was working on *Ohio State Murders*, her son Adam Kennedy was beaten and arrested by a white police officer, then accused of striking him. The made-up charges against Adam were dismissed, and he later won a civil lawsuit. Kennedy wrote "Letter to My Students on My Sixty-First Birthday by Suzanne Alexander" about her anxieties during that process. This prose piece dramatically intersperses memory narrative with documents, letters, and depositions.

Motherhood 2000 (1994), produced at the McCarter Theater in Princeton, continues Kennedy's dramatic rumination about the senseless beating that her son received in 1991. Set in the near future, the play brings the responsible policeman right to Kennedy's New York neighborhood, and the miracle play that unfolds ends when the writer strikes the policeman's head with a hammer.

The Adrienne Kennedy Reader ends with a series of recent, previously unpublished prose pieces. "A Letter to Flowers" represents refractions of the past and is a perfect companion piece to Kennedy's dramas. "Secret Paragraphs about My Brother" examines the fate of a brother who disappeared; after an oddly funny beginning, reflections turn to memories, and Kennedy explores the different ways of feeling loss. "Sisters Etta and Ella," an excerpt from a narrative, resumes themes from *Ohio State Murders* and alludes to several of Kennedy's earlier works. Set in contemporary New York, this is a classic doppelgänger tale as well as a ghost story with a surprise ending. "Grendel and Grendel's Mother," the last prose piece in this collection, interweaves readings in *Beowulf* with violent urges and fantasies that ultimately merge with the language of the poem. All these prose pieces are intimately, and at times mysteriously, connected with Kennedy's plays, as they draw on settings and motifs from her previous work (Ghana, Italy, London, Ohio, flowers, remembering, the Upper West Side, English literature, issues of race and violence) while also incorporating new material about teaching and writing in the 1990s.

Robert Brustein, director of the American Repertory Theater at Harvard University, where *Ohio State Murders* was staged in 2000, says Kennedy's plays are "strong dreams that reveal us in our most vulnerable moments." Kennedy goes beyond revealing her characters' and her audience members' vulnerable moments: she connects to them by revealing her own. Hers is the quintessential modern voice on the American stage.

Michael Feingold writes, "With Beckett gone, Adrienne Kennedy is probably the boldest artist now writing for the theater." More than thirty-five years after *Funnyhouse,* Kennedy still awaits full recognition by a wider national audience as a full-fledged modern American creator of "out-of-kilter, lyrical, and drop-dead brilliant work for the American theater" (as Lisa Jones put it). This collection finally gives Kennedy the visibility that she deserves.

The Adrienne Kennedy Reader

Because of the King of France

When my brother and I were children we had a cousin who ran away to the Virgin Islands. His name was Sidney.

It was a great joke. Often at night when we'd be sitting telling ghost stories my brother would giggle and say, "suddenly from the haunted house there appeared Sidney back from the Virgin Islands." My mother who would be sitting embroidering crisscrosses on towels, in absurd solemnity never failed to say, "I wonder why on earth that boy went to the Virgin Islands? Of all the places in the world." This stately perplexity always collapsed my brother and me further into wild giggles that lasted at least a quarter of an hour. One time when my brother and I were sitting in the attic playing monopoly Sidney's father came to see us. He was a thin little Negro in denim overalls and a great cap. He drove a mustard colored moving van and looked very sad. My brother and I came to the top of the stairs and peeped at him. I thought he was one of my father's patients (my father was a doctor). When he left my mother said the poor man was so unhappy, his wife dead and Sidney gone. She told my father that night and they talked about it. My father said he would go and see him. But my brother and I rarely saw Mr. Carter. He lived on the other side of town.

One day many years later, when I was in college, I was in a department store. It was a Saturday afternoon in September and I believe I was buying something silly, a cashmere sweater or socks with my initials on them (they were popular that year), when I felt someone watching me, I turned. And staring at me was a forlorn thin stooped figure. I knew right away that it was Sidney: the sallow skin, the elongated head, the black spiritual eyes. But he was so much older than I remembered. He looked almost thirty. He wore a battered hat, skimpy cotton trousers and

a baggy poplin jacket. I didn't give him a chance to speak but uncon-
sciously put down my packages on the counter, looked at him saying in
perfect imitation of my mother.

"Sidney," I demanded as only a spoiled college girl can, "why on
earth did you run away to the Virgin Islands. Of all places." And then
as if to atone for my impudence I hastily added, "and you who could
play the piano so well." He looked at me not in the least humiliated by
my rudeness and answered in a clear sweet earnestness which I have
never forgotten, "Because of the King of France."

I went back to school that fall. I was very happy in those days and
never thought of anything except my cashmere sweaters. I doubt if Sidney or our encounter ever crossed my mind.

Then one day toward the Christmas holidays a letter came. My
room-mate and I had a joke of taking each other's mail and gluing it to
the ceiling. When I came in for lunch I saw a grey envelope waiting for
me there. It was late afternoon before I got the desk chair and the umbrella and took the letter down, examining the tiny squarish handwriting
and the dim postmark reading St. Thomas, Virgin Islands. For some reason I clutched at the letter then suddenly threw it across the room, went
out and left it. I wondered what was in that letter. I could not explain it
but I did not want to open that damn thing. Perhaps I would go back
and throw it in the wastepaper basket. Inexplicably against my will I
began to remember things about Sidney. His mother had died. Willa
was her name. She was a distant cousin of my father's. (I hadn't liked
their house because it smelled of turnip greens. I had told my mother
and she said dear you mustn't be like that, those are your father's cousins.
But I hadn't liked being cousins to poor people. My father was a doctor.) Then there had been a girl named Sylvia. My mother had seen her
once at a piano recital where Sidney played, later recalling her she said
the girl had looked deathly... very homely. She was a Jew with kinky
blonde hair and according to Willa Sidney's first love. They studied
music together at the Cleveland Institute where Sidney had gotten a
scholarship. (It was after his first year there that Willa died.) And right
after that that all that trouble began. Mr. Carter came to see my father
late one night and had Sidney with him. Mr. Carter was crying. But Sidney sat almost immobile and withdrawn, repeating over and over, it was
the whole world let me in, finally the whole world let me in. It seemed
that Sylvia Klein was pregnant with Sidney's baby and her father had
come to the house and before Mr. Carter could reach him had beat Sidney
in the face with a lead pipe. My father asked him did he know the seri-

ousness of such a thing. But Sidney only sat then looked directly into my father's eyes, "Did you know there's love in the world," he said. "Did you know it? Did you know that even though Mama's gone there's love in this world." And the next thing I heard Sidney was dismissed from his beloved institute and Mr. Klein who was a little Jewish grocer took his family to Sandusky.

Of course my mother didn't believe it. How on earth she would exclaim. Sidney, of all people, so intelligent, so artistic, "always playing the piano," she'd add bewilderingly. It seemed impossible to me; too embarrassing to even discuss with my brother.

"Willa's to blame," my father said. "She's dead and in her grave but she's to blame for all this. She babied that boy so, making him think he was a genius, put all those ideas into his head about him being a piano player, giving him music lessons, sending him to the Institute. Why that boy thinks he's white and he's colored. He's nothing but a poor little colored boy. I feel sorry for him Mildred" (that was my mother's name). "It is a shame," my mother replied.

I came back to the room that night. The letter was still there under the bed where I had thrown it. I picked it up and looked at it for a long time. Then I went over and latched the door and sat down at the desk, took out a cigarette and read. This is what it said.

It was because of the King of France I came away. You see after I left the Institute I went to live at Versailles. Louis XIV asked me to. Chopin was due to arrive soon. Of course Louis XIV was not a Negro. Neither was Chopin or Mr. Rosen my teacher at the Institute. But I am. And everyone at the Institute knows that Negroes are people who were brought to America from Africa and Africa is a black jungle where black pygmies with rings in their noses sit banging drums and distorting their pygmy bodies. Everyone at the Institute knows that Negroes are stupid people with woolen hair who shuffle and say Lawsy me and I gwine and black. Very black. Everyone except Sylvia Klein. And if I were not a Negro then her father would not yell at her when I walked her to the store that day. Her father would not scream at her about the niggers, niggers, everywhere and the kinkiness of nigger hair and the flatness of nigger noses and the blackness of their skin. Nobody would yell. And my mother would not keep saying to me, Sidney baby, it's the Lord's will you're black and she's white. If he had wanted you white and living on Ridge Street he would have made it so.

"But I love her. I love her mama," I cry. "I'm sixteen years old and I know what I feel."

"You can't go against the Lord, Sidney," she says. "You can't go against Him."

"I love her," I cry.

But all that was past and now I had my life at the Palace. I lived in a white walled salon with a balcony overlooking the Palace gardens. I was happy there, myself and the Royal Family, when one day Louis XIV came to see me. He had been away for a long while. He came striding into the rooms and asked me to play a concert for him that Sunday at the Hall of Mirrors. I agreed. For we were great friends. As we stood talking on the balcony overlooking the fountains the King went on to tell me of the concert. I would play anything I chose. And also playing would be the amusing Monsieur Philipe. He had commanded him. I had not heard of this Philipe before and mentioned this to the King. He's an inconsequential fellow, he shrugged and with that the King disappeared off to the Throne Room or perhaps hunting. I practiced that week, read my books and composed pieces for Sylvia for even at the Palace I had not been able to forget the sorrow. The King had never visited me but that week he came in often to remark about the amusing Monsieur Philipe. It seemed he was an ugly fellow, small, stunted, sallow skinned with a large nose and besides he was a Corsican, and spent hours in his room cursing his vile Corsican face and his stunted body. And besides the most amusing part he was in love with his daughter. The vile stunted thing loved his daughter. Louis XIV giggled. Then Sunday came and the Concert in the Hall of Mirrors. I played well and the Royal Family applauded. I was a great success. Then Monsieur Philipe came on.

He was ugly. And crippled too. He limped onto the stage and turned to us. His face was hideous. He looked like a filthy beggar. When he turned to look at the Princess she averted her face in disgust. He seated his crippled body at the piano and began to play. I saw tears in his eyes. And he played. And from those ugly fingers came all the longings, all the tenderness, all the loveliness that comes from dreaming alone in shuttered rooms that smell of turnips, all the fierceness that comes from being convicted to disgrace and inequity by God's will . . . the rage, the annihilation, the grief of race and the unchangingness, the eternity of it all.

The King of France laughed.

Adrienne Kennedy in One Act

For my sons, Adam and Joe

ACKNOWLEDGMENTS

For encouragement and support I really want to thank Dr. Joseph Kennedy, Michael Kahn, Edward Albee, Ellen Stewart, Mr. and Mrs. Fredrick Eberstadt, Joseph Papp, Robert Brustein, Werner Sollors, Joseph Chaikin, William Gaskill, Gaby Rodgers, The Rockefeller Foundation, the Guggenheim Foundation, and Juilliard. I also want to acknowledge the work in these plays of so many brilliant and dedicated actors, among them being Billie Allen, Ellen Holly, Joan Harris, Mary Alice, Robbie McCauley, Roger Robinson, Moses Gunn, Yaphet Kotto, and Ruby Dee.

And I'd especially like to thank my editors, Terry Cochran and Craig Carnahan, for their tremendous enthusiasm for putting these plays in one volume. For the entire volume I would like to give special thanks to University of Minnesota Press marketing director Kathryn Grimes.

A.K.

PREFACE

More than anything I remember the days surrounding the writing of each of these plays . . . the places . . . Accra Ghana and Rome for *Funnyhouse of a Negro* . . . the shuttered guest house surrounded by gardens of sweet-smelling frangipani shrubs . . . in Rome, the sunny roof of the apartment on Via Reno . . . the beginnings of *The Owl Answers,* also in Ghana . . . the lines of the play growing on trips to the North, as I sought refuge from the heat at the desks of guest houses . . . our wonderful brand-new apartment in New York in the Park West Village for *A Rat's Mass* and the enchanting Primrose Hill in London for *Sun* (sitting in the dining room overlooking Chalcot Crescent). Hadn't Sylvia Plath lived across the way in Chalcot Square? And again the Upper West Side of Manhattan for *A Movie Star Has to Star in Black and White* and *Electra* and *Orestes.*

Without exception the days when I am writing are days of images fiercely pounding in my head and days of walking . . . in Ghana across the campus of Legon, in Rome through the Forum, in New York along Columbus Avenue, and in London, Primrose Hill (hadn't Karl Marx walked there?). Walks and coffee, all which seem to put me under a spell of sorts. . . . I am at the typewriter almost every waking moment and suddenly there is a play. It would be impossible to say I wrote them. Somehow under this spell they become written.

A.K.
New York City
Upper West Side, 1987

Funnyhouse of a Negro

CHARACTERS

NEGRO-SARAH
DUCHESS OF HAPSBURG   One of herselves
QUEEN VICTORIA REGINA   One of herselves
JESUS   One of herselves
PATRICE LUMUMBA   One of herselves
SARAH'S LANDLADY   Funnyhouse Lady
RAYMOND   Funnyhouse Man
THE MOTHER

AUTHOR'S NOTE

Funnyhouse of a Negro is perhaps clearest and most explicit when the play is placed in the girl Sarah's room. The center of the stage works well as her room, allowing the rest of the stage as the place for herselves. Her room should have a bed, a writing table and a mirror. Near her bed is the statue of Queen Victoria; other objects might be her photographs and her books. When she is placed in her room with her belongings, then the director is free to let the rest of the play happen around her.

BEGINNING: *Before the closed Curtain a* WOMAN *dressed in a white nightgown walks across the Stage carrying before her a bald head. She moves as one in a trance and is mumbling something inaudible to herself. Her hair is wild, straight and black and falls to her waist. As she moves, she gives the effect of one in a dream. She crosses the Stage from Right to Left. Before she has barely vanished, the CURTAIN opens. It is a white satin Curtain of a cheap material and a ghastly white, a material that brings to mind the interior of a cheap casket, parts of it are frayed and look as if it has been gnawed by rats.*

SCENE: TWO WOMEN *are sitting in what appears to be a Queen's chamber. It is set in the middle of the Stage in a strong white LIGHT, while the rest of the Stage is in unnatural BLACKNESS. The quality of the white light is unreal and ugly. The Queen's chamber consists of a dark monumental bed resembling an ebony tomb, a low, dark chandelier with candles, and wine-colored walls. Flying about are great black* RAVENS. QUEEN VICTORIA *is standing before her bed holding a small mirror in her hand. On the white pillow of her bed is a dark, indistinguishable object. The* DUCHESS OF HAPSBURG *is standing at the foot of the bed. Her back is to us as is the* QUEEN'S. *Throughout the entire scene, they do not move.* BOTH WOMEN *are dressed in royal gowns of white, a white similar to the white of the Curtain, the material cheap satin. Their headpieces are white and of a net that falls over their faces. From beneath both their headpieces springs a headful of wild kinky hair. Although in this scene we do not see their faces, I will describe them now. They look exactly alike and will wear masks or be made up to appear a whitish yellow. It is an alabaster face, the skin drawn tightly over the high cheekbones, great dark eyes that seem gouged out of the head, a high forehead, a full red mouth and a head of frizzy hair. If the characters do not wear a mask, then the face must be highly powdered and possess a hard expressionless quality and a stillness as in the face of death. We hear KNOCKING.*

VICTORIA. *(Listening to the knocking.)* It is my father. He is arriving again for the night. *(The* DUCHESS *makes no reply.)* He comes through the jungle to find me. He never tires of his journey.

DUCHESS. How dare he enter the castle, he who is the darkest of them all, the darkest one? My mother looked like a white woman, hair as straight as any white woman's. And at least I am yellow, but he is black, the blackest one of them all. I hoped he was dead. Yet he still comes through the jungle to find me.

> *(The KNOCKING is louder.)*

VICTORIA. He never tires of the journey, does he, Duchess? *(Looking at herself in the mirror.)*

DUCHESS. How dare he enter the castle of Queen Victoria Regina, Monarch of England? It is because of him that my mother died. The wild black beast put his hands on her. She died.

VICTORIA. Why does he keep returning? He keeps returning forever, coming back ever and keeps coming back forever. He is my father.

DUCHESS. He is a black Negro.

VICTORIA. He is my father. I am tied to the black Negro. He came when I was a child in the south, before I was born he haunted my conception, diseased my birth.

DUCHESS. Killed my mother.

VICTORIA. My mother was the light. She was the lightest one. She looked like a white woman.

DUCHESS. We are tied to him unless, of course, he should die.

VICTORIA. But he is dead.

DUCHESS. And he keeps returning.

(The KNOCKING is louder; BLACKOUT. The LIGHTS go out in the Chamber. Onto the Stage from the Left comes the FIGURE *in the white nightgown carrying the bald head. This time we hear her speak.)*

MOTHER. Black man, black man, I never should have let a black man put his hands on me. The wild black beast raped me and now my skull is shining. *(She disappears to the Right.)*

(Now the LIGHT is focused on a single white square wall that is to the Left of the Stage, that is suspended and stands alone, of about five feet in dimension and width. It stands with the narrow part facing the audience. A CHARACTER *steps through. She is a faceless, dark character with a hangman's rope about her neck and red blood on the part that would be her face. She is the* NEGRO. *The most noticeable aspect of her looks is her wild kinky hair. It is a ragged head with a patch of hair missing from the crown which the* NEGRO *carries in her hand. She is dressed in black. She steps slowly through the wall, stands still before it and begins her monologue:)*

NEGRO. Part of the time I live with Raymond, part of the time with God, Maxmillian and Albert Saxe Coburg. I live in my room. It is a small room on the top floor of a brownstone in the West Nineties in New York, a room filled with my dark old volumes, a narrow bed and on the wall old photographs of castles and monarchs of England. It is also Victoria's chamber. Queen Victoria Regina's. Partly because it is consumed by a gigantic plaster statue of Queen Victoria who is my idol and partly for other reasons; three steps that I contrived out of boards lead to the statue which I have placed opposite the door as I enter the room. It is a sitting figure, a replica of one in London, and a thing of astonishing whiteness. I found it in a dusty shop on Morningside Heights. Raymond says it is a thing of terror, possessing the quality of nightmares, suggesting large and probable deaths. And of course he is right. When I am the Duchess of Hapsburg I sit opposite Victoria in my headpiece and we talk. The other time I wear the dress of a student, dark clothes and dark stockings. Victoria always wants me to tell her of whiteness. She wants me to tell her of a royal world where everything and everyone is white and there are no unfortunate black ones. For as we of royal blood know, black is evil and has been from the beginning. Even before my mother's hair started to fall out. Before she was raped by a wild black beast. Black was evil.

As for myself I long to become even a more pallid Negro than I am now; pallid like Negroes on the covers of American Negro magazines; soulless, educated and irreligious. I want to possess no moral value, particularly value as to my being. I want not to be. I ask nothing except anonymity. I am an English major, as my mother was when she went to school in Atlanta. My father majored in social work. I am graduated from a city college and have occasional work in libraries, but mostly spend my days preoccupied with the placement and geometric position of words on paper. I write poetry filling white page after white page with imitations of Edith Sitwell. It is my dream to live in rooms with European antiques and my Queen Victoria, photographs of Roman ruins, walls of books, a piano, oriental carpets and to eat my meals on a white glass table. I will visit my friends' apartments which will contain books, photographs of Roman ruins, pianos and oriental carpets. My friends will be white.

I need them as an embankment to keep me from reflecting too much upon the fact that I am a Negro. For, like all educated Negroes—out of life and death essential—I find it necessary to maintain a stark fortress against recognition of myself. My white friends, like myself, will be shrewd, intellectual and anxious for death. Anyone's death. I will mistrust them, as I do myself, waver in their opinion of me, as I waver in the opinion of myself. But if I had not wavered in my opinion of myself, then my hair would never have fallen out. And if my hair hadn't fallen out, I wouldn't have bludgeoned my father's head with an ebony mask.

In appearance I am good-looking in a boring way; no glaring Negroid features, medium nose, medium mouth and pale yellow skin. My one defect is that I have a head of frizzy hair, unmistakably

Negro kinky hair; and it is indistinguishable. I would like to lie and say I love Raymond. But I do not. He is a poet and is Jewish. He is very interested in Negroes.

(*The* NEGRO *stands by the wall and throughout her following speech, the following characters come through the wall, disappearing off into varying directions in the darkened night of the Stage:* DUCHESS, QUEEN VICTORIA, JESUS, PATRICE LUMUMBA. JESUS *is a hunchback, yellow-skinned dwarf, dressed in white rags and sandals.* PATRICE LUMUMBA *is a black man. His head appears to be split in two with blood and tissue in eyes. He carries an ebony mask.*)

SARAH (NEGRO). The rooms are my rooms; a Hapsburg chamber, a chamber in a Victorian castle, the hotel where I killed my father, the jungle. These are the places myselves exist in. I know no places. That is, I cannot believe in places. To believe in places is to know hope and to know the emotion of hope is to know beauty. It links us across a horizon and connects us to the world. I find there are no places only my funnyhouse. Streets are rooms, cities are rooms, eternal rooms. I try to create a space for myselves in cities, New York, the midwest, a southern town, but it becomes a lie. I try to give myselves a logical relationship but that too is a lie. For relationships was one of my last religions. I clung loyally to the lie of relationships, again and again seeking to establish a connection between my characters. Jesus is Victoria's son. Mother loved my father before her hair fell out. A loving relationship exists between myself and Queen Victoria, a love between myself and Jesus but they are lies.

(*Then to the Right front of the Stage comes the* WHITE LIGHT. *It goes to a suspended stairway. At the foot of it, stands the* LANDLADY. *She is a tall, thin, white woman dressed in a black and red hat and appears to be talking to someone in a suggested open doorway in a corridor of a rooming house. She laughs like a mad character in a funnyhouse throughout her speech.*)

LANDLADY. (*Who is looking up the stairway.*) Ever since her father hung himself in a Harlem hotel when Patrice Lumumba was murdered she hides herself in her room. Each night she repeats: He keeps returning. How dare he enter the castle walls, he who is the darkest of them all, the darkest one? My mother looked like a white woman, hair as straight as any white woman's. And I am yellow but he, he is black, the blackest one of them all. I hoped he was dead. Yet he still comes through the jungle.

I tell her: Sarah, honey, the man hung himself. It's not your blame.
But, no, she stares at me: No, Mrs. Conrad, he did not hang himself,
that is only the way they understand it, they do, but the truth is that
I bludgeoned his head with an ebony skull that he carries about with
him. Wherever he goes, he carries black masks and heads.

She's suffering so till her hair has fallen out. But then she did always
hide herself in that room with the walls of books and her statue. I
always did know she thought she was somebody else, a Queen or
something, somebody else.

BLACKOUT

SCENE: *Funnyman's place.*

The next scene is enacted with the DUCHESS *and* RAYMOND. *Raymond's
place is suggested as being above the* NEGRO's *room and is etched in with a
prop of blinds and a bed. Behind the blinds are mirrors and when the
blinds are opened and closed by Raymond this is revealed.* RAYMOND *turns
out to be the funnyman of the funnyhouse. He is tall, white and ghostly
thin and dressed in a black shirt and black trousers in attire suggesting an
artist. Throughout his dialogue he laughs. The* DUCHESS *is partially dis-
robed and it is implied from their attitudes of physical intimacy—he is
standing and she is sitting before him clinging to his leg. During the scene*
RAYMOND *keeps opening and closing the blinds.*

DUCHESS. *(Carrying a red paper bag.)* My father is arriving and what
am I to do?

    *(*RAYMOND *walks about the place opening the blinds and
laughing.)*

FUNNYMAN. He is arriving from Africa, is he not?

DUCHESS. Yes, yes, he is arriving from Africa.

FUNNYMAN. I always knew your father was African.

DUCHESS. He is an African who lives in the jungle. He is an African
who has always lived in the jungle. Yes, he is a nigger who is an
African who is a missionary teacher and is now dedicating his life to
the erection of a Christian mission in the middle of the jungle. He is
a black man.

FUNNYMAN. He is a black man who shot himself when they murdered
Patrice Lumumba.

DUCHESS. *(Goes on wildly.)* Yes, my father is a black man who went to
Africa years ago as a missionary teacher, got mixed up in politics,

was revealed and is now devoting his foolish life to the erection of a Christian mission in the middle of the jungle in one of those newly freed countries. Hide me. *(Clinging to his knees.)* Hide me here so the nigger will not find me.

FUNNYMAN. *(Laughing.)* Your father is in the jungle dedicating his life to the erection of a Christian mission.

DUCHESS. Hide me here so the jungle will not find me. Hide me.

FUNNYMAN. Isn't it cruel of you?

DUCHESS. Hide me from the jungle.

FUNNYMAN. Isn't it cruel?

DUCHESS. No, no.

FUNNYMAN. Isn't it cruel of you?

DUCHESS. No. *(She screams and opens her red paper bag and draws from it her fallen hair. It is a great mass of dark wild hair. She holds it up to him. He appears not to understand. He stares at it.)* It is my hair. *(He continues to stare at her.)* When I awakened this morning it had fallen out, not all of it but a mass from the crown of my head that lay on the center of my pillow. I arose and in the greyish winter morning light of my room I stood staring at my hair, dazed by my sleeplessness, still shaken by nightmares of my mother. Was it true, yes, it was my hair. In the mirror I saw that, although my hair remained on both sides, clearly on the crown and at my temples my scalp was bare. *(She removes her black crown and shows him the top of her head.)*

FUNNYMAN. *(Staring at her.)* Why would your hair fall out? Is it because you are cruel? How could a black father haunt you so?

DUCHESS. He haunted my very conception. He was a wild black beast who raped my mother.

FUNNYMAN. He is a black Negro. *(Laughing.)*

DUCHESS. Ever since I can remember he's been in a nigger pose of agony. He is the wilderness. He speaks niggerly groveling about wanting to touch me with his black hand.

FUNNYMAN. How tormented and cruel you are.

DUCHESS. *(As if not comprehending.)* Yes, yes, the man's dark, very dark-skinned. He is the darkest, my father is the darkest, my mother is the lightest. I am in between. But my father is the darkest. My father is a nigger who drives me to misery. Any time spent with him evolves itself into suffering. He is a black man and the wilderness.

FUNNYMAN. How tormented and cruel you are.

DUCHESS. He is a nigger.

FUNNYMAN. And your mother, where is she?

DUCHESS. She is in the asylum. In the asylum bald. Her father was a white man. And she is in the asylum.

(He takes her in his arms. She responds wildly.)
BLACKOUT

KNOCKING is heard; it continues, then somewhere near the Center of the Stage a FIGURE *appears in the darkness, a large dark faceless* MAN *carrying a mask in his hand.*

MAN. It begins with the disaster of my hair. I awaken. My hair has fallen out, not all of it, but a mass from the crown of my head that lies on the center of my white pillow. I arise and in the greyish winter morning light of my room I stand staring at my hair, dazed by sleeplessness, still shaken by nightmares of my mother. Is it true? Yes. It is my hair. In the mirror I see that although my hair remains on both sides, clearly on the crown and at my temples my scalp is bare. And in my sleep I had been visited by my bald crazy mother who comes to me crying, calling me to her bedside. She lies on the bed watching the strands of her own hair fall out. Her hair fell out after she married and she spent her days lying on the bed watching the strands fall from her scalp, covering the bedspread until she was bald and admitted to the hospital. Black man, black man, my mother says, I never should have let a black man put his hands on me. She comes to me, her bald skull shining. Black diseases, Sarah, she says. Black diseases. I run. She follows me, her bald skull shining. That is the beginning.
BLACKOUT

SCENE: *Queen's Chamber.*

Her hair is in a small pile on the bed and in a small pile on the floor, several other small piles of hair are scattered about her and her white gown is covered with fallen out hair. QUEEN VICTORIA *acts out the following scene: She awakens (in pantomime) and discovers her hair has fallen. It is on her pillow. She arises and stands at the side of the bed with her back toward us, staring at hair. The* DUCHESS *enters the room, comes around, standing behind* VICTORIA, *and they stare at the hair.* VICTORIA *picks up a mirror. The* DUCHESS *then picks up a mirror and looks at her own hair. She opens the red paper bag that she is carrying and takes out her hair, attempting to place it back on her head (for unlike* VICTORIA, *she does not wear her headpiece now.) The LIGHTS remain on. The unidentified* MAN *returns out of the darkness and speaks. He carries the mask.*

MAN. *(Patrice Lumumba.)* I am a nigger of two generations. I am Patrice Lumumba. I am a nigger of two generations. I am the black shadow that haunted my mother's conception. I belong to the generation born at the turn of the century and the generation born before the depression. At present I reside in New York City in a brownstone in the West Nineties. I am an English major at a city college. My nigger father majored in social work, so did my mother. I am a student and have occasional work in libraries. But mostly I spend my vile days preoccupied with the placement and geometric position of words on paper. I write poetry filling white page after white page with imitations of Sitwell. It is my vile dream to live in rooms with European antiques and my statue of Queen Victoria, photographs of Roman ruins, walls of books, a piano and oriental carpets and to eat my meals on a white glass table. It is also my nigger dream for my friends to eat their meals on white glass tables and to live in rooms with European antiques, photographs of Roman ruins, pianos and oriental carpets. My friends will be white. I need them as an embankment to keep me from reflecting too much upon the fact that I am Patrice Lumumba who haunted my mother's conception. They are necessary for me to maintain recognition against myself. My white friends, like myself, will be shrewd intellectuals and anxious for death. Anyone's death. I will despise them as I do myself. For if I did not despise myself then my hair would not have fallen and if my hair had not fallen then I would not have bludgeoned my father's face with the ebony mask.

(The LIGHT remains on him. Before him a BALD HEAD is dropped on a wire, SOMEONE screams. Another wall is dropped, larger than the first one was. This one is near the front of the Stage facing thus. Throughout the following monologue, the CHARACTERS: DUCHESS, VICTORIA, JESUS go back and forth. As they go in their backs are to us but the NEGRO faces us, speaking:)

I always dreamed of a day when my mother would smile at me. My father . . . his mother wanted him to be Christ. From the beginning in the lamp of their dark room she said—I want you to be Jesus, to walk in Genesis and save the race. You must return to Africa, find revelation in the midst of golden savannas, nim and white frankopenny trees, white stallions roaming under a blue sky, you must walk with a white dove and heal the race, heal the misery, take us off the cross. She stared at him anguished in the kerosene light . . . At dawn he watched her rise, kill a hen for him to eat at breakfast, then go to work down at the big house till dusk, till she died.

His father told him the race was no damn good. He hated his father and adored his mother. His mother didn't want him to marry my mother and sent a dead chicken to the wedding. I DON'T want you marrying that child, she wrote, she's not good enough for you, I want you to go to Africa. When they first married they lived in New York. Then they went to Africa where my mother fell out of love with my father. She didn't want him to save the black race and spent her days combing her hair. She would not let him touch her in their wedding bed and called him black. He is black of skin with dark eyes and a great dark square brow. Then in Africa he started to drink and came home drunk one night and raped my mother. The child from the union is me. I clung to my mother. Long after she went to the asylum I wove long dreams of her beauty, her straight hair and fair skin and grey eyes, so identical to mine. How it anguished him. I turned from him, nailing him on the cross, he said, dragging him through grass and nailing him on a cross until he bled. He pleaded with me to help him find Genesis, search for Genesis in the midst of golden savannas, nim and white frankopenny trees and white stallions roaming under a blue sky, help him search for the white doves, he wanted the black man to make a pure statement, he wanted the black man to rise from colonialism. But I sat in the room with my mother, sat by her bedside and helped her comb her straight black hair and wove long dreams of her beauty. She had long since begun to curse the place and spoke of herself trapped in blackness. She preferred the company of night owls. Only at night did she rise, walking in the garden among the trees with the owls. When I spoke to her she saw I was a black man's child and she preferred speaking to owls. Nights my father came from his school in the village struggling to embrace me. But I fled and hid under my mother's bed while she screamed of remorse. Her hair was falling badly and after a while we had to return to this country.

He tried to hang himself once. After my mother went to the asylum he had hallucinations, his mother threw a dead chicken at him, his father laughed and said the race was no damn good, my mother appeared in her nightgown screaming she had trapped herself in blackness. No white doves flew. He had left Africa and was again in New York. He lived in Harlem and no white doves flew. Sarah, Sarah, he would say to me, the soldiers are coming and a cross they are placing high on a tree and are dragging me through the grass and nailing me upon the cross. My blood is gushing. I wanted to live in Genesis in the midst of golden savannas, nim and white frankopenny trees and white stallions roaming under a blue sky. I wanted to walk with a white dove. I wanted to be a Christian. Now I am Judas. I betrayed my mother. I sent your mother to the asylum. I created a yellow child who hates me. And he tried to hang himself in a Harlem hotel.

> *BLACKOUT*
> *(A BALD HEAD is dropped on a string. We hear LAUGHING.)*

SCENE: ÐUCHESS'S *place.*

The next scene is done in the DUCHESS OF HAPSBURG'*s place which is a chandeliered ballroom with SNOW falling, a black and white marble floor, a bench decorated with white flowers, all of this can be made of obviously fake materials as they would be in a funnyhouse. The* DUCHESS *is wearing a white dress and as in the previous scene a white headpiece with her kinky hair springing out from under it. In the scene are the* DUCHESS *and* JESUS. JESUS *enters the room, which is at first dark, then suddenly BRILLIANT, he starts to cry out at the* DUCHESS, *who is seated on a bench under the chandelier, and pulls his hair from the red paper bag holding it up for the* DUCHESS *to see.*

JESUS. My hair. *(The* DUCHESS *does not speak,* JESUS *again screams.)* My
   hair. *(Holding the hair up, waiting for a reaction from the* DUCHESS.*)*
DUCHESS. *(As if oblivious.)* I have something I must show you. *(She goes
   quickly to shutters and darkens the room, returning standing before* JE-
   SUS. *She then slowly removes her headpiece and from under it takes a
   mass of her hair.)* When I awakened I found it fallen out, not all of it
   but a mass that lay on my white pillow. I could see, although my
   hair hung down at the sides, clearly on my white scalp it was missing.
   (Her baldness is identical to JESUS'.*)*
   BLACKOUT

The LIGHTS come back up. They are BOTH *sitting on the bench
examining each other's hair, running it through their fingers, then
slowly the* DUCHESS *disappears behind the shutters and returns
with a long red comb. She sits on the bench next to* JESUS *and
starts to comb her remaining hair over her baldness. (This is done
slowly.)* JESUS *then takes the comb and proceeds to do the same to*

the DUCHESS OF HAPSBURG*'s hair. After they finish they place the* DUCHESS*'s headpiece back on and we can see the strands of their hair falling to the floor.* JESUS *then lies down across the bench while the* DUCHESS *walks back and forth, the* KNOCKING *does not cease. They speak in unison as the* DUCHESS *walks about and* JESUS *lies on the bench in the falling snow, staring at the ceiling.*

DUCHESS and JESUS. *(Their hair is falling more now, they are both hideous.)* My father isn't going to let us alone. *(KNOCKING.)* Our father isn't going to let us alone, our father is the darkest of us all, my mother was the fairest, I am in between, but my father is the darkest of them all. He is a black man. Our father is the darkest of them all. He is a black man. My father is a dead man.

(Then they suddenly look up at each other and scream, the LIGHTS go to their heads and we see that they are totally bald. There is a KNOCKING. LIGHTS go to the stairs and the LANDLADY.*)*

LANDLADY. He wrote to her saying he loved her and asked her forgiveness. He begged her to take him off the cross *(He had dreamed she would.)*, stop them from tormenting him, the one with the chicken and his cursing father. Her mother's hair fell out, the race's hair fell out because he left Africa, he said. He had tried to save them. She must embrace him. He said his existence depended on her embrace. He wrote her from Africa where he is creating his Christian center in the jungle and that is why he came here. I know that he wanted her to return there with him and not desert the race. He came to see her once before he tried to hang himself, appearing in the corridor of my apartment. I had let him in. I found him sitting on a bench in the hallway. He put out his hand to her, tried to take her in his arms, crying out—Forgiveness, Sarah, is it that you never will forgive me for being black? Sarah, I know you were a child of torment. But forgiveness. That was before his breakdown. Then, he wrote her and repeated that his mother hoped he would be Christ but he failed. He had married her mother because he could not resist the light. Yet, his mother from the beginning in the kerosene lamp of their dark rooms in Georgia said: I want you to be Jesus, to walk in Genesis and save the race, return to Africa, find revelation in the black. He went away.

But Easter morning, she got to feeling badly and went into Harlem to see him; the streets were filled with vendors selling lilies. He had checked out of that hotel. When she arrived back at my brownstone he was here, dressed badly, rather drunk, I had let him in again. He sat on a bench in the dark hallway, put out his hand to her, trying to take her in his arms, crying out—forgiveness, Sarah, forgiveness for my being black, Sarah. I know you are a child of torment. I know on dark winter afternoons you sit alone weaving stories of your mother's beauty. But Sarah, answer me, don't turn away, Sarah. Forgive my blackness. She would not answer. He put out his hand to her. She ran past him on the stairs, left him there with his hand out to me, repeating his past, saying his mother hoped he would be Christ. From the beginning in the kerosene lamp of their dark rooms, she said, "Wally, I want you to be Jesus, to walk in Genesis and save the race. You must return to Africa, Wally, find revelation in the midst of golden savannas, nim and white frankopenny trees and white stallions roaming under a blue sky. Wally, you must find the white dove and heal the pain of the race, heal the misery of the black man, Wally, take us off the cross, Wally." In the kerosene light she stared at me anguished from her old Negro face—but she ran past him leaving him. And now he is dead, she says, now he is dead. He left Africa and now Patrice Lumumba is dead.

(The next scene is enacted back in the DUCHESS OF HAPSBURG'S *place.* JESUS *is still in the Duchess's chamber, apparently he has fallen asleep and as we see him he awakens with the* DUCHESS *by his side, and sits here as in a trance. He rises terrified and speaks.)*

JESUS. Through my apocalypses and my raging sermons I have tried so to escape him, through God Almighty I have tried to escape being black. *(He then appears to rouse himself from his thoughts and calls:)* Duchess, Duchess. *(He looks about for her, there is no answer. He gets up slowly, walks back into the darkness and there we see that she is hanging on the chandelier, her bald head suddenly drops to the floor and she falls upon* JESUS. *He screams.)* I am going to Africa and kill this black man named Patrice Lumumba. Why? Because all my life I believed my Holy Father to be God, but now I know that my father is a black man. I have no fear for whatever I do, I will do in the name of God, I will do in the name of Albert Saxe Coburg, in the name of Victoria, Queen Victoria Regina, the monarch of England, I will.

BLACKOUT

SCENE: *In the jungle, RED SUN, FLYING THINGS, wild black grass. The effect of the jungle is that it, unlike the other scenes, is over the entire stage. In time this is the longest scene in the play and is played the slowest, as the slow, almost standstill stages of a dream. By lighting the desired effect would be—suddenly the jungle has overgrown the chambers and all the other places with a violence and a dark brightness, a grim yellowness.*

JESUS *is the first to appear in the center of the jungle darkness. Unlike in previous scenes, he has a nimbus above his head. As they each successively appear, they all too have nimbuses atop their heads in a manner to suggest that they are saviours.*

JESUS. I always believed my father to be God.
> *(Suddenly they all appear in various parts of the jungle.* PATRICE LUMUMBA, *the* DUCHESS, VICTORIA, *wandering about speaking at once. Their speeches are mixed and repeated by one another:)*

ALL. He never tires of the journey, he who is the darkest one, the darkest one of them all. My mother looked like a white woman, hair as straight as any white woman's. I am yellow but he is black, the darkest one of us all. How I hoped he was dead, yet he never tires of the journey. It was because of him that my mother died because she let a black man put his hands on her. Why does he keep returning? He keeps returning forever, keeps returning and returning and he is my father. He is a black Negro. They told me my Father was God but my father is black. He is my father. I am tied to a black Negro. He returned when I lived in the south back in the twenties, when I was a child, he returned. Before I was born at the turn of the century, he haunted my conception, diseased my birth . . . killed my mother. He killed the light. My mother was the lightest one. I am bound to him unless, of course, he should die.

But he is dead.

And he keeps returning. Then he is not dead.

Then he is not dead.

Yet, he is dead, but dead he comes knocking at my door.

> *(This is repeated several times, finally reaching a loud pitch and then* ALL *rushing about the grass. They stop and stand perfectly still.* ALL *speaking tensely at various times in a chant.)*

I see him. The black ugly thing is sitting in his hallway, surrounded by his ebony masks, surrounded by the blackness of himself. My mother comes into the room. He is there with his hand out to me, groveling, saying—Forgiveness, Sarah, is it that you will never forgive me for being black.

Forgiveness, Sarah, I know you are a nigger of torment.

Why? Christ would not rape anyone.

You will never forgive me for being black.

Wild beast. Why did you rape my mother? Black beast, Christ would not rape anyone.

He is in grief from that black anguished face of his. Then at once the room will grow bright and my mother will come toward me smiling while I stand before his face and bludgeon him with an ebony head.

Forgiveness, Sarah, I know you are a nigger of torment.
(Silence. Then they suddenly begin to laugh and shout as though they are in victory. They continue for some minutes running about laughing and shouting.)
BLACKOUT

Another WALL drops. There is a white plaster statue of Queen Victoria which represents the NEGRO*'s room in the brownstone, the room appears near the staircase highly lit and small. The main prop is the statue but a bed could be suggested. The figure of Victoria is a sitting figure, one of astonishing repulsive whiteness, suggested by dusty volumes of books and old yellowed walls.*

The Negro SARAH *is standing perfectly still, we hear the KNOCKING, the LIGHTS come on quickly, her* FATHER*'s black figure with bludgeoned hands rushes upon her, the LIGHT GOES BLACK and we see her hanging in the room.*

LIGHTS come on the laughing LANDLADY. *And at the same time remain on the hanging figure of the* NEGRO.

LANDLADY. The poor bitch has hung herself. *(*FUNNYMAN RAYMOND *appears from his room at the commotion.)* The poor bitch has hung herself.

RAYMOND. *(Observing her hanging figure.)* She was a funny little liar.

LANDLADY. *(Informing him.)* Her father hung himself in a Harlem hotel when Patrice Lumumba died.

RAYMOND. Her father never hung himself in a Harlem hotel when Patrice Lumumba was murdered. I know the man. He is a doctor, married to a white whore. He lives in the city in rooms with European antiques, photographs of Roman ruins, walls of books and oriental carpets. Her father is a nigger who eats his meals on a white glass table.

END

On the Writing of *Funnyhouse of a Negro*

Funnyhouse of a Negro was completed in Rome, Italy, the week before our second son Adam was born in Salvator Mundi hospital. I was twenty-nine. And I believed if I didn't complete this play before my child's birth and before my thirtieth birthday I would never finish it.

My son Joe Jr. and I lived in a beautiful tranquil apartment about fifteen minutes from Piazza di Spagna. Hall steps led to a miniature living room that opened onto a terrace that overlooked Rome. I sat at the dark desk in the cool miniature room with pages I had started in Ghana on the campus of Legon (Achimota Guest House). They seemed a disjointed raging mass of paragraphs typed on thin transparent typing paper I had bought at the campus of Legon's bookstore. The entire month of July each morning when my son Joe went to Fregene with a play group of children run by an American couple, I tried to put the pages in order.

Ten months earlier at the end of September 1960 my husband Joe and I left New York on the *Queen Elizabeth*. It was my first sight of Europe and Africa. We stopped in London, Paris, Madrid, Casablanca and lived in Monrovia, Liberia before we settled in Accra, Ghana.

The imagery in *Funnyhouse of a Negro* was born by seeing those places: Queen Victoria, the statue in front of Buckingham Palace, Patrice Lumumba on posters and small cards all over Ghana, murdered just after we arrived in Ghana, fall 1960; the savannahs in Ghana, the white frankopenny trees; the birth of Ghana newly freed from England, scenes of Nkrumah on cloth murals and posters. And this was the first time in my life that it was impossible to keep my hair straightened. In Ghana and for the rest of the thirteen month trip I stopped straightening my hair.

After Ghana in February 1961 I had chosen Rome to wait for my husband to finish his work in Nigeria. Rome was the land my high school Latin teacher had sung of: the Forum, the Tiber, the Palatine, Caesar. When my son Joe was at the Parioli Day School I walked in the Forum for hours that spring of 1961. I rode the bus on the Appian Way, the rhythms of my teacher speaking out loud in my mind. Wandering through Rome while Joe was at school I was more alone than I had ever been. At noon I returned to the Pensioni Sabrina for lunch, often a pasta soup made of star-shaped pasta, then went into our room while waiting for my son to return on the bus at the American Embassy and stared at the pages. There were paragraphs about Patrice Lumumba and Queen Victoria. I had always liked the Duchess of Hapsburg since I'd seen the Chapultapec Palace in Mexico. There were lines about her. But the main character talked in monologues about her hair and savannahs in Africa. At that moment *Funnyhouse of a Negro* and *The Owl Answers* were all a part of one work. It wasn't until late July and the impetus of my son's impending birth that the two works split apart and my character Sarah (with her selves Queen Victoria, Patrice Lumumba, Duchess of Hapsburg and Jesus) was born.

In May, two months earlier, my mother had written me that my father had left Cleveland and returned to Georgia to live after thirty five years. I cried when I read the letter, walking from American Express up the Piazza di Spagna steps. So Jesus (who I had always mixed with my social worker father) and the landscape and memories of Georgia and my grandparents became intertwined with the paragraphs on the Ghanian savannahs and Lumumba and his murder.

So trying (for the first time in my life) to comb my unstraightened hair, trying to out race the birth of my child, rereading the divorce news letters from my mother . . . in the July Italian summer mornings, alone in the miniature room, near the Roman Forum, I finished *Funnyhouse of a Negro* the last week of July 1961. Our son Adam was born August 1.

The Owl Answers

SHE who is CLARA PASSMORE who is the VIRGIN MARY who is the
   BASTARD who is the OWL.
BASTARD'S BLACK MOTHER who is the REVEREND'S WIFE who is
   ANNE BOLEYN.
GODDAM FATHER who is the RICHEST WHITE MAN IN THE TOWN
   who is the DEAD WHITE FATHER who is REVEREND PASSMORE.
THE WHITE BIRD who is REVEREND PASSMORE'S CANARY who is
   GOD'S DOVE.
THE NEGRO MAN.
SHAKESPEARE, CHAUCER, WILLIAM THE CONQUEROR.

The characters change slowly back and forth into and out of themselves, leaving some garment from their previous selves upon them always to remind us of the nature of She who is Clara Passmore who is
the Virgin Mary who is the Bastard who is the Owl's world.

SCENE: *The scene is a New York subway is the Tower of London is a Harlem
hotel room is St. Peter's. The scene is shaped like a subway car. The sounds
are subway sounds and the main props of a subway are visible—poles.
Two seats on the scene are like seats on the subway, the seat in which* SHE
WHO IS *sits and* NEGRO MAN*'s seat.*
   Seated is a plain, pallid NEGRO WOMAN, *wearing a cotton summer
dress that is too long, a pair of white wedged sandals. She sits staring into
space. She is* CLARA PASSMORE *who is the* VIRGIN MARY *who is the* BAS-
TARD *who is the* OWL. SHE WHO IS *speaks in a soft voice as a Negro school-*

teacher from Savannah would. SHE WHO IS *carries white handkerchiefs,* SHE WHO IS *carries notebooks that throughout the play like the handkerchiefs fall. She will pick them up, glance frenziedly at a page from a notebook, be distracted, place the notebooks in a disorderly pile, drop them again, etc. The scene should lurch, lights flash, gates slam. When* THEY *come in and exit they move in the manner of people on a train, too there is the noise of the train, the sound of moving steel on the track. The* WHITE BIRD'S *wings should flutter loudly. The gates, the High Altar, the ceiling and the Dome are like St. Peter's, the walls are like the Tower of London.*

The music which SHE WHO IS *hears at the most violent times of her experience should be Haydn's "Concerto for Horn in D" (Third Movement).*

Objects on the stage (beards, wigs, faces) should be used in the manner that people use everyday objects such as spoons or newspapers. The Tower Gate should be black, yet slam like a subway door. The GATES SLAM. Four people enter from different directions. They are SHAKESPEARE, WILLIAM THE CONQUEROR, CHAUCER *and* ANNE BOLEYN. *They are dressed in costumes of Shakespeare, William the Conqueror, Chaucer and Anne Boleyn but too they are strangers entering a subway on a summer night, too they are the guards in the Tower of London. Their lines throughout the play are not spoken specifically by one person but by all or part of them.*

THEY. Bastard. *(They start at a distance, eventually crowding her. Their lines are spoken coldly.* SHE WHO IS *is only a prisoner to them.)*
> You are not his ancestor.
> Keep her locked there, guard.
> Bastard.

SHE. You must let me go down to the chapel to see him. He is my father.

THEY. Your father? *(Jeering.)*

SHE. He is my father.

THEY. Keep her locked there, guard.
> *(*SHAKESPEARE *crosses to gate and raises hands. There is a SLAM as if great door is being closed.)*

SHE. We came this morning. We were visiting the place of our ancestors, my father and I. We had a lovely morning, we rose in darkness, took a taxi past Hyde Park through the Marble Arch to Buckingham Palace, we had our morning tea at Lyons then came out to the Tower. We were wandering about the gardens, my father leaning on my arm, speaking of you, William the Conqueror. My father loved you, William. . . .

THEY. *(Interrupting.)* If you are his ancestor why are you a Negro?

Yes, why is it you are a Negro if you are his ancestor? Keep her locked there.

SHE. You must let me go down to the Chapel to see him.

(SUBWAY STOPS. Doors open. CHAUCER *exits.* ANNE BOLEYN *and* WILLIAM THE CONQUEROR *remain staring at* HER. CHAUCER *and* SHAKESPEARE *return carrying a stiff dead man in a black suit. The most noticeable thing about him is his hair, long, silky, white hair that hangs as they bring him through the gate and place him at her feet.)*

THEY. Here is your father.

(They then all exit through various gate entrances. SHE *picks up the dead man, drags him to a dark, carved high-backed chair on the Right. At the same time a dark* NEGRO MAN, *with a dark suit and black glasses on, enters from the Right gate and sits on the other subway seat. Flashing, movement, slamming the gate. The scene revolves one and one-quarter turns as next action takes place. The* NEGRO MAN *sits up very straight and proceeds to watch* SHE WHO IS. *Until he speaks to her he watches her constantly with a wild, cold stare. The* DEAD FATHER *appears dead. He is dead. Yet as* SHE *watches, he moves and comes to life. The* DEAD FATHER *removes his hair, takes off his white face, from the chair he takes a white church robe and puts it on. Beneath his white hair is dark Negro hair. He is now* REVEREND PASSMORE. *After he dresses he looks about as if something is missing. SUBWAY STOPS, doors open.* FATHER *exits and returns with a gold bird cage that hangs near the chair and a white battered Bible. Very matter-of-factly he sits down in the chair, stares for a moment at the cage, then opens the Bible, starting to read.* SHE *watches, highly distracted, until he falls asleep. Scene revolves one turn as* ANNE BOLEYN *throws red rice at* SHE WHO IS *and the* DEAD FATHER *who is now* REVEREND PASSMORE. *They see her.* SHE *exits and returns with a great black gate and places the gate where the pole is.* SHE WHO IS *runs to* ANNE BOLEYN.)*

SHE. Anne, Anne Boleyn. *(Throws rice upon* SHE WHO IS CLARA PASS-MORE *who is the* VIRGIN MARY *who is the* BASTARD *who is the* OWL.)* Anne, you know so much of love, won't you help me? They took my father away and will not let me see him. They locked me in this tower and I can see them taking his body across to the Chapel to be buried and see his white hair hanging down. Let me into the Chapel. He is my blood father. I am almost white, am I not? Let me into St. Paul's

Chapel. Let me please go down to St. Paul's Chapel. I am his daughter. (ANNE *appears to listen quite attentively but her reply is to turn into the* BASTARD'S BLACK MOTHER. *She takes off part of her own long dress and puts on a rose-colored, cheap lace dress. While she does this there is a terrific SCREECH.* SHE WHO IS*'s reaction is to run back to her subway seat. She drops her notebooks. The* BASTARD'S BLACK MOTHER *opens her arms to* SHE WHO IS. SHE *returns to the gate.*) Anne. (*As if trying to bring back* ANNE BOLEYN.)

BBM (BASTARD'S BLACK MOTHER). (*Laughs and throws a white bridal bouquet at her.*) Clara, I am not Anne. I am the Bastard's Black Mother, who cooked for somebody. (*Still holding out her arms, she kneels by the gate, her kinky hair awry. Eyes closed, she stares upward, praying. Suddenly she stops praying and pulls at* SHE WHO IS *through the gate.*)

(*The* WHITE BIRD, *with very loud fluttering wings, flies down from St. Peter's Dome and goes into the cage.* REVEREND PASSMORE *gets up and closes the cage door.*)

SHE. Anne, it is I.

BBM. Clara, you were conceived by your Goddam Father who was the Richest White Man in the Town and somebody that cooked for him. That's why you're an owl. (*Laughs.*) That's why when I see you, Mary, I cry. I cry when I see Marys, cry for their deaths.

(WHITE BIRD *flies.* REVEREND *reads. The* BASTARD'S BLACK MOTHER *stands at the gate, watches, then takes off rose lace dress and black face [beneath her black face is a more pallid Negro face], pulls down her hair, longer dark hair, and puts on a white dress. From a fold in the dress she takes out a picture of Christ, then kneels and stares upward. She is the* REVEREND'S WIFE. *While she does this the scene revolves one turn.*)

REVEREND'S WIFE. (*Kneeling.* REVEREND *stands and watches her.* REVEREND'S WIFE *takes a vial from her gown and holds it up.*) These are the fruits of my maidenhead, owl blood Clara who is the Bastard Clara Passmore to whom we gave our name, see the Owl blood, that is why I cry when I see Marys, cry for their deaths, Owl Mary Passmore. (SHE *gets up, exits from a side gate. SUBWAY STOPS, gates open, they come in, gates close. SUBWAY STARTS.* SHE WHO IS *goes to the* REVEREND *as if to implore him. He then changes into the* DEAD FATHER, *resuming his dirty white hair.* THEY *stand about.*)

SHE. Dear Father, My Goddam Father who was the Richest White Man in the Town, who is Dead Father—you know that England is the home of dear Chaucer, Dickens and dearest Shakespeare. Winters we spent here at the Tower, our chambers were in the Queen's House, summers we spent at Stratford with dearest Shakespeare. It was all so lovely. I spoke to Anne Boleyn, Dead Father. She knows so much of love and suffering and I believe she is going to try to help me. *(Takes a sheaf of papers from her notebooks; they fall to the floor.)* Communications, all communications to get you the proper burial, the one you deserve in St. Paul's Chapel, they are letting you rot, my Goddam Father who was the Richest White Man in the Town—they are letting you rot in that town in Georgia. I haven't been able to see the king. I'll speak again to Anne Boleyn. She knows so much of love. *(Shows the papers to the* DEAD FATHER *who sits with his hair hanging down, dead, at which point scene revolves clock-wise one-half turn. There are* SCREECHES, *and bird flaps wings. The* REVEREND'S WIFE *enters and prays at gate.)*

DEAD FATHER. If you are my ancestor why are you a Negro, Bastard? What is a Negro doing at the Tower of London, staying at the Queen's House? Clara, I am your Goddam Father who was the Richest White Man in the Town and you are a schoolteacher in Savannah who spends her summers in Teachers College. You are not my ancestor. You are my bastard. Keep her locked there, William.

SHE. *(They stare at her like passengers on a subway, standing, holding the hand straps.)* We were wandering about the garden, you leaning on my arm, speaking of William the Conqueror. We sat on the stone bench to rest, when we stood up you stumbled and fell onto the walk—dead. Dead. I called the guard. Then I called the Warder and told him my father had just died, that we had been visiting London together, the place of our ancestors and all the lovely English, and my father just died. *(She reaches out to touch him.)*

DEAD FATHER. You are not my ancestor.

SHE. They jeered. They brought me to this tower and locked me up. I can see they're afraid of me. From the tower I saw them drag you across the court...your hair hanging down. They have taken off your shoes and you are stiff. You are stiff. *(Touches him.)* My dear father. *(MUSIC: Haydn.)*

DEAD FATHER. Daughter of somebody that cooked for me. *(Smiles. He then ignores* SHE WHO IS, *changes into the* REVEREND, *takes the Bible and starts to read. The* WHITE BIRD *flies into the cage. Wings flutter. The* REVEREND'S WIFE *prays, lights a candle. The* REVEREND *watches the* BIRD. REVEREND'S WIFE *then puts on her black face, rose dress.*

Some of the red rice has fallen near her, she says, "Oww," and starts to peck at it like a bird. SHE WHO IS *wanders about, then comes to speak to the* BASTARD'S BLACK MOTHER *who remains seated like an owl. END MUSIC.)*

SHE. It was you, the Bastard's Black Mother, who told me. I asked you where did Mr. William Mattheson's family come from and you, my Black Mother, said: I believe his father came from England. England, I said. England is the Brontës' home. Did you know, Black Bastard's Mother, who cooked for somebody, in the Reverend's parlor—there in a glass bookcase are books and England is the home of Chaucer, Dickens and Shakespeare. Black Mother who cooked for somebody, Mr. William Mattheson died today. I was at the College. The Reverend's Wife called me, Clara who is the Bastard who is the Virgin Mary who is the Owl. Clara, who is the Bastard who is the Virgin Mary who is the Owl, Clara, she said, the Reverend told me to call you and tell you Mr. William Mattheson died today or it was yesterday he died yesterday. It was yesterday. The Reverend told me to tell you it was yesterday he died and it is today they're burying him. Clara who is the Bastard, you mustn't come. Don't do anything foolish like come to the funeral, Mary. You've always been such a fool about that white man, Clara. But I am coming, the Black Bastard's Mother. I am coming, my Goddam Father who was the Richest White Man in Jacksonville, Georgia. When I arrive in London, I'll go out to Buckingham Palace, see the Thames at dusk and Big Ben. I'll go for lovely walks through Hyde Park, and to innumerable little tearooms with great bay windows and white tablecloths on little white tables and order tea. I will go all over and it will be June. Then I'll go out to the Tower to see you, my father.

(SUBWAY STOPS. Doors open. THEY *enter.)*

THEY. If you are his ancestor, what are you doing on the subway at night looking for men?

What are you doing looking for men to take to a hotel room in Harlem?

Negro men?

Negro men, Clara Passmore?

(GATES CLOSE, SUBWAY STARTS, BIRD*'s wings flap.)*

SHE. *(Runs to the* BIRD.*)* My dead father's bird: God's Dove. My father died today.

BIRD. *(Mocking.)* My father died today, God's Dove.

SHE. He was the Richest White Man in our Town. I was conceived by him and somebody that cooked for him.

BIRD. What are you doing in the Tower of London then?
(The REVEREND *becomes the* DEAD FATHER *who comes forward, pantomimes catching the* BIRD, *puts him in the cage, shuts the door.)*

SHE. My father. *(He turns, stares at her and comes toward her and dies. There is a CLANG.)* What were you saying to William, my father, you loved William so? *(She holds him in her arms. He opens his eyes.)*

DEAD FATHER. *(Waking.)* Mary, at last you are coming to me. *(MUSIC: Haydn.)*

SHE. I am not Mary, I am Clara, your daughter, Reverend Passmore— I mean Dead Father. *(*BIRD *flies in the cage.)*

DEAD FATHER. Yes, my Mary, you are coming into my world. You are filled with dreams of my world. I sense it all.
(Scene revolves counterclockwise one and one-quarter turns. LIGHTS FLASH. SHE WHO IS, *trying to escape, runs into* NEGRO MAN.)*

NEGRO MAN. At last you are coming to me. *(Smiles.)*

DEAD FATHER. Mary, come in here for eternity. Are you confused? Yes, I can see you are confused. *(*THEY *come on.)*

THEY. Are you confused? *(One of them,* CHAUCER, *is now dressed as the* REVEREND. *He comes, falls down onto the empty high-backed chair and sits staring into the Bible.)*

DEAD FATHER. So at last you are coming to me, Bastard.
*(*BASTARD'S BLACK MOTHER *exits from gate, returns, part owl with owl feathers upon her, dragging a great dark bed through the gate.)*

BBM. Why be confused? The Owl was your beginning, Mary. *(There is a GREAT CLANG. Begins to build with the bed and feathers the High Altar. Feathers fly.)*

SHE. He came to me in the outhouse, he came to me under the porch, in the garden, in the fig tree. He told me you are an owl, ow, oww, I am your beginning, ow. You belong here with us owls in the fig tree, not to somebody that cooks for your Goddam Father, oww, and I ran to the outhouse in the night crying oww. Bastard they say, the people in the town all say Bastard, but I—I belong to God and the owls, ow, and I sat in the fig tree. My Goddam Father is the Richest White Man in the Town, but I belong to the owls, till Reverend Passmore adopted me they all said Bastard . . . then my father was a reverend. He preached in the Holy Baptist Church on the top of the hill, on the top of the Holy Hill and everybody in the town knew then my name was Mary. My father was the Baptist preacher and I was Mary. *(SUBWAY STOPS, GATES OPEN.* THEY *enter. GATES CLOSE. SUBWAY STARTS.* SHE *sits next to* NEGRO MAN.*)* I who am the ancestor of Shakespeare, Chaucer and William the Conqueror, I went to London—the Queen Elizabeth. London. They all said who ever heard of anybody going to London but I went. I stayed in my cabin the whole crossing, solitary. I was the only Negro there. I read books on subjects like the History of London, the Life of Anne Boleyn, Mary Queen of Scots and Sonnets. When I wasn't in the cabin I wrapped myself in a great sweater and sat over the dark desks in the writing room and wrote my father. I wrote him every day of my journey. I met my father once when my mother took me to visit him and we had to go into the back door of his house. I was married once briefly. On my wedding day the Reverend's Wife came to me and said when I see Marys I cry for their deaths, when I see brides, Clara, I cry for their deaths. But the past years I've spent teaching alone in Savannah. And alone I'm almost thirty-four, I who am the ancestor of somebody that cooked for somebody and William the Conqueror. *(DEAD FATHER rises, goes to her, then dies again. GREAT CLANG.* BASTARD'S BLACK MOTHER *shakes a rattle at* SHE. SHE *screams at the* DEAD FATHER *and the* MOTHER.*)* You must know how it is to be filled with yearning.

　(THEY laugh. BASTARD'S BLACK MOTHER *bangs at the bed.)*
NEGRO MAN. *(Touches her.)* And what exactly do you yearn for?
SHE. You know.
NEGRO MAN. No, what is it?
SHE. I want what I think everyone wants.
NEGRO MAN. And what is that?
SHE. I don't know. Love or something, I guess.
NEGRO MAN. Out there Owl?
DEAD FATHER. In St. Paul's Chapel Owl?
THEY. Keep her locked there, guard. *(GREAT CLANG.)*
BBM. Is this love to come from out there?
SHE. I don't know what you mean.
DEAD FATHER. I know you don't.
THEY. We know you don't.
SHE. Call me Mary.
NEGRO MAN. Mary?

THEY. Keep her locked there.

DEAD FATHER. If you are Mary what are you doing in the Tower of London?

NEGRO MAN. Mary?

> *(The* REVEREND *gets up, goes to chair, puts on robe, sits. The* BASTARD'S BLACK MOTHER *reappears on the other side of the gate, owl feathers about her, bearing a vial, still wearing the long black hair of the* REVEREND'S WIFE.*)*

BBM. When I see sweet Marys I cry for their deaths, Clara. The Reverend took my maidenhead and I am not a Virgin anymore and that is why you must be Mary, always be Mary, Clara.

SHE. Mama. *(*BASTARD'S BLACK MOTHER *rises. Steps in costume of* ANNE BOLEYN.*)* Mama. *(Watches her change to* ANNE BOLEYN. *They watch.)*

BBM. What are you doing on the subway if you are his ancestor?

> *(*ANNE *makes circular cross around stage until she is back in same position she started at.)*

SHE. I am Clara Passmore. I am not His ancestor. I ride, look for men to take to a Harlem hotel room, to love, dress them as my father, beg to take me.

THEY. Take you?

SHE. Yes, take me, Clara Passmore.

THEY. Take you, Bastard?

SHE. There is a bed there.

> *(The* WHITE BIRD *laughs like the mother.)*

WILL. And do they take you?

SHE. No, William.

WILL. No?

SHE. Something happens.

WILL. Happens?

CHAUCER. Happens?

SHE. Something strange always happens, Chaucer.

CHAUCER. Where?

SHE. In the hotel room. It's how I've passed my summer in New York, nights I come to the subway, look for men. It's how I've passed my summer. If they would only take me! But something strange happens.

ANNE. Take you, Mary. Why, Mary? *(*ANNE *has now reached gate.)*

> *(*BASTARD'S BLACK MOTHER *steps out of costume, crosses to bed.* SHE *talks to* ANNE *as if she were there.)*

SHE. Anne, you must help me. They, my Black Mother and my God-dam Father and the Reverend and his wife, they and the teachers at the school where I teach, and Professor Johnson, the principal to whom I'm engaged, they all say, "London, who in the hell ever heard of anybody going to London?" Of course I shouldn't go. They said I had lost my mind, read so much, buried myself in my books. They said I should stay and teach summer school to the kids up from Oglethorpe. But I went. All the way from Piccadilly Circus out there in the black taxi, my cold hands were colder than ever. Then it happened. No sooner than I left the taxi and passed down a grey walk through a dark gate and into a garden where there were black ravens on the grass when I broke down. I broke down and started to cry, oh the Tower, winters in Queen's House, right in front of everybody. People came and stared. I was the only Negro there. The Guard came and stared, the ravens flew and finally a man with a black hat on helped me out through the gate into the street. I am never going back, Anne. Anne, I am never going back. I will not go.

  (SUBWAY STOPS, GATES OPEN.)

THEY. Keep her locked there, guard.

  (LIGHT comes through gates as if opened. SHE *makes crown of paper, and places on* NEGRO MAN*'s head.)*

SHE. God, do you see it? Do you see? They are opening the cell door to let me go.

NEGRO MAN. See it, Mary?

SHE. They are opening the cell door to let me go down to St. Paul's Chapel where I am yearning to go. Do you see it?

NEGRO MAN. Love? Love Mary?

SHE. Love?

NEGRO MAN. Love in St. Paul's Chapel? *(He tries to grab at her.)*

SHE. No, no, the love that exists between you and me. Do you see it?

NEGRO MAN. Love Mary? *(He takes her hand, with his other hand, he tries to undress her.)*

SHE. Love God.

NEGRO MAN. Love Mary?

SHE. Love God.

THEY. *(Simultaneously.)* Bastard, you are not His ancestor, you are not God's ancestor. *(There is a SCREECH as* THEY *bring the* DEAD FATHER *and leave him at her feet.)*

NEGRO MAN. Love Mary?

SHE. Love God. Yes.

BBM. *(Calls.)* Clara. Clara. *(The* REVEREND *watching.)*

THEY. Open the door. Let her go, let her go, guards. Open the cell door. (THEY *exit, leaving the gates open.*)

  (NEGRO MAN *will not release* SHE WHO IS CLARA *who is the* BASTARD *who is the* VIRGIN MARY *who is the* OWL.)

SHE. Go away. Go away. (*The* NEGRO MAN *will not release her.*)

  (*The* REVEREND'S WIFE *goes on building the High Altar with owl feathers, prays, builds, prays, stops, holds out her hand to* SHE WHO IS, *puts up candles, puts up owl feathers, laughs, puts more candles on the High Altar.*)

REVEREND'S WIFE. (*Calls.*) Owl, come sit by me. (*The* REVEREND'S WIFE *does not look at* SHE WHO IS, *but rather stares feverishly upward, her gestures possessing the fervent quality of biblical images. Sitting on the High Altar, she holds one of her hands over her shoulder as though she drew near the fingers of a deity. Suddenly her hand reaches inside her gown and she pulls up a butcher knife.*) Clara. (*Staring upward, holding the knife.*)

SHE. Yes, the Reverend's Wife who came to me on my wedding day and said I cry for the death of brides. Yes?

REVEREND'S WIFE. I told the Reverend if he ever came near me again . . . (*She turns the butcher knife around.*) Does he not know I am Mary, Christ's bride? What does he think? Does he think I am like your black mother who was the biggest whore in town? He must know I'm Mary. Only Mary would marry the Reverend Passmore of the church on the top of the Holy Hill. (*Turns the knife around, staring at it.* SHE *is leaving with* NEGRO MAN. REVEREND'S WIFE *is pulling her.*) We adopted you, took you from your bastard birth, Owl.

  (SHE *and* NEGRO MAN *exit. GATES CLOSE. SUBWAY STARTS.* REVEREND'S WIFE *drags bed onto Center Stage. She enters with* NEGRO MAN *Down Center.*)

SHE. Home, God, we're home. Did you know we came from England, God? It's the Brontës' home too. Winters we spent here at the Tower. Our chambers were in the Queen's House. Summers we spent at Stratford. It was so lovely. God, do you remember the loveliness? (*LIGHTS FLASH. Scene revolves clockwise one and one-quarter turns.* BIRD *flaps wings. LIGHT comes up on him.*)

BIRD. If you are the Virgin, what are you doing with this Negro in a Harlem hotel room? Mary?

SHE. My name is Clara Passmore.

BIRD. Mary. *(*WHITE BIRD *laughs like the* BASTARD'S BLACK MOTHER. *The* REVEREND'S WIFE *lights candles.)*

NEGRO MAN. *(Going to her.)* What is it?

SHE. Call me Mary, God.

NEGRO MAN. Mary?

SHE. God, do you remember the loveliness?

REVEREND'S WIFE. *(Lights more candles and moves closer with the butcher knife, calling:)* Clara. *(The* BIRD *flies wildly, the* REVEREND *sits in the chair reading the white tattered Bible.)*

NEGRO MAN. What is it? What is it? What is wrong? *(He tries to undress her. Underneath her body is black. He throws off the crown she has placed on him. She is wildly trying to get away from him.)* What is it? *(The* WHITE BIRD *flies toward them and about the green room.)* Are you sick?

SHE. *(Smiles.)* No, God. *(She is in a trance.)* No, I am not sick. I only have a dream of love. A dream. Open the cell door and let me go down to St. Paul's Chapel. *(The blue crepe shawl is half about her. She shows the* NEGRO MAN *her notebooks, from which a mass of papers fall. She crazily tries to gather them up. During this* SHE *walks around bed. He follows her.)* Communications, God, communications, letters to my father. I am making it into my thesis. I write my father every day of the year.

God, I who am the Bastard who is the Virgin Mary who is the Owl, I came here this morning with my father. We were visiting England, the place of our ancestors, my father and I who am the Bastard who is the Virgin Mary who is the Owl. We had a lovely morning. We rose in darkness, took a taxi past Hyde Park, through the Marble Arch to Buckingham Palace. We had our morning tea at Lyons and then we came out to the Tower.

And I started to cry and a man with a black hat on helped me out of the gate to the street. I was the only Negro here.

They took him away and would not let me see him. They who are my Black Mother and my Goddam Father locked me in the fig tree and took his body away and his white hair hung down.

Now they, my Black Mother and my Goddam Father who pretend to be Chaucer, Shakespeare and Eliot and all my beloved English, come to my cell and stare and I can see they despise me and I despise them.

They are dragging his body across the green his white hair hanging down. They are taking off his shoes and he is stiff. I must get into the chapel to see him. I must. He is my blood father. God, let me into his burial. *(He grabs her Down Center.* SHE, *kneeling.)* I call God and the Owl answers. *(Softer.)* It haunts my Tower calling, its feathers are blowing against the cell wall, speckled in the garden on the fig tree, it comes, feathered, great hollow-eyed with yellow skin and yellow eyes, the flying bastard. From my Tower I keep calling and the only answer is the Owl, God. *(Pause. Stands.)* I am only yearning for our kingdom, God.

> *(The* WHITE BIRD *flies back into the cage,* REVEREND *reads smiling, the* DEAD FATHER *lies on cell floor. The* MOTHER, *now part the black mother and part the* REVEREND'S WIFE *in a white dress, wild kinky hair, part feathered, comes closer to* CLARA.)

MOTHER. Owl in the fig tree, owl under the house, owl in outhouse. *(Calling cheerfully the way one would call a child, kissing* SHE WHO IS.) There is a way from owldom. *(Kissing her again.)* Clara who is the Bastard who is the Virgin who is the Owl.

SHE. *(Goes to* MOTHER.*)* My Black Mother who cooked for somebody who is the Reverend's Wife. Where is Anne Boleyn?

MOTHER. Owl in the fig tree, do you know it? Do you? Do you know the way to St. Paul's Chapel, Clara? *(Takes her hand.)* I do. Kneel, Mary, by the gate and pray with me who is your black mother who is Christ's Bride. *(She holds up the butcher knife.)* Kneel by the High Altar and pray with me. *(They kneel; she smiles.)* Do you know it, Clara, do you, Clara Bastard? *(Kisses her.)* Clara, I know the way to St. Paul's Chapel. I know the way to St. Paul's Chapel, Clara.

> *(*MOTHER *lifts knife. She stabs herself. At this moment,* BIRD *flaps wings, scene moves counterclockwise one turn. There is a SCREECH of a SUBWAY. Then the Haydn plays. When revolve stops,* NEGRO MAN *tries to kiss her and pin her down on bed.* SHE *is fighting him off. The* WHITE BIRD *descends steps.)*

SHE. God, say, "You know I love you, Mary, yes, I love you. That love is the oldest, purest testament in my heart." Say, "Mary, it was a testament imprinted on my soul long before the world began. I pray to you, Mary." God, say, "Mary, I pray to you. Darling, come to my kingdom. Mary, leave owldom—come to my kingdom. I am awaiting you." *(The* NEGRO MAN *tries again to kiss her. The* WHITE BIRD *picks up the* DEAD MOTHER *and takes her to the top of St. Peter's Dome. They remain there, watching down. The* REVEREND *reads the Bible, smiling.)*

NEGRO MAN. What is wrong?

SHE. Wrong, God?

NEGRO MAN. God?

SHE. Wrong, God?

NEGRO MAN. God? *(They are upon the burning High Altar. He tries to force her down, yet at the same time he is frightened by her. The* DEAD FATHER *who has been holding the candles smiles.)*

SHE. Negro! *(MUSIC ENDS.)* Keep her locked there, guard. *(They struggle.)* I cry for the death of Marys.

(They struggle. SHE *screeches.)* Negro! *(*SHE *tries to get out of the room, but he will not let her go.)* Let me go to St. Paul's Chapel. Let me go down to see my Goddam Father who was the Richest White Man in the Town. *(They struggle, he is frightened now.)* God, God, call me, Mary. *(*SHE *screeches louder.)* God!! *(Suddenly* SHE *breaks away, withdraws the butcher knife, still with blood and feathers upon it, and very quickly tries to attack him, holds the knife up, aiming it at him, but then dropping it just as suddenly in a gesture of wild weariness. He backs farther.* SHE *falls down onto the side of the burning bed. The* NEGRO MAN *backs farther out through the gate.* SHE, *fallen at the side of the altar burning, her head bowed, both hands conceal her face, feathers fly, green lights are strong. Altar burning,* WHITE BIRD *laughs from the Dome.* SHE WHO IS CLARA *who is the* BASTARD *who is the* VIRGIN MARY *suddenly looks like an owl, and lifts her bowed head, stares into space and speaks:)* Ow... oww. *(*FATHER *rises and slowly blows out candles on bed.)*

CURTAIN

A Lesson in Dead Language

The scene is a classroom, bright. A great WHITE DOG—*the teacher*—*is seated at a great dark desk. Seven girl* PUPILS *are seated at ordinary school desks. They wear white organdy dresses, white socks and black shoes. The* PUPILS *move stiffly. When the* PUPILS *write, they write with their arms on imaginary tablets. There are three blackboards, Stage Front, Left and Right.*

The statues of Jesus, Joseph, Mary, two Wise Men and a shepherd are on a ridge around the room. The statues are highly colored, wooden, and larger than the PUPILS. *(The* WHITE DOG *also appears larger than the* PUPILS.*) Three statues are situated at the front of the classroom, one on each side, and one at the rear of the classroom.*

The DOG *appears to be in a position of a dog begging; great, stiff, white. The actress who plays this role should be costumed as a dog from the waist up.*

The WHITE DOG *sits at the desk. Her speech is unaccompanied by any movement of the mouth, since she should be wearing what resembles a mask.*

The PUPILS *are seated, backs to audience, facing the* WHITE DOG.

WHITE DOG. *(Woman's voice.)* Lesson I bleed.

> *(The* PUPILS *write in unison with their arms on imaginary tablets. What they write they speak aloud.)*

PUPILS. *(Slowly, dully.)* I bleed.

WHITE DOG. The day the white dog died, I started to bleed. Blood came out of me.

PUPILS. Teacher, the white dog died, I started to bleed. The white dog died, I started to bleed. Where are the lemons? I am bleeding, Mother.

(They put down their imaginary pens, sit erect with folded hands.)

WHITE DOG. Now, will the one who killed the white dog please come forward from the senate? *(The* PUPILS *turn their heads mechanically at each other to see who will come forward; they then turn back to the teacher, erect.)* Will the one who killed the white dog please come forward. . . . And Caesar too, the one who killed Caesar.

(A silence. No one moves. Then one PUPIL *raises her hand. The* WHITE DOG *nods recognition.)*

PUPIL. I bleed, Teacher. I bleed. I am bleeding, Mother.

WHITE DOG. *(Ignores the* PUPIL.*)* I said will the one who killed the white dog please come forward. . . . And Caesar, at the foot of Pompey's statue . . .

(A silence. A PUPIL *raises her hand.)*

PUPIL. I bleed, Teacher, I bleed. It started when my white dog died. It was a charming little white dog. He ran beside me in the sun when I played a game with lemons on the green grass. And it started when I became a woman. My mother says it is because I am a woman that I bleed. Why, Mother, why do I bleed?

(They raise their hands.)

PUPILS. *(In unison.)* My mother says it is because I am a woman that I bleed. Blood comes out of me.

(They giggle tensely. Then they fold their hands. Silence. The PUPILS *stare at the* WHITE DOG—*the* WHITE DOG *stares at the* PUPILS.*)*

WHITE DOG. Since we do not know the one that killed the sun, we will all be punished. We will all bleed, since we do not know the one, we will all be punished. *(The* PUPILS *stand in the aisle, backs to audience. Silence. They each have a great circle of blood on the back of their dresses. They go stiffly to the three boards, three* PUPILS *at one board, two* PUPILS *at the other two.)* Write one hundred times, "Who killed the white dog and why do I bleed? I killed the white dog and that is why I must bleed. And the lemons and the grass and the sun. It was at the Ides of March."

(They pick up great white chalk and write on the boards "Who killed.")

PUPILS. I killed the white dog and that is why I must bleed for Caesar. Dear Caesar.

(They write "I killed." Then the PUPILS *turn and face the* TEACHER. *One* PUPIL *raises her hand. The* WHITE DOG *nods recognition.)*

PUPIL. He ran beside me and the sky was blue and so was Mary's robe.

PUPILS. *(In unison.)* This bleeding started when Jesus and Joseph and Mary, the two Wise Men, and my shepherd died, and now Caesar. *(The* PUPILS *look up at the statues in the room. The statues are bright.)*

STATUES. *(Voices from offstage.)* It started when Jesus and Joseph, Mary, the two Wise Men and the shepherd died. I found their bodies in the yard of my house. One day they disappeared and I found their bodies in the yard of my house tumbled down.

PUPIL. *(Raises her hand.)* I played a game with lemons in the green grass. I bleed too, Caesar. Dear Caesar.

PUPILS. My mother says it is because I am a woman.

STATUES. *(Offstage voices again.)* That I found the bodies on the grass at the Capitol at the foot of Pompey's statue.

PUPIL. They were the friends of my childhood. I bleed too, Caesar.

(A silence. No one writes. The WHITE DOG *stares at the* PUPILS. *The* PUPILS *stare at the* WHITE DOG. *Then the* WHITE DOG *stares at the empty desks.)*

WHITE DOG. Calpurnia dreamed. Dear Caesar, I bleed too. *(A silence. The* PUPILS *stare at the* WHITE DOG.)* Calpurnia dreamed a pinnacle was tumbling down. *(Another silence. The* WHITE DOG *stares at the pupils.)* Calpurnia dreamed. I am bleeding, Mother. Does no one know where the lemons are? Since no one knows, then we will all bleed and continue to bleed.

*(*PUPILS *return to their seats, turn and face the* WHITE DOG. *We again see the greater circle of blood on their dresses. They stand silently, then sit and fold their hands. A silence. A* PUPIL *raises her hand. The* WHITE DOG *nods.)*

PUPIL. Does no one know where we played a game of lemons in the sunshine is? Is it in the senate?

(A silence. The PUPILS *stare at each other.)*

SAME PUPIL. Teacher, why does no one know who killed the white dog? Mother, why does no one know? Why doesn't Caesar know who the conspirators are? *(A silence. The* PUPILS *stare at each other. The* SAME PUPIL *raises her hand.)* Teacher, my mother is sending me to the Asylum if I don't stop talking about my white dog that died and my bleeding and Jesus and the game in the green grass. I asked her who made me bleed. The conspirators, she said.

PUPILS. *(In unison.)* Who?

SAME PUPIL. The conspirators. And she said everything soon bleeds away and dies. Caesar, too.

PUPILS. Everything. And now Caesar, too. Dear Mother.

(A silence. The WHITE DOG *stares at the* PUPILS.)

WHITE DOG. Calpurnia dreamed a pinnacle was tumbling down.

(The PUPILS *stare at the* WHITE DOG; *they fold their hands. Suddenly the* WHITE DOG *raps on the desk. The* WHITE DOG *rises, dims the room [imaginary light], stands in front of her desk.)*

PUPILS. *(Loud whispering.)* Calpurnia dreamed . . . *(Loud rapid whispering. The whispering stops. The* WHITE DOG *starts to walk through the aisles.)* Dear Caesar played a game of lemons in the sun on the green grass and my white dog ran beside. Jesus and Joseph and Mary, two Wise Men and the shepherd were friends of my childhood. Dear Mother.

(They look up at the statues. They put their heads down. The WHITE DOG *walks and comes to the end of the aisle; stands before the desk. A silence. Heads down. Another long silence.)*

WHITE DOG. Calpurnia dreamed.

PUPILS. *(Suddenly lift their heads and say:)* I bleed. I bleed. Ever since I became a woman. I bleed. Like Caesar will I bleed away and die? Since I became a woman blood comes out of me. I am a pinnacle tumbled down.

(Silence. They stand slowly. Their skirts are covered with blood. They stare at the WHITE DOG, *who stares at them. They hang their heads wearily. The stage becomes darker. Then a light comes slowly and fixes on a* PUPIL *to the right, rear, a* PUPIL *wearing a school dress. Her back is to us, her hands folded. Then a light to the* WHITE DOG, *who turns slowly about a full circle, revealing a blank human face. She holds a great Latin book. The statues are revealed as statues of Romans.* PUPILS *still stand, skirts covered with bright blood, heads hung. A silence. A bright light.)*

WHITE DOG. And what is the answer? Translate what I read.

(A silence. The PUPIL *raises her hand. The* WHITE DOG *nods recognition. A long pause.)*

PUPIL. *(Very slowly, as if translating.)* Calpurnia dreamed a pinnacle was tumbling down.

BLACKOUT

A Rat's Mass

CHARACTERS

ROSEMARY
BROTHER RAT
SISTER RAT
JESUS, JOSEPH, MARY, TWO WISE MEN, SHEPHERD

BROTHER RAT *has a rat's head, a human body, a tail.* SISTER RAT *has a rat's belly, a human head, a tail.* ROSEMARY *wears a Holy Communion dress and has worms in her hair. Mass said in prayer voices that later turn to gnawing voices. They were two pale Negro children.*

SCENE: *The rats' house. The house consists of a red carpet runner and candles. The light is the light of the end of a summer day.*
BROTHER RAT *is kneeling facing the audience.*
At the far left of the house stands a procession of JESUS, JOSEPH, MARY, TWO WISE MEN, *and a* SHEPHERD.
SISTER RAT *stands at the end of the red aisle.*

BROTHER RAT. Kay within our room I see our dying baby, Nazis, screaming girls and cursing boys, empty swings, a dark sun. There are worms
  in the attic beams. *(Stands.)* They scream and say we are damned. I
  see dying and grey cats walking. Rosemary is atop the slide. Exalted!
  (Kneels again.) Kay within our room I see a dying baby, Nazis, again
  they scream. *(Stands again.)* and say we are damned. Within our
  once Capitol I see us dying. Rosemary is atop the slide exalted.
SISTER RAT. We swore on Rosemary's Holy Communion book.
BROTHER RAT. Did you tell? Does anyone know?

(The procession watches.)

SISTER RAT. Blake, we swore on our father's Bible the next day in the attic.

BROTHER RAT. Did you tell Sister Rat, does anyone know? *(Kneels.)* It was Easter and my fear of holy days, it was because it was Easter I made us swear.

SISTER RAT. Brother Rat, it was not Easter. It was night after Memorial Day.

BROTHER RAT. No, it was not after Memorial Day. It was the beginning of winter. Bombs fell. It was the War.

SISTER RAT. It was the War.

BROTHER RAT. Our fathers said everything was getting hung and shot in Europe. America wouldn't be safe long. *(Remains kneeling; procession marches across the house to center.)*

SISTER RAT. Remember... we lived in a Holy Chapel with parents and Jesus, Joseph, Mary, our Wise Men and our Shepherd. People said we were the holiest children. *(BROTHER RAT turns face front. SISTER RAT comes down the aisle. Procession is still. SISTER RAT walking.)* Blake, our parents send me to Georgia. It is a house with people who say they are relatives and a garden of great sunflowers. Be my brother's keeper, Blake. I hide under the house, my rat's belly growing all day long I eat sunflower petals, I sit in the garden Blake and hang three gray cats. *(Stands before BROTHER RAT.)* Blake, I'm going to have a baby. I got our baby on the slide. *(Falls.)* Gray cats walk this house all summer I bury my face in the sand so I cannot bear the rats that hide in our attic beams. Blake, why did the War start? I want to hang myself.

BROTHER RAT. Kay, stop sending me the petals from Georgia. Stop saying our mother says you have to go to the State Hospital because of your breakdown. Stop saying you have a rat's belly.

(Procession marches across sound of rats.)

BROTHER AND SISTER RAT. The Nazis! *(Marching.)* The Nazis have invaded our house. *(Softer.)* Why did the War start? We want to hang ourselves. The rats. *(Sound.)* The rats have invaded our Cathedral. *(They rapidly light more candles. Procession returns, marches to the center.)* Our old Rosemary songs. Weren't they beautiful! Our Rosemary Mass. *(Procession watches; silence.)* Yet we weren't safe long. *(They look at procession.)* Soon we will be getting shot and hung. Within our house is a giant slide. Brother and Sister Rat we are.

SISTER RAT. Blake, remember when we lived in our house with Jesus and Joseph and Mary?

BROTHER RAT. Now there are rats in the church books behind every face in the congregation. They all have been on the slide. Every sister bleeds and every brother has made her bleed. The Communion wine.

BROTHER AND SISTER RAT. The Communion wine. Our father gives out the Communion wine and it turns to blood, a red aisle of blood. Too something is inside the altar listening. (SISTER RAT *kneels.*) When we were children we lived in our house, our mother blessed us greatly and God blessed us. Now they listen from the rat beams. (*Sound rats. They remain kneeling. Sound rats.*) It is our mother.

Rosemary, Rosemary was the first girl we ever fell in love with. She lived next door behind a grape arbor her father had built. She often told us stories of Italy and read to us from her Holy Catechism book. She was the prettiest girl in our school. It is one of those midwestern neighborhoods, Italians, Negroes and Jews. Rosemary always went to Catechism and wore Holy Communion dresses.

BROTHER RAT. Where are you going Rosemary? we say. And she says, "I have to go to Catechism." Why do you always go to Catechism? "Because I am Catholic"; then thinking, she says, "Colored people are not Catholics, are they?"

SISTER RAT. I don't think many.

BROTHER RAT. "Well I am. I am a descendant of the Pope and Julius Caesar and the Virgin Mary." Julius Caesar? "Yes, Caesar was the Emperor of all Italia." And are you his descendant? "Yes," she said.

BROTHER AND SISTER RAT. We wish we were descendants of this Caesar, we said, how holy you are, how holy and beautiful. She smiled.

BROTHER RAT. Our school had a picnic in the country and she took my hand. We walked to a place of white birch trees. It is our Palatine, she said. We are sailing to Italy, I said. She was the prettiest girl— the only thing, she has worms in her hair.

SISTER RAT. Great Caesars my brother and I were. Behold us singing greatly walking across our Palatine, my brother holding my hand and I holding his and we are young before the War O Italia. Rosemary was our best friend and taught us Latin and told us stories of Italy. O Rosemary songs.

BROTHER AND SISTER RAT. My sister and I when we were young before the War, and Rosemary our best friend, O Rosemary songs. Now we live in Rat's Chapel. My sister and I.

(BROTHER RAT stares down the aisle.)

BROTHER RAT. It is Rosemary. *(Stares.)* Did you tell? Does anyone know? Did you tell? Does anyone know? You started to cry Kay and I struck you in the face with our father's rifle. It was the beginning of summer. Just getting dark, we were playing and Rosemary said let's go to the playground. After you lay down on the slide so innocently Rosemary said if I loved her I would do what she said. Oh Kay. After that our hiding in the attic rats in the beam. Now there is snow on the playground, ambulances are on every street and within every ambulance is you Kay going to the hospital with a breakdown.

SISTER RAT. Blake, perhaps God will marry us in the State Hospital. Our fellow rats will attend us. Every day I look under our house to see who is listening. *(Aisle bright. Procession marches out.)* I cry all the time now...not sobbing...Blake, did we really go on that slide together? What were those things she made us do while she watched?

BROTHER RAT. We hide in the attic like rats.

SISTER RAT. I cry all the time now.

BROTHER RAT. Within every ambulance is you, Kay. Sister, all the time.

SISTER RAT. *(Sound rats.)* I am waiting for you Blake under the hospital so the Nazis won't see me.

(Procession marches to center.)

BROTHER RAT. The rat comes to the attic crying softly with her head down. She thinks she's going to have a baby. If I were a Nazi I'd shoot her. On the slide she said, Blake I am bleeding. Now there is blood on the aisle of our church. Before rat blood came onto the slide we sailed. We did not swing in chains before blood, we sang with Rosemary. Now I must go to battle. *(Heil. Salutes procession.)* Will you wait for me again at last spring? *(Procession does not answer. BROTHER and SISTER RAT fall down and light candles. BROTHER RAT stands. Stares down aisle.)* Will they wait for me at last spring Rosemary?

(ROSEMARY comes down red aisle in her Holy Communion dress.)

ROSEMARY. Blake the Nazis will get you on the battlefield.

(ROSEMARY and BROTHER RAT stand before each other. SISTER remains kneeling.)

BROTHER RAT. Rosemary atone us, take us beyond the Nazis. We must sail to the Capitol. Atone us. Deliver us unto your descendants.

ROSEMARY. The Nazis are going to get you.

BROTHER RAT. If you do not atone us Kay and I will die. We shall have to die to forget how every day this winter gray cats swing with sunflowers in their mouths because my sister thinks I am the father of a baby. Rosemary will you not atone us?

ROSEMARY. I will never atone you. Perhaps you can put a bullet in your head with your father's shotgun, then your holy battle will be done.
(The procession is at the edge of the house.)

SISTER RAT. *(Kneeling.)* O Holy Music return.
(The procession marches to center.)

ROSEMARY. Come with me, Blake.

BROTHER RAT. How can I ever reach last spring again if I come with you, Rosemary? I must forget how every day this winter gray cats swing with sunflowers in their mouths.

ROSEMARY. Perhaps you can put a bullet in your head.

SISTER RAT. I have a rat's belly.

BROTHER RAT. How can I ever again reach last spring if I come with you, Rosemary?

ROSEMARY. You must damn last spring in your heart. You will never see last spring again.

BROTHER AND SISTER RAT. Then we must put a bullet in our heads.
(Procession marches out. Silence. They stare at ROSEMARY. Procession returns.)

PROCESSION. Goodbye Kay and Blake. We are leaving you.

BROTHER AND SISTER RAT. Jesus, Joseph, Mary, Wise Men and Shepherd, do not leave. Great Caesars, we will be again, you will behold us as we were before Rosemary with the worms in her hair, a spring can come after the War.

PROCESSION. What Kay and Blake?

BROTHER AND SISTER RAT. A spring can come after the War when we grow up we will hang you so that we can run again, walk in the white birch trees. Jesus, Joseph, Wise Men, Shepherd, do not leave us.

PROCESSION. We are leaving because it was Easter.

BROTHER RAT. No, no, it was not Easter, it was the beginning of June.

PROCESSION. In our minds it was Easter. Goodbye Kay and Blake.
(They walk out. A gnawing sound. SISTER RAT *kneels,* BROTHER RAT *and* ROSEMARY *face each other. A gnawing sound.)*

ROSEMARY. In my mind was a vision of us rats all.

BROTHER RAT. If only we could go back to our childhood.

SISTER RAT. Now there will always be rat blood on the rat walls of our rat house just like the blood that came onto the slide.

BROTHER RAT. Beyond my rat head there must remain a new Capitol where Great Kay and I will sing. But no within my shot head I see the dying baby Nazis and Georgia relatives screaming girls cursing boys a dark sun and my grave. I am damned. No . . . when I grow up I will swing again in white trees because beyond this dark rat run and gnawed petals there will remain a Capitol.

SISTER RAT. A Cathedral.

BROTHER RAT. Now within my mind I forever see dying rats. And gray cats walking. Rosemary worms in her hair atop the slide. Our Holy songs in our parents' house weren't they beautiful.

BROTHER AND SISTER RAT. Now it is our rat's mass. *(From now on their voices sound more like gnaws.)* She said if you love me you will. It seemed so innocent. She said it was like a wedding. Now my sister Kay sends me gnawed petals from sunflowers at the State Hospital. She puts them in gray envelopes. Alone I go out to school and the movies. No more do I call by for Rosemary. She made me promise never to tell if you love me she screamed you'll never tell. And I do love her. I found my father's rifle in the attic. Winter time . . . gray time dark boys come laughing starting a game of horseshoes gnawing in the beams. The winter is a place of great gnawed sunflowers. I see them in every street in every room of our house. I pick up gnawed great yellow petals and pray to be atoned.

BROTHER RAT. I am praying to be atoned. I am praying to be atoned dear God. I am begging dear God to be atoned for the Holy Communion that existed between my sister and me and the love that I have for Rosemary. I am praying to be atoned. *(He kisses* ROSEMARY. *He comes down aisle, movements more rat-like . . . voice more like gnawing.)* Bombs fall I am alone in our old house with an attic full of dead rat babies. I must hide.

BROTHER AND SISTER RAT. God we ask you to stop throwing dead rat babies.

*(*BROTHER RAT *kneels.)*

BROTHER RAT. When I asked you yesterday the day they brought my sister Kay home from the State Hospital, you said God, Blake perhaps you must put a bullet in your head then your battle will be done. God, I think of Rosemary all the time. I love her. I told myself afterward it was one of the boys playing horseshoes who had done those horrible things on the slide with my sister. Yet I told Kay I am her keeper yet I told Rosemary I love her. It is the secret of my battlefield.

SISTER RAT. Here we are again in our attic where we once played games, but neither of us liked it because from time to time you could hear the rats. But it was our place to be alone, Blake now that I am home from the hospital we must rid our minds of my rat's belly. Can you see it? You did not visit me in the hospital Brother Rat. Blake I thought you were my brother's keeper.

BROTHER RAT. Everywhere I go I step in your blood. Rosemary I wanted you to love me. (*He turns—aisles bright—gnawing sound—battlefield sounds.*)

BROTHER AND SISTER RAT. God is hanging and shooting us.

SISTER RAT. Remember Brother Rat before I bled, before descending bombs and death on our capitol we walked the Palatine . . . we went to the movies. Now the Germans and Caesar's army are after us, Blake.

(*He goes back to* ROSEMARY *whose back is to him and starts.*)

ROSEMARY. The Nazis are after you. My greatest grief was your life together. My greatest grief.

BROTHER AND SISTER RAT. (*Look up.*) Now every time we will go outside we will walk over the grave of our dead baby Red aisle runners will be on the street when we come to the playground Rosemary will forever be atop the slide exalted with worms in her hair. (*They kneel, then rise, kneel, then rise.*) We must very soon get rid of our rat heads so dying baby voices on the beams will no more say we are our lost Caesars.

ROSEMARY. It is our wedding now, Blake.

BROTHER AND SISTER RAT. Brother and Sister Rat we are very soon we must.

SISTER RAT. We are rats in the beam now.

ROSEMARY. My greatest grief was your life together. The Nazis will come soon now.

BROTHER AND SISTER RAT. Every time we go out red blood runners will be on the street. (*They kneel, then rise, kneel, then rise.*) At least soon very soon we will get rid of our rat heads and rat voices in beams will say no more we are your lost Caesars.

ROSEMARY. It is our wedding, Blake. The Nazis have come. (*Marching.*) Brother and Sister Rat you are now soon you will become headless and all will cease the dark sun will be bright no more and no more sounds of shooting in the distance. *(Marching procession appears bearing shotguns.)*

BROTHER AND SISTER RAT. We will become headless and all will cease the dark sun will be bright no more and no more sounds of shooting in the distance. It will be the end. *(The procession shoots, they scamper, more shots, they fall,* ROSEMARY *remains.)*

CURTAIN

Sun

Dedicated to Malcolm X

NOTE: MOVEMENTS

Movements of the Man
His orbiting
Sun's orbiting
Movements of the Moon
Movements of the Sun
Wire
Revolving of the head
MAN. Flowers and Water
    (Steel wire appears encircling them.)
The adoration of kings and a
kneeling youth
    (Red flashes.)
A madonna and a child, a man
A madonna and a child, a man
a madonna and a child and a
unicorn a study of a kneeling angel
    (Red sun flashes top left. Moon image moves. MAN *watches the red*
    sun, tries to move his arms upward toward it.)
there exist landscapes flowers
and water views of the coast of
Italy cloudbursts lilies a
mountain a mountain of lilies
    (A purple light. MAN *tries to move his arms.)*
and the heart,

(Red sun revolves. HE *watches it and tries to move. A yellow light. Half of the moon vanishes.* HE *watches it fearfully over his shoulder as the half slowly drifts away. Then before him* HE *watches red sun revolving. It disappears in front of him, lower left.* MAN *is still, then looks again at vanished half moon.)*

Yes, and the heart and the tendons
of the neck a landscape with a
view over a valley mountains
beyond a drawing of a square castle

(Orange sun appears top right. Greater hope.)

Yes, my heart and tendons
of the neck landscapes mountains
a drawing of a square castle

(Moon still in half. Orange sun spins. MAN *watches greatly fearful as if the spinning sun held a grim omen, but goes on speaking hopefully.)*

the head of a man, yes a man's
head a man's shoulders the
organs of a woman an embryo
in the uterus the heart a
nude man a nude man
with his arms stretched out

(Pause. Intently watches orange sun spin.)

As a young man I felt myself
to be in the midst of sun

(Orange sun spins. Yellow sun now appears, spins. Beautiful sound. Could be this spinning.)

I liked to think my heart
led to light. Yet I discerned
coming dishonor.

(Sound and yellow and orange suns vanish. As always, when things vanish, MAN *is greatly perturbed. A black sun flashes top center then goes downward.* HE *watches its downward descent. Silence. Behind him the moon loses a quarter.* HE *watches it over his shoulder. The quarter vanishes slowly, moving away from him.)*

Yes the position of my blood vessels
the blood vessels in my face
a nude man with his arms
stretched out my lungs my
main arteries. *(Pause.)*

a branch of blackberry
> *(Black sun that has remained grows larger, a purple light.* MAN *watches black sun grow large.)*

Yes, water in motion a
spray of a plant a domed
church, a flying machine
horses horses and riders
> *(A yellow sun flashes orbits the wire vanishes. Moon still at quarter. Now at lower right the* MAN*'s disembodied head appears. Large black sun vanishes wire starts to move slowly in a circle. Long silence.* MAN *speaks looking at dismembered head before him.)*

My head, the head of Christ
the head of an apostle head
of St. Anne Head of the Virgin
Head of the infant St. John
Head of the infant Jesus. *(Pause.)*
my head dismembered
> *(Staring at his dismembered head disbelieving.)*

No, I still dream children
children, the body and arms
of a child. *(Pause.)*
Yet my head. Dead
> *(*HE *goes on staring at his head as a black sun orbits twice. New light comes onto the whole scene. Full moon comes again, but a slightly different texture, more disturbing. Wire still slowly moving.* MAN *waits. The position of the moon,* MAN, *wire, head and all slightly change position so now less symmetry exists. The expression on the face of the head changes. All of these changes seem to be felt within the* MAN *since they are his inner state. The* MAN*'s own head grows distorted as* HE *watches the wire move around him. His head watches him, comes closer, smiles. Wire closer. Then a long waiting. Great imbalance of objects. Then loudly the moon fragments slowly and completely to pieces. Long fragmentation.* HE *tries to watch from his angular position.* HE *waits. Long fragmentation. Red sun appears top right. As the moon loudly totally fragments behind him* HE *looks up at the new red sun.)*

When a new sun appears
I think before I was born
my mother dreamed she saw
me in the sun then the

sun went down and at
night I appear within
the moon. . . . And as the moon
fragments and all is imbalanced
I keep on thinking landscapes
flowers and water views
of the coast of Italy
cloudbursts lilies, a
mountain of lilies the heart
>   *(Moon fragments again. Red sun revolves closer to* MAN*'s face.*
>   *Orange sun appears, drops across him, disappears. Head watches*
>   MAN *as* MAN *watches all. Fragmented moon, red sun, vanished*
>   *orange sun.)*

Yet all is in imbalance
no I must think of
trees, a tree, a tree
no a tree, a tree.
Water in motion
>   *(Red sun revolves rapidly, closer to his own face and starts to spin*
>   *mysteriously, before his face.)*

No rocks and streams
and flowers and violas
and sketches of landscapes
a river with a canal
alongside and a castle
on a hill flower rushes
>   *(His dismembered head vanishes.)*

star of Bethlehem
and other plants . . .
a spray of brambles
>   *(Sun passes through his face leaving a light before him. Loud noise*
>   *of the moon fragmenting on his ear.)*

No rocks and streams
and flowers and violas
and sketches of landscapes
a river with a canal
alongside and a castle
on a hill
>   *(Louder fragmenting.)*

flowering rushes, a star
of Bethlehem and other
plants . . . a spray of brambles
> *(A smell of spray of brambles fills the air.* MAN*'s arms appear more disjointed.* MAN *continues loudly fragmenting, an orange spinning sun appears lower left dismembered head appears top left and starts to orbit wire still revolving slowly a disembodied arm appears lower right.)*

the sun is now myself
dismembered in darkness
my blood my dismembered
self at sundown on the moon.
> *(*HE *watches his arm. The sun slowly vanishes moving upward beyond his vision.* HE *understands that his own arms are growing more disjointed. Noises of spattering. Suddenly blood starts to run out of the fragmented moon. Smell of blood.* MAN *grows more disjointed while his head orbits and while blood runs out of the dark fragmented moon. Great smell of blood, noises of spattering as if the blood were falling against his head.)*

No the head of this man
a man's head and shoulders
the organs of my woman
as embryo in the uterus
its heart
this nude man
this nude man with his
arms stretched out
> *(*HE *tries to stretch his arms. Suddenly many suns explode over the* MAN. *More blood pours out of the fragmented moon. More suns explode. Wire revolves closer to his head. His dismembered head. Still orbiting. A disembodied leg appears, vanishes. In the third time suns explode over the whole scene very slowly blood stops pouring out of the fragmented moon. Very slowly suns stop exploding and very slowly the fragmented moon changes into the* MAN *very slowly limb by limb the limbs slightly bloodied. Very slowly. At the same time his head silently revolves and at the same time very slowly blood comes onto his own face and* HE *becomes blotted out by it.* HE *lowers his blotted head. Silence. Head revolves. His own head blotted blank by blood.)*

When I was young I did
dream myself to be in the
midst of suns now fragmented
in the moon I am the head
of a bear the paws of a
dog the paws of a wolf
heads of monsters, a dragon . . .
a lizard symbolizing this truth
Now where is my head the
head of Christ the head of
an apostle head of St. Anne
Head of the Virgin head of
the infant St. John, head
of the infant Jesus. Where?
> (*Silence. Revolving head stops. Orange spinning sun appears, lower
> right.* MAN, *now more disjointed, with blotted head.*)

I still dream of a woman
wearing a bodice of interlaced
ribbons a young woman
the head of a girl a girl's
braided hair the human
figure in a circle, man
man carrying earth
As my head moves
dead as the bones
and tendons of
my arms move dead I still dream
Still I dream of the heart
> (*The whole scene starts moving into imbalance.*)

The position of the blood vessels
in the neck and the face
> (*Dark blue and purple suns appear, revolve.*)

A crowned eagle standing on a globe
> (*The moon, the* MAN, *the wire the head all moving to a new
> imbalance. Then limb by limb the* MAN*'s body becomes blotted by
> blood.*)

Yes the heart
the head and shoulder of a man
muscles of the face and arms
a nude man

organs of a woman
an embryo in the uterus
the heart
Tuscany
A tree

> *(The* MAN*'s body becomes more blotted by blood while the
> symmetry of the scene is lost. Disembodied legs appear then vanish.)*

Arezzo
Borgho
San Sepulchro
Perugia
Chiusi and Siena

> *(The whole scene moves violently. The boundaries of the moon
> vanish. Black suns revolve. In the moon* MAN*'s body falls apart.)*

Two trees on the
bank of a stream
I still dream

> *(His body in the moon falls apart as the moon totally loses
> boundaries and all parts of his body fly into space.)*

A river with a rope ferry.

> *(Wire breaks. Flashing grey and black suns. Collision of objects.
> Great collision, then the* MAN *who is blotted out by blood becomes
> smaller and smaller. Great collision of his flying limbs.* MAN
> *becomes smaller and smaller and vanishes into a tiny red sun.)*
>
> *Vanished* MAN*'s voice:*

The Arno

> *(*MAN *has vanished into a tiny red sun. Red sun turns black.)*
>
> *Vanished* MAN*'s voice:*

A river with a canal alongside.

> *(Flying limbs become still, vanish. Wire vanishes. All vanishes.
> Except tiny black sun.)*
>
> *Vanished* MAN*'s voice:*

And a castle on a hill
flowering rushes.
I still

DARKNESS

A Movie Star Has to Star
in Black and White

A Movie Star Has to Star in Black and White was done as a work in progress at the New York Shakespeare Festival in New York on November 5, 1976, with the following cast:

Wallace	*Frank Adu*
Marlon Brando	*Ray Barry*
Eddie	*Robert Christian*
Paul Henreid	*Richard Dow*
Hattie	*Gloria Foster*
Montgomery Clift	*C. S. Hayward*
Jean Peters/Columbia Pictures Lady	*Karen Ludwig*
Clara	*Robbie McCauley*
Bette Davis	*Avra Petrides*
Shelley Winters	*Ellin Ruskin*

Director: Joseph Chaikin
Lights: Beverly Emmons
Costumes: Kate Carmel
Music: Peter Golub

NOTES: The movie music throughout is romantic.

The ship, the deck, the railings and the dark boat can all be done with lights and silhouettes.

All the colors are shades of black and white.

These movie stars are romantic and moving, never camp or farcical, and the attitudes of the supporting players to the movie stars is deadly serious.

The movie music sometimes plays at intervals when CLARA*'s thought is still.*

CHARACTERS

CLARA

"Leading Roles" are played by actors who look exactly like:

BETTE DAVIS

PAUL HENREID

JEAN PETERS

MARLON BRANDO

MONTGOMERY CLIFT

SHELLEY WINTERS

(They all look exactly like their movie roles.)

Supporting roles by

THE MOTHER

THE FATHER

THE HUSBAND

> *(They all look like photographs* CLARA *keeps of them except when they're in the hospital.)*

SCENES:

I. Hospital lobby and *Now Voyager*

II. Brother's room and *Viva Zapata*

III. Clara's old room and *A Place in the Sun*

Dark stage. From darkness center appears the COLUMBIA PICTURES LADY *in a bright light.*

COLUMBIA PICTURES LADY. Summer, New York, 1955. Summer, Ohio, 1963. The scenes are *Now Voyager, Viva Zapata,* and *A Place in the Sun.*

The leading roles are played by Bette Davis, Paul Henreid, Jean Peters, Marlon Brando, Montgomery Clift and Shelley Winters. Supporting roles are played by the mother, the father, the husband. A bit role is played by Clara.

Now Voyager takes place in the hospital lobby.

Viva Zapata takes place in the brother's room.

A Place in the Sun takes place in Clara's old room.

June 1963.

My producer is Joel Steinberg. He looks different from what I once thought, not at all like that picture in *Vogue.* He was in *Vogue* with a group of people who were going to do a musical about Socrates. In the photograph Joel's hair looked dark and his skin smooth. In real life his skin is blotched. Everyone says he drinks a lot.

Lately I think often of killing myself. Eddie Jr. plays outside in the playground. I'm very lonely. . . . Met Lee Strasberg: the members of the playwrights unit were invited to watch his scene. Geraldine Page, Rip Torn and Norman Mailer were there. . . . I wonder why I lie so much to my mother about how I feel. . . . My father once said his life has been nothing but a life of hypocrisy and that's why his photograph smiled. While Eddie Jr. plays outside I read Edith Wharton, a book on Egypt and Chinua Achebe. LeRoi Jones, Ted Joans and Allen Ginsburg are reading in the Village. Eddie comes every evening right before dark. He wants to know if I'll go back to him for the sake of our son.

> (*She fades. At the back of the stage as in a distance a dim light goes on a large doorway in the hospital. Visible is the foot of the white hospital bed and a figure lying upon it. Movie music.* CLARA *stands at the doorway of the room. She is a Negro woman of thirty-three wearing a maternity dress. She does not enter the room but turns away and stands very still. Movie music.*)

CLARA. (*Reflective; very still facing away from the room.*) My brother is the same . . . my father is coming . . . very depressed.

Before I left New York I got my typewriter from the pawnshop. I'm terribly tired, trying to do a page a day, yet my play is coming together.

Each day I wonder with what or with whom can I co-exist in a true union?

> (*She turns and stares into her brother's room. Scene fades out; then bright lights that convey an ocean liner in motion.*)

SCENE I

Movie music. On the deck of the ocean liner from "Now Voyager" are BETTE DAVIS *and* PAUL HENREID. *They sit at a table slightly off stage center.* BETTE DAVIS *has on a large white summer hat and* PAUL HENREID *a dark summer suit. The light is romantic and glamorous. Beyond backstage left are deck chairs. It is bright sunlight on the deck.*

BETTE DAVIS. (*To Paul.*) June 1955.

When I have the baby I wonder will I turn into a river of blood and die? My mother almost died when I was born. I've always felt sad that I couldn't have been an angel of mercy to my father and mother and saved them from their torment.

I used to hope when I was a little girl that one day I would rise above them, an angel with glowing wings and cover them with peace. But I failed. When I came among them it seems to me I did not bring them peace . . . but made them more disconsolate. The crosses they bore always made me sad.

The one reality I wanted never came true . . . to be their angel of mercy to unite them. I keep remembering the time my mother threatened to kill my father with the shotgun. I keep remembering my father's going away to marry a girl who talked to willow trees.

(Onto the deck wander the MOTHER, *the* FATHER, *and the* HUSBAND. *They are Negroes. The parents are as they were when young in 1929 in Atlanta, Georgia. The* MOTHER *is small, pale and very beautiful. She has on a white summer dress and white shoes. The* FATHER *is small and dark skinned. He has on a Morehouse sweater, knickers and a cap. They both are emotional and nervous. In presence both are romanticized. The* HUSBAND *is twenty-eight and handsome. He is dressed as in the summer of 1955 wearing a seersucker suit from Kleins that cost thirteen dollars.)*

BETTE DAVIS. In the scrapbook that my father left is a picture of my mother in Savannah, Georgia in 1929.

MOTHER. *(Sitting down in a deck chair, takes a cigarette out of a beaded purse and smokes nervously. She speaks bitterly in a voice with a strong Georgia accent.)* In our Georgia town the white people lived on one side. It had pavement on the streets and sidewalks and mail was delivered. The Negroes lived on the other side and the roads were dirt and had no sidewalk and you had to go to the post office to pick up your mail. In the center of Main Street was a fountain and white people drank on one side and Negroes drank on the other.

When a Negro bought something in a store he couldn't try it on. A Negro couldn't sit down at the soda fountain in the drug store but had to take his drink out. In the movies at Montefore you had to go in the side and up the stairs and sit in the last four rows.

When you arrived on the train from Cincinnati the first thing you saw was the WHITE and COLORED signs at the depot. White people had one waiting room and we Negroes had another. We sat in only two cars and white people had the rest of the train.

(She is facing PAUL HENREID *and* BETTE DAVIS. *The* FATHER *and the* HUSBAND *sit in deck chairs that face the other side of the*

sea. The FATHER *also smokes. He sits hunched over with his head down thinking. The* HUSBAND *takes an old test book out of a battered briefcase and starts to study. He looks exhausted and has dark circles under his eyes. His suit is worn.)*

BETTE DAVIS. My father used to say John Hope Franklin, Du Bois and Benjamin Mays were fine men.

(Bright sunlight on FATHER *sitting on other side of deck.* FATHER *gets up and comes toward them . . . to* BETTE DAVIS.*)*

FATHER. Cleveland is a place for opportunity, leadership, a progressive city, a place for education, a chance to come out of the back woods of Georgia. We Negro leaders dream of leading our people out of the wilderness.

(He passes her and goes along the deck whistling. Movie music. BETTE DAVIS *stands up looking after the* FATHER . . . *then distractedly to* PAUL HENREID.*)*

BETTE DAVIS. *(Very passionate.)* I'd give anything in the world if I could just once talk to Jesus.

Sometimes he walks through my room but he doesn't stop long enough for us to talk . . . he has an aureole. *(Then to the* FATHER *who is almost out of sight on the deck whistling.)* Why did you marry the girl who talked to willow trees? *(To* PAUL HENREID.*)* He left us to marry a girl who talked to willow trees.

*(*FATHER *is whistling,* MOTHER *is smoking, then the* FATHER *vanishes into a door on deck.* BETTE DAVIS *walks down to railing.* PAUL HENREID *follows her.)*

BETTE DAVIS. June 1955.

My mother said when she was a girl in the summers she didn't like to go out. She'd sit in the house and help her grandmother iron or shell peas and sometimes she'd sit on the steps.

My father used to come and sit on the steps. He asked her for her first "date." They went for a walk up the road and had an ice cream at Miss Ida's Icecream Parlor and walked back down the road. She was fifteen.

My mother says that my father was one of the most well thought of boys in the town, Negro or white. And he was so friendly. He always had a friendly word for everybody.

He used to tell my mother his dreams how he was going to go up north. There was opportunity for Negroes up north and when he was finished at Morehouse he was going to get a job in someplace like New York.

And she said when she walked down the road with my father people were so friendly.

He organized a colored baseball team in Montefore and he was the Captain. And she used to go and watch him play baseball and everybody called him "Cap."

Seven more months and the baby.

Eddie and I don't talk too much these days.

Very often I try to be in bed by the time he comes home.

Most nights I'm wide awake until at least four. I wake up about eight and then I have a headache.

When I'm wide awake I see Jesus a lot.

My mother is giving us the money for the doctor bill. Eddie told her he will pay it back.

Also got a letter from her; it said I hope things work out for you both. And pray, pray sometimes. Love Mother.

We also got a letter from Eddie's mother. Eddie's brother had told her that Eddie and I were having some problems. In her letter which was enclosed in a card she said when Eddie's sister had visited us she noticed that Eddie and I don't go to church. She said we mustn't forget the Lord, because God takes care of everything. . . . God gives us peace and no matter what problems Eddie and I were having if we trusted in Him God would help us. It was the only letter from Eddie's mother that I ever saved.

Even though the card was Hallmark.
July 1955.

Eddie doesn't seem like the same person since he came back from Korea. And now I'm pregnant again. When I lost the baby he was thousands of miles away. All that bleeding. I'll never forgive him. The Red Cross let him send me a telegram to say he was sorry. I can't believe we used to be so in love on the campus and park the car and kiss and kiss. Yet I was a virgin when we married. A virgin who was to bleed and bleed . . . when I was in the hospital all I had was a photograph of Eddie in GI clothes standing in a woods in Korea. *(Pause.)* Eddie and I went to the Thalia on 95th and Broadway. There's a film festival this summer. We saw *Double Indemnity, The Red Shoes* and *A Place in the Sun*. Next week *Viva Zapata* is coming. Afterwards we went to Reinzis on Macdougal Street and had Viennese coffee. We forced an enthusiasm we didn't feel. We took the subway back up to 116th Street and walked to Bencroft Hall. In the middle of the night I woke up and wrote in my diary.

(A bright light at hospital doorway. CLARA *younger, fragile, anxious. Movie music. She leaves hospital doorway and comes onto the deck from the door her father entered. She wears maternity dress, white wedgies, her hair is straightened as in the fifties. She has a passive beauty and is totally preoccupied. She pays no attention to anyone, only writing in a notebook. Her movie stars speak for her.* CLARA *lets her movie stars star in her life.* BETTE DAVIS *and* PAUL HENREID *are at the railing. The* MOTHER *is smoking. The* HUSBAND *gets up and comes across the deck carrying his battered briefcase. He speaks to* CLARA *who looks away.* PAUL HENREID *goes on staring at the sea.)*

HUSBAND. Clara, please tell me everything the doctor said about the delivery and how many days you'll be in the hospital.

(Instead of CLARA, BETTE DAVIS *replies.* PAUL HENREID *is oblivious of him.)*

BETTE DAVIS. *(Very remote.)* I get very jealous of you Eddie. You're do-ing something with your life.

(He tries to kiss CLARA. *She moves away and walks along the deck and writes in notebook.)*

BETTE DAVIS. *(To Eddie.)* Eddie, do you think I have floating anxiety? You said everyone in Korea had floating anxiety. I think I might have it. *(Pause.)* Do you think I'm catatonic?

EDDIE. *(Staring at* CLARA.*)* I'm late to class now. We'll talk when I come home. *(He leaves.)* When I get paid I'm going to take you to Birdland. Dizzy's coming back.

(Movie music.)

CLARA. July.

I can't sleep. My head always full of thoughts night and day. I feel so nervous. Sometimes I hardly hear what people are saying. I'm writing a lot of my play, I don't want to show it to anyone though. Suppose it's no good. *(Reads her play.)*

They are dragging his body across the green his white hair hang-ing down. They are taking off his shoes and he is stiff. I must get into the chapel to see him. I must. He is my blood father. God, let me in to his burial. *(He grabs her down center. She, kneeling.)* I call God and the Owl answers. *(Softer.)* It haunts my Tower calling, its feathers are blowing against the cell wall, speckled in the garden on the fig tree, it comes, feathered, great hollow-eyed with yellow skin and yellow eyes, the flying bastard. From my Tower I keep calling

and the only answer is the Owl, God. *(Pause. Stands.)* I am only
yearning for our kingdom, God.
   (Movie music.)
BETTE DAVIS. *(At railing.)* My father tried to commit suicide once
   when I was in High School. It was the afternoon he was presented
   an award by the Mayor of Cleveland at a banquet celebrating the
   completion of the New Settlement building. It had taken my father
   seven years to raise money for the New Settlement which was the
   center of Negro life in our community. He was given credit for being the one without whom it couldn't have been done. It was his
   biggest achievement.
      I went upstairs and found him whistling in his room. I asked
   him what was wrong. I want to see my dead mama and papa he
   said, that's all I really live for is to see my mama and papa. I stared at
   him. As I was about to leave the room he said I've been waiting to
   jump off the roof of the Settlement for a long time. I just had to
   wait until it was completed . . . and he went on whistling.
      He had tried to jump off the roof but had fallen on a scaffold.
      (Movie music. The deck has grown dark except for the light on
      BETTE DAVIS *and* PAUL HENREID *and* CLARA.*)*
CLARA. I loved the wedding night scene from *Viva Zapata* and the
   scene where the peasants met Zapata on the road and forced the soldiers to take the rope from his neck . . . when they shot Zapata at the
   end I cried.
      (Deck darker. She walks along the deck and into door, leaving
      PAUL HENREID *and* BETTE DAVIS *at railing. She arrives at the*
      hospital doorway, then enters her brother's room, standing at the
      foot of his bed. Her brother is in a coma.)
CLARA. *(To her brother.)* Once I asked you romantically when you came
   back to the United States on a short leave, how do you like Europe
   Wally? You were silent. Finally you said, I get into a lot of fights
   with the Germans. You stared at me. And got up and went into the
   dining room to the dark sideboard and got a drink.
      (Darkness. Movie music.)

SCENE II

Hospital room and Viva Zapata. *The hospital bed is now totally visible. In*
it lies WALLY *in a white gown. The light of the room is twilight on a sum-*
mer evening. CLARA*'s brother is handsome and in his late twenties. Beyond*

the bed is steel hospital apparatus. CLARA *stands by her brother's bedside. There is no real separation from the hospital room and* Viva Zapata *and the ship lights as there should have been none in* Now Voyager. *Simultaneously brighter lights come up stage center. Wedding night scene in* Viva Zapata. *Yet it is still the stateroom within the ship. Movie music.* MARLON BRANDO *and* JEAN PETERS *are sitting on the bed. They are both dressed as in* Viva Zapata.

JEAN PETERS. *(To Brando.)* July 11.

I saw my father today. He's come from Georgia to see my brother. He lives in Savannah with his second wife. He seemed smaller and hunched over. When I was young he seemed energetic, speaking before civic groups and rallying people to give money to the Negro Settlement.

In the last years he seems introspective, petty and angry. Today he was wearing a white nylon sports shirt that looked slightly too big . . . his dark arms thin. He had on a little straw sport hat cocked slightly to the side.

We stood together in my brother's room. My father touched my brother's bare foot with his hand. My brother is in a coma. *(Silent.)*

Eddie and I were married downstairs in this house. My brother was best man. We went to Colorado, but soon after Eddie was sent to Korea. My mother has always said that she felt if she and my father hadn't been fighting so much maybe I wouldn't have lost the baby. After I lost the baby I stopped writing to Eddie and decided I wanted to get a divorce when he came back from Korea. He hadn't been at Columbia long before I got pregnant again with Eddie Jr.

(MARLON BRANDO listens. They kiss tenderly. She stands up. She is bleeding. She falls back on her bed. BRANDO *pulls a sheet out from under her. The sheets are black. Movie music.)*

JEAN PETERS. The doctor says I have to stay in bed when I'm not at the hospital.

(From now until the end MARLON BRANDO *continuously helps* JEAN PETERS *change sheets. He puts the black sheets on the floor around them.)*

CLARA. *(To her brother, at the same time.)* Wally, you just have to get well. I know you will, even though you do not move or speak.

(Sits down by his bedside watching him. Her MOTHER *enters. She is wearing a rose colored summer dress and small hat. The mother is in her fifties now. She sits down by her son's bedside and holds his*

*hand. Silence in the room. The light of the room is constant
twilight. They are in the constant dim twilight while* BRANDO
and PETERS *star in a dazzling wedding night light. Mexican
peasant wedding music, Zapata remains throughout compassionate,
heroic, tender. While* CLARA *and her* MOTHER *talk* BRANDO *and*
PETERS *sit on the bed, then enact the Zapata teach-me-to-read
scene in which* BRANDO *asks* PETERS *to get him a book and teach
him to read.)*

MOTHER. What did I do? What did I do?

CLARA. What do you mean?

MOTHER. I don't know what I did to make my children so unhappy.
   *(*JEAN PETERS *gets book for* BRANDO.*)*

CLARA. I'm not unhappy mother.

MOTHER. Yes you are.

CLARA. I'm not unhappy. I'm very happy. I just want to be a writer.
   Please don't think I'm unhappy.

MOTHER. Your family's not together and you don't seem happy. *(They
   sit and read.)*

CLARA. I'm very happy mother. Very. I've just won an award and I'm
   going to have a play produced. I'm very happy.
   (Silence. The MOTHER *straightens the sheet on her son's bed.)*

MOTHER. When you grow up in boarding school like I did, the thing
   you dream of most is to see your children together with their families.

CLARA. Mother you mustn't think I'm unhappy because I am, I really
   am, very happy.

MOTHER. I just pray you'll soon get yourself together and make some
   decisions about your life. I pray for you every night. Shouldn't you
   go back to Eddie especially since you're pregnant?
   (There are shadows of the ship's lights as if Now Voyager *is still in
   motion.)*

CLARA. Mother, Eddie doesn't understand me.
   (Silence. Twilight dimmer, MOTHER *holds* WALLY*'s hand. Movie
   light bright on* JEAN PETERS *and* MARLON BRANDO.*)*

JEAN PETERS. My brother Wally's still alive.

CLARA. *(To her diary.)* Wally was in an accident. A telegram from my
   mother. Your brother was in an automobile accident...has been
   unconscious since last night in St. Luke's hospital. Love, Mother.

JEAN PETERS. Depressed.

CLARA. Came to Cleveland. Eddie came to La Guardia to bring me
   money for my plane ticket and to say he was sorry about Wally who

was best man at our wedding. Eddie looks at me with such sadness. It fills me with hatred for him and myself.

(BRANDO *is at the window looking down on the peasants. Mexican wedding music.*)

JEAN PETERS. Very depressed, and afraid at night since Eddie and I separated. I try to write a page a day on another play. It's going to be called a Lesson In Dead Language. The main image is a girl in a white organdy dress covered with menstrual blood.

(CLARA *is writing in her diary. Her* MOTHER *sits holding* WALLY's *hand,* BRANDO *stares out the window,* JEAN PETERS *sits on the bed.* Now Voyager *ship, shadows and light.*)

CLARA. It is twilight outside and very warm. The window faces a lawn, very green, with a fountain beyond. Wally does not speak or move. He is in a coma. *(Twilight dims.)*

It bothers me that Eddie had to give me money for the ticket to come home. I don't have any money of my own: the option from my play is gone and I don't know how I will be able to work and take care of Eddie Jr. Maybe Eddie and I should go back together.

(FATHER *enters the room, stands at the foot of his son's bed. He is in his fifties now and wears a white nylon sports shirt a little too big, his dark arms thin, baggy pants and a little straw sports hat cocked to the side. He has been drinking. The moment he enters the room the mother takes out a cigarette and starts to nervously smoke. They do not look at each other. He speaks to* CLARA, *then glances in the direction of the* MOTHER. *He then touches his son's bare feet.* WALLY *is lying on his back, his hands to his sides.* CLARA *gets up and goes to the window.* BRANDO *comes back and sits on the bed next to* JEAN PETERS. *They all remain for a long while silent. Suddenly the* MOTHER *goes and throws herself into her daughter's arms and cries.*)

MOTHER. The doctor said he doesn't see how Wally has much of a chance of surviving: his brain is damaged.

(*She clings to her daughter and cries. Simultaneously.*)

JEAN PETERS. *(To* BRANDO.*)* I'm writing on my play. It's about a girl who turns into an Owl. Ow. *(Recites from her writings.)* He came to me in the outhouse, in the fig tree. He told me, You are an owl, I am your beginning. I call God and the Owl answers. It haunts my tower, calling.

(*Silence.* FATHER *slightly drunk goes toward his former wife and his daughter. The* MOTHER *runs out of the room into the lobby.*)

MOTHER. I did everything to make you happy and still you left me for another woman.

(CLARA *stares out of the window.* FATHER *follows the* MOTHER *into the lobby and stares at her.* JEAN PETERS *stands up. She is bleeding. She falls back on the bed.* MARLON BRANDO *pulls a sheet out from under her. The sheets are black. Movie music.*)

JEAN PETERS. The doctor says I have to stay in bed when I'm not at the hospital.

(*From now until the end* MARLON BRANDO *continuously helps* JEAN PETERS *change sheets. He puts the black sheets on the floor around them.*)

JEAN PETERS. This reminds me of when Eddie was in Korea and I had the miscarriage. For days there was blood on the sheets. Eddie's letters from Korea were about a green hill. He sent me photographs of himself. The Red Cross, the letter said, says I cannot call you and I cannot come.

For a soldier to come home there has to be a death in the family.

MOTHER. (*In the hallway she breaks down further.*) I have never wanted to go back to the south to live. I hate it. I suffered nothing but humiliation and why should I have gone back there?

FATHER. You ought to have gone back with me. It's what I wanted to do.

MOTHER. I never wanted to go back.

FATHER. You yellow bastard. You're a yellow bastard. That's why you didn't want to go back.

MOTHER. You black nigger.

JEAN PETERS. (*Reciting her play.*) I call God and the Owl answers, it haunts my tower, calling, its feathers are blowing against the cell wall, it comes feathered, great hollow-eyes... with yellow skin and yellow eyes, the flying bastard. From my tower I keep calling and the only answer is the Owl.

July 8 I got a telegram from my mother. It said your brother has been in an accident and has been unconscious since last night in St. Luke's hospital. Love, Mother. I came home.

My brother is in a white gown on white sheets.

(*The* MOTHER *and the* FATHER *walk away from one another. A sudden bright light on the Hospital Lobby and on* WALLY's *room.* CLARA *has come to the doorway and watches her parents.*)

MOTHER. (*To both her former husband and her daughter.*) I was asleep and the police called and told me Wally didn't feel well and would I please come down to the police station and pick him up. When I arrived at the police station they told me they had just taken him to the hospital because he felt worse and they would drive to the hospital. When I arrived here the doctor told me the truth: Wally's car had crashed into another car at an intersection and Wally had been thrown from the car, his body hitting a mail box and he was close to death.

(Darkness.)

SCENE III

JEAN PETERS *and* BRANDO *are still sitting in* Viva Zapata *but now there are photographs above the bed of* CLARA's *parents when they were young, as they were in* Now Voyager. WALLY's *room is dark. Lights of the ship from* Now Voyager.

JEAN PETERS. Wally is not expected to live. *(She tries to stand.)* He does not move. He is in a coma. *(Pause.)* There are so many memories in this house. The rooms besiege me.

My brother has been living here in his old room with my mother. He is separated from his wife and every night has been driving his car crazily around the street where she now lives. On one of these nights was when he had the accident.

*(*JEAN PETERS *and* BRANDO *stare at each other. A small dark boat from side opposite* WALLY's *room. In it are* SHELLEY WINTERS *and* MONTGOMERY CLIFT. CLARA *sits behind* SHELLEY WINTERS *writing in her notebook.* MONTGOMERY CLIFT *is rowing. It is* A Place in the Sun. *Movie music.* BRANDO *and* JEAN PETERS *continue to change sheets.)*

CLARA. I am bleeding. When I'm not at the hospital I have to stay in bed. I am writing my poems. Eddie's come from New York to see my brother. My brother does not speak or move.

*(*MONTGOMERY CLIFT *silently rows dark boat across.* CLARA *has on a nightgown and looks as if she has been very sick, and heartbroken by her brother's accident.* MONTGOMERY CLIFT, *as were* HENREID *and* BRANDO, *is mute. If they did speak they would speak lines from their actual movies. As the boat comes across* BRANDO *and* PETERS *are still. Movie music.* EDDIE *comes in room with* JEAN PETERS *and* BRANDO. *He still has his textbook and briefcase.* SHELLEY WINTERS *sits opposite* MONTGOMERY CLIFT *as in* A Place in the Sun. CLARA *is writing in her notebook.)*

EDDIE. *(To* JEAN PETERS; *simultaneously* CLARA *is writing in her diary.)* Are you sure you want to go on with this?

JEAN PETERS. This?

EDDIE. You know what I mean, this obsession of yours?

JEAN PETERS. Obsession?

EDDIE. Yes, this obsession to be a writer?

JEAN PETERS. Of course I'm sure.

(BRANDO *is reading.* CLARA *from the boat.)*

CLARA. I think the Steinbergs have lost interest in my play. I got a letter from them that said they have to go to Italy and would be in touch when they came back.

EDDIE. I have enough money for us to live well with my teaching. We could all be so happy.

CLARA. *(From boat.)* Ever since I was twelve I have secretly dreamed of being a writer. Everyone says it's unrealistic for a Negro to want to write.

Eddie says I've become shy and secretive and I can't accept the passage of time, and that my diaries consume me and that my diaries make me a spectator watching my life like watching a black and white movie.

He thinks sometimes . . . to me my life is one of my black and white movies that I love so . . . with me playing a bit part.

EDDIE. *(To* JEAN PETERS *looking up at the photographs.)* I wonder about your obsession to write about your parents when they were young. You didn't know them. Your mother's not young, your father's not young and we are not that young couple who came to New York in 1955, yet all you ever say to me is Eddie you don't seem the same since you came back from Korea.

(EDDIE *leaves.* MONTGOMERY CLIFT *rows as* SHELLEY WINTERS *speaks to him. Lights on* BRANDO *and* PETERS *start slowly to dim.)*

SHELLEY WINTERS. *(To* MONTGOMERY CLIFT.*)* A Sunday Rain . . . our next door neighbor drove me through the empty Sunday streets to see my brother. He's the same. My father came by the house last night for the first time since he left Cleveland and he and my mother got into a fight and my mother started laughing. She just kept saying see I can laugh ha ha nothing can hurt me anymore. Nothing you can ever do, Wallace, will ever hurt me again, no one can hurt me since my baby is lying out there in that Hospital and nobody knows whether he's going to live or die. And very loudly again she said ha ha and started walking in circles in her white shoes. My father said how goddamn crazy she was and they started pushing each other. I begged them to stop. My father looked about crazily.

I hate this house. But it was my money that helped make a down payment on it and I can come here anytime I want. I can come here and see my daughter and you can't stop me, he said.

CLARA. *(To diary.)* The last week in March I called up my mother and I told her that Eddie and I were getting a divorce and I wanted to come to Cleveland right away.

She said I'm coming up there.

When, I said. When?

It was four o'clock in the afternoon.

When can you come I said.

I'll take the train tonight. I'll call you from the station.

Should I come and meet you?

No, I'll call you from the station.

She called at 10:35 that morning. She said she would take a taxi. I went down to the courtyard and waited. When she got out of the taxi I will never forget the expression on her face. Her face had a hundred lines in it. I'd never seen her look so sad.

CLARA. *(Reciting her play.)* They said: I had lost my mind, read so much, buried myself in my books. They said I should stay and teach summer school. But I went. All the way to London. Out there in the black taxi my cold hands were colder than ever. No sooner than I left the taxi and passed down a gray walk through a dark gate and into a garden where there were black ravens on the grass, when I broke down. Oow... oww.

SHELLEY WINTERS. This morning my father came by again. He said Clara I want to talk to you. I want you to know my side. Now, your mother has always thought she was better than me. You know Mr. Harrison raised her like a white girl, and your mother, mark my word, thinks she's better than me. (It was then I could smell the whiskey on his breath... he had already taken a drink from the bottle in his suitcase.)

(She looks anxiously at MONTGOMERY CLIFT *trying to get him to listen.)*

CLARA. *(Reading from her notebook.)* He came to me in the outhouse, in the garden, in the fig tree. He told me you are an owl, ow, oww, I am your beginning, ow. You belong here with us owls in the fig tree, not to somebody that cooks for your Goddamn Father, oww, and I ran to the outhouse in the night crying oww. Bastard they say, the people in the town all say Bastard, but I—I belong to God and the owls, ow, and I sat in the fig tree. My Goddamn Father is the Richest White Man in the Town, but I belong to the owls.

(Putting down her notebook. Lights shift back to PETERS *and* BRANDO *on the bed.)*

JEAN PETERS. When my brother was in the army in Germany, he was involved in a crime and was court-martialled. He won't talk about it. I went to visit him in the stockade.

It was in a Quonset hut in New Jersey.

His head was shaven and he didn't have on any shoes. He has a vein that runs down his forehead and large brown eyes. When he was in high school he was in All City track in the two-twenty dash. We all thought he was going to be a great athlete. His dream was the Olympics. After high school he went to several colleges and left them; Morehouse (where my father went), Ohio State (where I went), and Western Reserve. I'm a failure he said. I can't make it in those schools. I'm tired. He suddenly joined the army.

After Wally left the army he worked nights as an orderly in hospitals; he liked the mental wards. For a few years every fall he started to school but dropped out after a few months. He and his wife married right before he was sent to Germany. He met her at Western Reserve and she graduated cum laude while he was a prisoner in the stockade.

(Movie music. Dark boat with MONTGOMERY CLIFT *and* SHELLEY WINTERS *reappears from opposite side.* MONTGOMERY CLIFT *rows.* CLARA *is crying.)*

SHELLEY WINTERS AND CLARA. Eddie's come from New York because my brother might die. He did not speak again today and did not move. We don't really know his condition. All we know is that his brain is possibly badly damaged. He doesn't speak or move.

JEAN PETERS. I am bleeding.

(Lights suddenly dim on MARLON BRANDO *and* JEAN PETERS. *Quite suddenly* SHELLEY WINTERS *stands up and falls "into the water." She is in the water, only her head is visible, calling silently.* MONTGOMERY CLIFT *stares at her. She continues to call silently as for help, but* MONTGOMERY CLIFT *only stares at her. Movie music.* CLARA *starts to speak as* SHELLEY WINTERS *continues to cry silently for help.)*

CLARA. The doctor said today that my brother will live; he will be brain damaged and paralyzed.

After he told us, my mother cried in my arms outside the hospital. We were standing on the steps, and she shook so that I thought both of us were going to fall headlong down the steps.

(SHELLEY WINTERS *drowns. Light goes down on* MONTGOMERY CLIFT *as he stares at* SHELLEY WINTERS *drowning. Lights on* CLARA. *Movie music. Darkness. Brief dazzling image of* COLUMBIA PICTURES LADY.)

END

Electra (Euripides)

The scene is outside the peasant's cottage. It is night, a little before sunrise.

CHORUS: Our ancient city Argos. The river. Inachus.

It was here that King Agamemnon led his army forth and with ships of war set sail for Troy.

And having killed the King of Troy and sacked that noble city he returned here to Argos. And on our temple walls hung high his trophies.

Abroad he had had good fortune. But here in his own home he died by his wife Clytemnestra's treachery, and her lover Aegisthus's murderous hand.

Now Agamemnon is dead.

Aegisthus is king now. And Clytemnestra is now his wife.

As for the children left behind . . .

. . . the son of Orestes, Aegisthus resolved to kill, but an old slave took him off to Phocis,

Electra stayed in Argos and when she was of age nobles from all Hellas came to beg her hand.

Aegisthus, fearing if her husband were a prince, her noble son could avenge him for Agamemnon's death, kept her at home and let no one marry her.

But then he feared she might bear a son in secret by a nobleman so he planned to kill her.

Clytemnestra stopped him: She feared the hatred her child's death would bring on her.

So Aegisthus plotted a final scheme: He promised to anyone who killed Orestes . . . now in exile . . . a reward in gold.

And gave Electra in marriage to a peasant.

(Enter ELECTRA *from the cottage with a bucket. She puts it down.)*

PEASANT: Electra why do you rise at dawn. You are a princess. You must rest.

ELECTRA: I must go to the spring for water. I know you don't expect it of me but it's only right that I do my share and work with all the strength I have for our life.

PEASANT: Go then if you wish to the spring. I will work in the fields this morning. As soon as it grows lighter I will take the oxen out, and do some harrowing.

(Exit ELECTRA *and* PEASANT. *Enter* ORESTES *and* PYLADES.*)*

ORESTES: Ha! Pylades you're the man I trust above all others. I've shared your home. You're a true friend the only one who has honored me in spite of the condition to which I have fallen.

Now I have come, sent by Apollo's oracle home to shed the blood of those who shed my father's blood.
Last night I visited my father's grave, offered tears, a shorn lock and killed a lamb.

And now instead of entering the city, I have come to the border to secretly search for my sister who, I have heard, is married and lives near.

I must see her and get her help in executing our revenge.

Look, the dawn is rising. Let us find a ploughman whom we can ask whether Electra lives near by.

Wait, a slave come weeping along the road.
For the moment, let's keep out of sight.

ELECTRA: *(Weeping.)* Agamemnon was my father.
My mother was Clytemnestra.
And I am known to the people of Argos.
As "poor" Electra. My life is unbearable and you
my father lie dead, Agamemnon killed by Aegisthus.

My brother, what city holds you in bondage?
Sad in my room I dream of you.

a del femo pja pol i tia sek ra ta
deizmio lipi meni sto do mati omu
se oni revo me.

My cry of despair
Father I call to you in the deep Earth.
Hear my lamentation which fills my days,
Pateramu Pateramu
Cruel the axe's edge that cut your flesh.

Cruel the cunning that awaited you when you finished your journey from Troy and your wife welcomed you home not with a crown but with a two edged sword.

CHORUS: Electra our princess, we've come to visit you to tell you of the festival the day after tomorrow. All the unmarried girls are getting ready to walk in the procession to Hera's temple. We want you to come.

ELECTRA: I cannot come. Fine dresses and necklaces of gold my dear friends, make my heart sadder. I could not bear the sight of the girls of Argos dancing, nor would I want to dance with them.
Besides, look at me my hair is uncared for, my dresses are rags. My appearance would bring shame to Agamemnon's memory.

CHORUS: Electra do come. The goddess Hera may inspire you. We will get for you a lovely gown and a golden necklace.
Do you expect ever to overcome your enemies if you spend your time weeping instead of praying to the Gods.
Your day of happiness will come, not from weeping, but from praying on these feast and festival days. Come.

ELECTRA: But my friends I have prayed.
Year after year.
But no god hears.

I've prayed for the king who died.
I've prayed for the prince who lives
exiled in an unknown country.
Still I am banished from my ancestral palace while my mother
lies with Aegisthus in a bed stained with murder.
Fo nos.

(Suddenly ORESTES *and* PYLADES *approach accompanied by attendants.)*

ELECTRA: *(Behind chorus.)* min me az ji zis!

ORESTES: Perimene. Akuse. I bring news of your brother Orestes.

ELECTRA: Tu a del fumo?

ORESTES: Yes.

ELECTRA: Is he alive or dead?

ORESTES: He is alive.

ELECTRA: Alive. *(Overcome for a moment.)* In what land is he living?

ORESTES: He goes from city to city but allowed to be a citizen of none.

ELECTRA: Is he hungry?

ORESTES: He is not hungry but like a refugee and powerless.

ELECTRA: Did he send a message to me?

ORESTES: He yearned to know if you were alive and what kind of life you are living.

ELECTRA: I have been devastated by grief as you can see.

ORESTES: Yes, as I weep to see.

ELECTRA: I've shorn my hair like the victims of the Scythians to mark my grief.

ORESTES: To mark your grief for Orestes and for your father's death.

ELECTRA: They were and are still dearer to me than life itself.

ORESTES: Your brother loves you in that same way.

ELECTRA: I know he loves me wherever he is.

ORESTES: Tell me Electra, why do you live so distant from Argos?

ELECTRA: I was forced to come here when I married.
My husband is from Mycenae.

ORESTES: And this is your house?

ELECTRA: Yes.

ORESTES: It is very poor.

ELECTRA: My husband is poor but he has shown me great kindness, even reverence. He has never come near my bed. To him I am still the princess Electra.

ORESTES: Perhaps he thinks Orestes may return still and avenge him.

ELECTRA: I think not. I think he acts from his heart. He reveres my royal ancestry.

ORESTES: That will make Orestes happy. And Clytemnestra, did she stand back and let this cruelty be committed against you.

ELECTRA: My mother cares for Aegisthus and only for Aegisthus and he is the one she listens to.

ORESTES: What made Aegisthus do this to you?

ELECTRA: He did not want me to have noble sons who could avenge him.

ORESTES: Then you are powerless.

ELECTRA: Yes.

(Silence between them.)

ORESTES: These women around us. Are they friends?

ELECTRA: Yes. They are my trusted friends.

ORESTES: And I can speak openly?

ELECTRA: Yes.

ORESTES: Well then suppose Orestes comes, do you think he could carry out his killing?

ELECTRA: He would have to be strong, as our father's murderers were.

ORESTES: And Electra, would you be willing to help Orestes kill your mother?

ELECTRA: I would, with the same axe with which she killed my father.

ORESTES: I will tell him then that you are steadfast.

ELECTRA: When I have shed my mother's blood as payment for my father's death then I can die content.

ORESTES: I know these are words Orestes would want to hear you speak if he could see you.

ELECTRA: If I saw him I would not recognize him.

ORESTES: No, you were both young when you were parted.

ELECTRA: There's only one who would know Orestes now.

ORESTES: You mean the old slave who stole him away and saved his life.

ELECTRA: Yes, that old man was my father's tutor.

ORESTES: Tell me, was your father given a grave near his noble kin.

ELECTRA: His body lies now where it fell, thrown out of doors, and no one is allowed to touch it.

ORESTES: Orestes also yearns to know of the wrongs committed against you these past years.

ELECTRA: I do not want my brother to anguish unduly. It is enough to tell him that I live exiled here on the border of the city. I have friends but my grief is such that I live mostly in solitude with my husband. Meanwhile our mother lives surrounded by the spoils of Troy that my father brought home. And Aegisthus who killed him gets into my father's own chariot and rides back and forth swaggering, clasping in his bloody hand the very sceptre which my father carried when he led Hellas to war. On my father's grave no wine was poured, no wreath of myrtle laid, dishonored, bare, there it lies.

Aegisthus when he's drunk, I've heard, jumps on the grave and flings stones at my father's name inscribed there and shouts, Where is your son Orestes? Why does he not return to protect your tomb?

ELECTRA: So dear stranger I beg of you, tell Orestes everything I have said. I speak for myself and for his father. Agamemnon brought death to the Trojan nation. Ask him can he not kill one man?

(Enter the peasant.)

PEASANT: *(Frightened for* ELECTRA.*)*
> Strangers what do you want at our door?
> Electra you should not let strangers
> come so close to our door.

ORESTES: We bring great news,
> We would never harm the princess Electra.

ELECTRA: These two men have brought me word of Orestes.

PEASANT: Orestes?

ELECTRA: Yes.

PEASANT: Is Orestes still alive?

ELECTRA: Yes he is still alive and he has sent them word of me.

PEASANT: Is this true?

ORESTES: On my honor I swear it.

ELECTRA: *(To men.)* This is the man who is known as "poor Electra's husband."

PEASANT: For this great news, please come inside. Such that we have is yours.

ORESTES: Let us accept this house's hospitality.

> *(Exit* ORESTES *and* PYLADES *into the cottage.)*

ELECTRA: *(To her husband.)* You know how bare our house is. These two guests are far above our level. Why must you ask them in?

PEASANT: Why not? If they're as noble as they look they'll be at home in this cottage.

ELECTRA: Since you've done it now,
> Go quickly and find my father's old servant, who since they turned him out of Argos, tends a flock of sheep close to the Spartan frontier.
> Tell him we have guests and he must come and bring something that I can cook and give them. He'll be joyful to know my brother, the child he once saved, still lives. He'll bless the gods.

PEASANT: I'll go now to the old man and take your message. You go in now and get things ready.

(Exit ELECTRA *and* PEASANT.*)*

CHORUS: Long ago in the mountains of Argos,
    A soft young lamb was found by Pan,

    And the lamb had a lovely fleece of pure gold.
    And Pan, they say, brought it to Atreus king of Argos.

    And lovely songs rose loud
    In praise of the golden lamb.

    Then Thyestes lay secretly with Atreus' wife,
    And persuaded her and took the marvelous lamb to his own
        house.

    Then going forth to the assembled people he proclaimed
    That he held in his own house
    The lamb with the golden fleece.

    Then it was that Zeus turned back
    The glittering journeys of the stars,
    And from that day on, the blaze of divine fire

    Drives always toward the western sky;
    And the parched plains of Ammon languish untouched by
        dew.
    And Zeus withholds from them his sweet rain.

    That is the story.

    But I can hardly believe

    That the golden sun

    Changed his burning course,

    To requite a human sin.

    Nevertheless,

    frightening tales are useful:
    They promote a reverence for the gods.

    O Clytemnestra,

    Had you but remembered tales like these
    As you raised your hand to kill your husband.

(Enter OLD MAN *carrying flowers and a lamb.)*

OLD MAN: Electra my princess. Electra. *(*ELECTRA *appears at the door.)* I've brought you a lamb bred in my own flock, took it from the ewe this morning, flowers and cheese straight from the press. And here's some old rich-scented wine. Let someone take this into the strangers. For at this moment my eyes are full of tears.

ELECTRA: Why are you weeping Old Man?

OLD MAN: On my way here I passed your father's grave. I knelt and shed tears and then I opened this wineskin and poured wine as an offering.

When I saw there on the altar a black fleeced ewe just newly sacrificed, the blood still wet, and beside it a lock of hair. What man would dare visit that grave? No Argive would. Do you think your brother could have come here secretly and paid reverence to his father's desolate tomb? Electra go there. Match that hair with your very own, see if it is the same.

ELECTRA: Even if it were Orestes' hair it would not match mine. Orestes' hair was grown like an athlete's in the palaestra and mine like a woman's softened by combing.

And besides, I do not think my brave Orestes would come to Argos secretly.

OLD MAN: That may be true; but still, go and see if the size and shape of the footprints near the grave are like your own.

ELECTRA: How could there be footprints on rocky ground?

No, either a stranger pitied the sad grave and laid the lock there or some Argive dared the guards and made these offerings.

OLD MAN: Well, where are these strangers? I want to see them.

ELECTRA: Here they come.

(Enter PYLADES *and* ORESTES.*)*

OLD MAN: My greetings to you strangers.

ORESTES *and* PYLADES: Greetings Old Man.

ORESTES: Electra whose friend is this man's?

ELECTRA: This man was my father's tutor.

ORESTES: *(Strangely.)* The same man that got your brother safely away.

ELECTRA: Orestes owes his life to him.

ORESTES: Why does he stare at me? Perhaps he thinks I am like someone.

(The OLD MAN *stares at* ORESTES.)

OLD MAN: Stranger, that scar on your brow. How did you come by it?

ORESTES: I fell and cut it once.

OLD MAN: You fell and cut it once when chasing a fawn.

ORESTES: Yes I fell and cut it once when chasing a fawn.

OLD MAN: You fell and cut it once when chasing a fawn with me.

ORESTES: I fell and cut it once when chasing a fawn with you.

(ELECTRA *stares at them.*)

OLD MAN: My princess look at this man before you.

ORESTES: Yes, Princess Electra, look closely at this man before you.

OLD MAN: Princess Electra it is your brother.
It is Orestes.

ELECTRA: O my brother. Is it you?

ORESTES: Yes. Electra.

(They run and embrace.)

ELECTRA: I thought you'd never come. O res ti mo

ORESTES: a ga pi me ni mu a del fi

ELECTRA: I had despaired.

ORESTES: I too.

ELECTRA: You really are Orestes.

ORESTES: Yes. Your one ally.
(To OLD MAN.*)* Now tell me old man, have I any friends in Argos?
Or am I bankrupt . . . as in fortune . . . so in all?
Shall I go by night or day?
What way shall I set out to meet my enemies?

OLD MAN: My son you are an exile: you have not one friend. In your old friends' eyes you are finished; no one pins his hopes on you.

ORESTES: I want to get back to Argos and my father's house.

OLD MAN: If that's your aim then you must kill Aegisthus and your mother.

ORESTES: That's the deed I've come for.

OLD MAN: As I see it, it's useless to think of getting inside the walls of the royal house. Aegisthus has sentries everywhere. He's greatly fearful, it is rumored, and cannot sleep at night. But listen. Fortune may have intervened. On my way here I saw Aegisthus.

ORESTES: Where? Pu je ron da

OLD MAN: Not far away in the pastures where his horses graze.

ORESTES: What was he doing?

OLD MAN: Preparing a banquet for the Nymphs. He had everything in hand to sacrifice a bull.

ORESTES: Were his men with him or had he just slaves?

OLD MAN: Only his slaves were there. No Argives.

ORESTES: Would there be some who would recognize me?

OLD MAN: No. They're slaves recently come to Argos. They've never seen you.

ORESTES: I wonder how I can get close to him.

OLD MAN: Perhaps you could just go and stand along the road near the sacrifice so he will see you.

ORESTES: And then.

OLD MAN: Often he can't resist playing the role of King. He may command you to join him.

ORESTES: I will go at once. Once I am there I will make my plan. Was my mother with him?

OLD MAN: She is in Argos still. She is afraid to go too much among the people. She is much hated.

ORESTES: Then it will be difficult to kill both of them.
And they must die at the same time.

ELECTRA: The killing of my mother I shall claim myself.

ORESTES: Then we shall succeed.

ELECTRA: Old Man will you help us?

OLD MAN: I will. What plan do you have for Clytemnestra's death?

ELECTRA: This: Go and tell her I have borne a child . . . a son. Say it was ten days ago.

OLD MAN: And how will this bring about your mother's death?

ELECTRA: When she is told of the birth of my son I know she will come.

OLD MAN: And why would she come, she who has disgraced you so.

ELECTRA: I know her well. She will come and pretend to weep over my son's lowly birth.

OLD MAN: Perhaps. And then once here?

ELECTRA: Once here, we will be ready.

OLD MAN: If I see Clytemnestra's death then I can die content.

ELECTRA: But first now you must show my brother where to go to find Aegisthus. And then go to my mother and tell her what I have said.

OLD MAN: I will speak your very words.

ELECTRA: Orestes. Our moment at last has come.

(They raise their hands in prayer.)

ORESTES: Zeus. Help us conquer our father's enemies and ours.

ELECTRA: And have pity on us for our days have been pitiable.

OLD MAN: Send strength to these dear children.

ORESTES: Bring the army of the dead to fight with us.

ELECTRA: Bring the brave who shared the victory over Troy.

OLD MAN: Bring all who hate impure hearts.

(Pause. ORESTES and OLD MAN rise.)

ELECTRA: Father, can you hear?

OLD MAN: He has heard all. I am certain. It is time to go.

(ELECTRA *rises.*)

ELECTRA: Orestes I give you my unbroken word. If in the struggle you lose your life, be sure I shall not live. I'll drive a sword into my heart.

ORESTES: I understand.

ELECTRA: Then take your courage in both hands.

(*Exit* ORESTES, PYLADES, OLD MAN.)

(*To women.*) My friends, your part will be to be beacons and to raise the cry for life or death. I'll be on watch too holding this sword. If Orestes is defeated, our enemies shall not wreak vengeance on his sister. (*She exits.*)

(CHORUS *assumes lookout positions; a death cry is heard.*)

CHORUS: What was that sound?
　　　　Electra, princess, come.

ELECTRA: What is it?

CHORUS: We heard a cry like death.

ELECTRA: I heard the cry too.

CHORUS: It comes from far off.

ELECTRA: That was my brother. This means the sword for me now.

CHORUS: Wait Electra, until we hear the cries once more.

ELECTRA: We have lost. I fear it.

CHORUS: Wait . . . here in the darkness comes a messenger.

(*They face him.*)

MESSENGER: Victory, women of Mycenae, Victory.
　　　　　　I proclaim Orestes' Victory.
　　　　　　Aegisthus, Agamemnon's murderer lies dead.
　　　　　　Praise be to the gods.

ELECTRA: di ke o si ni il thes epi tel lus
　　　　Tell me. Tell me of his death.

MESSENGER: After we left this cottage we reached a road and we followed this road to where Aegisthus was. He stood in a field cutting young myrtle leaves to make a garland for his head.

When he saw us he called out "Greetings Strangers. Where do you come from?"

And Orestes said "We are from Thessaly. We are on our way to Delphi to sacrifice to Zeus."

Then Aegisthus said, "Stay here, be my guests, I'm killing a bull in honor of the nymphs and you must share the banquet. I won't let you refuse.

"Slaves bring holy water for these guests. Come here to the purifying bowl."

Orestes answered, "We purified ourselves down the road there in holy water from a stream.

"So Aegisthus, if strangers may join in the sacrifice with Argive, we will not refuse you." The slaves guarding the King lay down their spears, being busy lighting fires, preparing the sacrificial bowl.

Then Aegisthus took barley and threw it on the altar.

"May evil suppress my enemies," he said, by which he meant you and Orestes. Then he said to Orestes,

"I've heard it said that Men of Thessaly are expert at cutting up a dead bull skillfully, friend, here's the sword.

Show us now if that's true."

It was a wellmade Dorian sword. Orestes grasped it firm
threw off his coat then took the bull-calf's leg
and with one stroke laid the bull's flesh bare,
severed the carcass then opened up the guts.
Aegisthus took augural parts and gazed at them.
The liver lobe was missing and the portal vein
and the gall bladder portended evil visitations.
The king's face grew dark.
Orestes said, "What has upset you?"

"Friend," replied Aegisthus, "I'm much in fear of treachery from abroad. Agamemnon's son is the most dangerous enemy to me and to my royal house."

Orestes said, "What you, a king, fear an exile's plots?
This Dorian knife's too small, bring me a Phythian sword.
I'll split the breast bone, and we can feast."
They brought one, and he cut bending over the augural parts.

Orestes then rose and struck him on the joint of his neck shattering his spine. His whole body writhed in agony and death.

The King's guard now seized their spears. But Pylades and Orestes stood their ground.

Orestes cried out, "I am Orestes. This man was my father's murderer whom I have punished."

At this they withdrew. At that instant he was recognized by an old man who had long served the royal house. "It is Orestes" he said.

And suddenly they started to cheer and shout with delight.

They put garlands on him. Now he's coming here bringing the body of Aegisthus.

CHORUS: Oh, Electra, blood has paid for blood.
      Set your feet dancing.
      Dance like the light. *(Piano in.)*
      O o res tis e ker vi se lam bri ko ro na
      e la te na ho rep su me

ELECTRA: o egistos kitete nekros ekinos
      pu katastrepse tinzoi tu pateramu
      Come friends.
      My finery that I possess that is
      stored in the cottage I will
      bring out.
      Too I will bring the crown
      for my brother's head.

CHORUS: Go Electra, bring the crown for Orestes.
      While we dance to the muses.

(Chant resumes under dance sequence. The dance comes to an end when sight of the dead body of AEGISTHUS *occurs.)*

ELECTRA: *(Placing a crown on* ORESTES' *head and then* PYLADES.*)*
      El a adelfumu afiseme nastere oso
      Sto ke falisu aftingorona
      Iltes piso fernondas to dikeo
      Pu mas a niki ke o eh trosmas
      Vris kete pj a ne kros sta podia mas
      je ne e mu niki ti

(To PYLADES.*)* Ke e si piladi
E pisis lave ap ta her jamu
Af to to niki ti rio stefani

ORESTES: Do what you wish: throw out his carcass to the dogs. Impale him on a stake to feed the birds of heaven. He's yours Electra, once your master, now your slave.

ELECTRA: *(To the body.)* You were the ruin of our life. My brother and I did you no harm but you made us fatherless.

ELECTRA: Take his body and put it out of sight. My mother must not see it before her throat is cut.

(ORESTES *sees* CLYTEMNESTRA *approaching in the distance.)*

ORESTES: Wait. There are other things we must decide.

ELECTRA: What is it? *(Looking in the same direction.)*
An armed force from Mycenae.

ORESTES: No it is our mother.

ELECTRA: Good, she is stepping into the trap. Look how fine she is . . .

A carriage, slaves, and her best gown.

ORESTES: What shall we do then? Are we really going to kill our mother?

ELECTRA: Have you grown soft as soon as you set eyes on her?

ORESTES: She bore me, she brought me up, how can I take her life?

ELECTRA: How? As she took our father's life.

ORESTES: It is wrong to kill my mother!

ELECTRA: You avenge your father.

ORESTES: Avenging him I am pure; but killing her condemned.

ELECTRA: If you neglect to avenge him you defy the gods.

ORESTES: But if I kill my mother shall I not be punished?

ELECTRA: He will pursue you if you let his vengeance go.

ORESTES: Some monster disguised as a god has commanded me. But I can't believe what the god told me is right.

ELECTRA: You cannot lose your nerve and be the coward now. You must use the same deception she used when with Aegisthus' help she struck our father down.

ORESTES: I'll go in. Every step is dreadful and the deed before me still more dreadful yet if heaven so wills, let it be done.

(Exit ORESTES *and* PYLADES *into the house; enter* CLYTEMNESTRA *attended by female slaves.)*

CLYTEMNESTRA: Set down the carriage, trojan slaves. Take my hand and help me to this place.

ELECTRA: Will you give me the privilege to hold your royal hand mother? I too am a slave who you took prisoner by sword.

CLYTEMNESTRA: Your father brought all this on you by wicked treachery. When I married I did not expect to see my children killed. He took my child to Aulis where the fleet lay bound, lured from home with lies about Achilles and cut her soft white throat. My Iphegenia. If he had done it to avert the capture of his city, or to exalt his house he could be forgiven but to sacrifice my child so that the fleet might have good winds that I cannot forgive. And that was Agamemnon's reason for murdering my daughter.

Even then as wicked as it was, I would not have turned savage or killed him. But he brought home with him the whore Cassandra and kept us both in one house. So I killed him. I took the only way open to me. I turned for help to his enemies. Well, what else could I do.

ELECTRA: You destroyed the life of the most noble man in Hellas. You pretend that you avenge your daughter with my father's blood.

There may be some who believe you but I know you.

Before Iphigenia's sacrifice was decided on . . . when Agamemnon was scarcely out of sight you began seeking what you should not. If Troy lost a battle your eyes clouded. Why? Because you didn't want Agamemnon to come back to Argos. I saw the way you looked at Aegisthus. Even if as you say, our father killed Iphigenia, what did my brother and I do to you? After you killed our father you exiled us from our house and bought yourself a lover with your dowry.

So if death demands justice then Orestes must kill you.

If one revenge is just so is the other.

CLYTEMNESTRA: Electra, I regret that revenge now.

ELECTRA: It is too late for regret. But Orestes lives. Why do you not bring him home?

CLYTEMNESTRA: I am frightened for myself. They say Orestes is mad with anger over his father's death.

ELECTRA: And why do you let Aegisthus still persecute me?

(CLYTEMNESTRA *turns away. Silence.*)

CLYTEMNESTRA: *(Abruptly.)* Why did you send for me?

ELECTRA: You were told of my confinement were you not?

CLYTEMNESTRA: I was. But why are you in this state, so ill-looking? The birth's well over now.

ELECTRA: Will you do this for me? Offer the tenth day sacrifice for a son.

CLYTEMNESTRA: It is usually done by the woman who delivered you.

ELECTRA: I was alone. I delivered myself.

CLYTEMNESTRA: What? In this house so far from any neighbor.

ELECTRA: We are poor; we don't have friends.

CLYTEMNESTRA: Well as a favor, I'll go in and pay the gods the respect for your son. And then I must go to where my husband's sacrificing to the nymphs out in the pasture. *(To servants.)* You there take the carriage away. And feed the horses. Give me as much time as I need to make this offering to the gods; then come for me. *(To* ELECTRA.*)* I have my husband to think of.

ELECTRA: Please come in. (CLYTEMNESTRA *goes in.*) All is prepared. The sword is sharpened for you. In the house of death you shall still be his bride whose bed you shared in life.

(ELECTRA *goes in.*)

CHORUS: Now retribution follows sin.
Through the fated house a new wind blows
Long ago my beloved Lord and King fell dead

Now retribution follows sin
Through the fated house a new wind blows
Long ago my beloved Lord and King fell dead

And through the rooms round the stone cornice
rang out his death cry.

O wicked wife why do you murder me,
returned after ten harvests
home to my country?

Now like a returning tide
justice comes to the reckless Clytemnestra.

CLYTEMNESTRA: Ped ya mu ya to o no ma ton te on
mi n sko to ne te tim mi ter as as
vo i thia ach ach
Soon or late heaven dispenses justice
Her revenge on her husband was unholy

CHORUS: Now Electra and Orestes come clothed
in fresh streams of their mother's blood.
Now Electra and Orestes come clothed
in fresh streams of their mother's blood.

i e lek tra ke o o re tis vu tij meni
sto fresko hye meno e: ma tis miterastus

(All together on last "miterastus." Enter ORESTES, ELECTRA, *and*
PYLADES *with body of* CLYTEMNESTRA.)

ORESTES: o: yi o zef e si puv le pis o la osa i an
tro pi ka non ki tak se af to af to to e ma ti ro
te a ma di o so mata hti pi me na a paf to to hye ri

ELECTRA: I am guilty too. I burned with desperate rage against her, yet
she was my mother. *(My mother in Greek repeated.)* i mi ter amu

ORESTES: O Apollo.
You have bestowed on me
a murderer's destiny.
To what city shall I go.
Will any friend, will any man who fears god,
Dare to look into my face . . . a son who has killed his mother?

ELECTRA: O what shall we do? O: ti fa ka no me.
Where shall we go? pu Oa pa me
(Repeat in Greek.)

ORESTES: Did you see how in her agony
　　　　she opened her gown, thrust forth her breast
　　　　and showed it to me as I struck.
　　　　The body that gave me birth sprawled on the ground.

ELECTRA: As she uttered a shriek she put her hand on my face.
　　　"My child I implore you" she said. Then she hung around my
　neck so that the sword fell out of my hand.

ORESTES: I held my cloak over my eyes
　　　　while with my sword I drove
　　　　the blade into my mother's throat.

ELECTRA: I urged you on and held the sword, my hand beside yours.

ORESTES: Come help me cover her limbs with her dress and close her
　wounds.

ELECTRA: As we wrap this cloak around her.
　　　　We loved you . . . although we hated you.

CHORUS: This is the prophetic end of great sorrow.

CURTAIN

Orestes (Euripides)

(ELECTRA *enters, haunted looking and wan, watching over* ORESTES. *Voices enter, sustained chord.*)

CHORUS: After the murder Orestes collapsed.
He lies in his bed seized by a raging fever.
And driven on to madness by his mother's ghost
and Eumenides who pursue him.

Six days since they sent her body to the pyre and six days he has not tasted food but lies there submerged in blankets.

Sometimes he madly rises from bed crying out. The Argives have forbidden anyone to speak to them or shelter them.

Today the Argives meet to decide whether they shall live or die and if they will die by stoning or the sword.

One single hope is left.
Their uncle Menelaus has come home from Troy. His fleet fills the harbor at Nauplia. He has brought Helen.

She so fears being killed by the fathers of those who died at Troy that Menelaus sent her ahead last night in darkness. She is in the palace weeping over her sister's, their mother's, death.

She has one consolation, her daughter Hermione, whom as a child she entrusted to their mother's care.

She has some comfort left but they do not so they sit watching the road in hope that Menelaus will come. Unless he helps them, they must die.

(Enter HELEN, *not young but vain of her beauty. She carries a pitcher for libations and small locks of her hair.)*

HELEN: *(To herself.)* Poor Clytemnestra. And to think I sailed for Troy without seeing her. Some god must have made me mad. *(Looking at* ORESTES.*)* When did he fall into this state?

ELECTRA: The day we spilt our mother's blood.

HELEN: *(Turning abruptly from* ORESTES.*)* I want you to help me Electra. I want you to go to my sister's grave.

ELECTRA: What? You want me to go to my mother's grave? But why?

HELEN: To pour libations on her grave and leave these shorn strands of my hair.

ELECTRA: But my mother was your sister. You go yourself.

HELEN: I am afraid.
I am afraid of the fathers of the soldiers who died at Troy.
Please go.
I do not want to walk the streets of Argos.
I am despised by the women here.

ELECTRA: No. I cannot bear the sight of my mother's grave.

HELEN: What can I do? I cannot send a servant.

ELECTRA: Then send Hermione.

HELEN: An unmarried girl cannot go alone to the grave.

ELECTRA: It is her duty. She owes it to my mother for caring for her.

*(*HELEN *pauses and then calls into the palace.)*

HELEN: Hermione. *(*HERMIONE, *a young girl, appears from the palace.)* Do as I say. Take this libation and this hair and go to Clytemnestra's grave. Pour this honey milk and wine over the grave and as you pour say these words; "Your sister Helen, stopped by the fear of the Argives from coming to your grave sends you these tokens." Then implore her to have mercy on my husband and me and on her poor children whom Apollo has destroyed. Hurry and come back quickly.

(Exit HERMIONE *with offerings.* HELEN *goes into the palace.)*

ELECTRA: *(Bitterly.)* Did you see how she cut only the tips of her curls for her offering?

(ELECTRA's friends enter playing mournful music.)

ELECTRA: Walk softly friends. Your music, keep it low.

CHORUS: He lies so still.

(ORESTES suddenly stirs and wakes.)

ORESTES: Sweet wizard sleep. How I needed you.

ELECTRA: How happy it made me to see you sleep at last.
Let me raise your head.

ORESTES: Yes, please help me up.

ELECTRA: Let me brush this poor matted hair.

ORESTES: The fever makes me weary.

ELECTRA: My brother lie back down and do not move.

(He lies down while she brushes his hair.)

ELECTRA: Now listen. Listen Orestes. Our uncle Menelaus is here in
Argos. His fleet lies at anchor at Nauplia.

ORESTES: What? Is it true?
Then our darkness has a dawn.
Our father did so much for him.
He will help us.

ELECTRA: There is more.
He has brought Helen home from Troy.

ORESTES: Then he has brought sorrow home.

(Suddenly ORESTES starts up wild eyed and screaming.)

ELECTRA: Orestes.

ORESTES: Take the snakes away.
Take the snakes with gorgon eyes away.

ELECTRA: Orestes there are no snakes.

ORESTES: They want to kill me.

ELECTRA: There are no snakes.

ORESTES: Let me go. Aseme. I know you, you're one of the Furies too.
You're holding me down to hurl me into hell.

Oh my poor sister, how wrong it is that my madness should hurt you so.

I think now if I had asked my dead father should I kill our mother he would have begged me, gone down on his knees and begged me not to take her life.

What had we to gain by murdering her?

Her death could never bring him back to life and I, by killing her, have to suffer as I suffer now.

It is hopeless.

But do not cry. And sometimes when you see me mad from desolation, comfort me and I in turn, when you despair, will comfort you.

Our love is all we have.

Now go inside.

And rest.

If you fall ill then I will die. You are my only help.

My only hope.

ELECTRA: I could never leave you Orestes. You are my hope too. What am I without you?

A woman brotherless, fatherless, alone. *(She kisses him.)* Rest if you can. *(She exits with bowl upper stage center.)*

CHORUS: Eumenides, women of darkness,
        avengers of murder,
        we implore you—
        release this boy,
        from his madness

        Happiness is brief.
        It will not stay.
        God batters at its sails,
        sorrow strikes,
        and happiness goes down,
        and glory sinks.

Hail to the king who led a thousand ships to Troy.

MENELAUS: Home at last. How happy I am to see this house once more—

But also sad for never have I seen a house more hedged about by suffering than this. Oh gods, is this some corpse I see?

ORESTES: It is I Uncle, your nephew.
I fall on my knees before you Menelaus.
and beg you to rescue us from death, you
who have led a thousand ships to Troy.

MENELAUS: That stare in your eyes. When did this madness start?

ORESTES: The day we built my mother's tomb. It came on me as I stood at the pyre.

MENELAUS: That you should suffer is hardly strange. In Nauplia the sailors told me of the murder of Clytemnestra.

ORESTES: It was Apollo who commanded my mother's murder.

MENELAUS: A callous, unjust and immoral order.

ORESTES: We obey the gods, whoever they may be.

MENELAUS: How do you stand in the city?

ORESTES: So hated and despised am I that not one person in Argos will speak to me. The city is voting on our sentence today.

MENELAUS: Will they let you keep your father's sceptre?

ORESTES: They do not want me to live.

MENELAUS: What is the punishment—banishment or death?

ORESTES: Death by stoning.

MENELAUS: You must try to escape.

ORESTES: Argos is surrounded by soldiers.
And that is why I turn to you, my father's brother.
You are our only hope.
Menelaus, we are desperate.
You have arrived in Argos prosperous and in your moment of glory: I implore you to help us.

CHORUS: Menelaus: Tyndareus of Sparta is on his way here.

ORESTES: O gods.
What can I do?
Of all the men on this earth that I dread to meet it is my grandfather Tyndareus who loved me more than his own sons Castor and Polydeuces and who I loved as much as my own father.

Where can I hide from my grandfather's eyes?

(Enter TYNDAREUS *gaunt in his seventies dressed in mourning black. He too has attendants.)*

TYNDAREUS: *(To women.)* Where can I find my daughter Helen's husband, Menelaus? I was pouring libations on my daughter's grave when I heard the news of his arrival home at Nauplia after these long years.

MENELAUS: *(Seeing him.)* Tyndareus!

TYNDAREUS: Menelaus my son!

(He stops abruptly as he sees ORESTES.*)*

TYNDAREUS: *(Staring at Orestes.)* o fon yas dis kor iz mo
            o fon yas dis kor iz mo
            o fon yas dis kor iz mo
            o fon yas dis kor iz mo

MENELAUS: Do not Tyndareus. Orestes is my brother's son.
And I loved my brother.

TYNDAREUS: This murderer. *(Pause.)* As a boy I held him in my arms.

MENELAUS: He is my brother's son in trouble.

TYNDAREUS: Foreigners, I see, have taught you their ways.

MENELAUS: It is a Greek custom, I think, to honor your kin.

TYNDAREUS: But not to put yourself above the laws.
Not once did Orestes weigh the justice of his cause or seek our courts.
When his father died he should have made Clytemnestra pay by legal action not murder.
Now if anything the evil he has done has surpassed her crime.
If a wife murders her husband and her son then kills her then his son must have his murder.
Then this chain of murder can never end since the last to kill is doomed to a permanent sentence of death by revenge.
Our ancestors banned murderers from sight forbidding them to speak or meet with anyone: and by this they purge their guilt by banishment not death and by so they stop the cycle of revenge.

There I take my stand, attacking with all my heart,
the brutal spirit of murder that is corrupting
our cities and destroying this country.
You heard me Orestes; brutal.

One thing I know.
These fits of madness are what you pay for murder.
Heaven itself has made you mad. *(He starts to leave.)*

ORESTES: Grandfather, please listen.
You who held me in your arms when I was a boy.
Listen.
I had every right to kill Clytemnestra.
She betrayed my father.
And I hated her.
She exiled my sister and me.
I had every right to kill her.

TYNDAREUS: I came from Sparta to lay flowers on your mother's grave
but now by god I have a stronger motive: your death.
I will go the Argives myself and hound them until they stone your
sister and you. Yes, your sister.
It was Electra with her malice, telling you of her dreams of Agamemnon's ghost and his cries from the grave that incited you against
your mother. *(Turning from* ORESTES.) I warn you Menelaus do not
oppose the gods by rescuing Orestes and Electra.

(He exits. ORESTES *starts after him but is stopped by* MENELAUS.)

ORESTES: *(Falls at* MENELAUS's *feet.)* Uncle, in honor of my dead father
in his grave help us.

CHORUS: Save them Menelaus.

MENELAUS: Orestes I know we are joined by a common bond of blood
and I am honor bound to come to your defense against your enemies.
I only wish I could. But I have arrived in Argos weakened.
My allies have dwindled away and I myself am exhausted from
this terrible ordeal.
We are weak and therefore our weapons must be diplomacy.
This is my plan.
I will go to the Argives and try to calm their fury and hope it will
burn itself out.

We have no other choice.
Be patient. The winds may shift. (MENELAUS *exits.*)

ORESTES: You traitor! What have you ever done but fight a war to bring
your wife back home? So now you turn your back and desert me.
This is the end.
This is the last of the house of Agamemnon.
My poor father deserted by his kin.
And now my last hope from death is lost . . . Menelaus.

(Enter PYLADES.*)*

PYLADES: I seem to have come none too soon Orestes.
As I was coming through the town I saw the Argives meeting
and heard them discussing a plan to execute Electra and you.

ORESTES: We are ruined.

PYLADES: As matters stand now our deaths are certain.

ORESTES: Our?

PYLADES: You, Electra, and I are one.

ORESTES: They vote on the sentence today.

PYLADES: Take Electra and try to escape.

ORESTES: Sentries are patrolling the streets.
We are surrounded like a city under siege.

PYLADES: I have suffered too.

ORESTES: Something else has happened?

PYLADES: My father has banished me from Phocis.

ORESTES: Heaven help us. *(Silence.)*

What am I supposed to do? Die without saying a word in my
own defense?

PYLADES: There is nothing to gain from staying here but if you go to
the meeting then something might be gained. But you may be killed.

ORESTES: But I must go. *(Pause.)*

My madness. What if I have an attack?
Madmen are hard to handle.

PYLADES: I will manage.

ORESTES: But if my madness strikes you too?

PYLADES: I am not afraid.

ORESTES: Then take me first to my father's grave.
I want to pray and implore his help.

PYLADES: Good.

ORESTES: But Pylades, don't let me see my mother's grave.

PYLADES: I will not.
We must go now.
Here lean on me.
Let the people jeer.
I'll lead you through the city unashamed.
What is friendship worth unless I prove it in this time of
trouble.

(They exit.)

CHORUS: Glory decays, and
greatness goes
from the happy house of Atreus.
Beneath the proud facade
the long stain spread
as the curse of blood began—
strife for a golden ram,
slaughter of little princes,
a table laid with horror,
a feast of murdered sons.
And still corruption swelled,
murder displacing murder,
to reach at last
the living heirs of Atreus.

What terror can compare with us?

Hands of a son,
Stained with his mother's blood.

*(ELECTRA appears from the palace and is frightened to find
ORESTES gone.)*

ELECTRA: *(To women.)* Where is Orestes? Has his madness come again?

CHORUS: No Electra. He went to the Argive meeting to speak in his own defense.

ELECTRA: But why? Who persuaded him?

CHORUS: Pylades.

(Enter MESSENGER.)

MESSENGER: Princess Electra.
I bring you sad news.

ELECTRA: *(Pause.)* Our sentence is death.

MESSENGER: Yes. The Argives voted that you and your brother must die today.

ELECTRA: And how are we to die my brother and I?

MESSENGER: Poor Orestes was just able to persuade them not to stone you both to death by promising that you and he would kill yourselves this day.
Pylades is bringing him home.
So bring out the sword for you must leave this light.
Apollo has destroyed you both.

ELECTRA: *(Trembling.)* Down and down my house.
Pelops line is ended.
Down and down
Greatness has gone from the house of Atreus
Ending with this curse on my brother and me.
i thei namas vo i thi sun

(Enter ORESTES supported by PYLADES. ELECTRA bursts into tears at the sight of him.)

ELECTRA: Orestimu Orestimu

(ORESTES kissing her.)

ORESTES: No more Electra.
What shame on earth can touch me anymore?
O my sister, this last sweet embrace is all we shall ever know of love and marriage.
Our time has come.
We must choose the sword or the rope.

ELECTRA: Kill me yourself Orestes.

ORESTES: I cannot my sister.

ELECTRA: If only one sword could kill us both. If we could only share one coffin together.

ORESTES: No . . . we must die as we were born . . . well . . . as the children of Agamemnon.
> I shall show Argos of what blood I come by
> falling on my sword and you must follow and die bravely.
> Pylades lay us out and make us both one grave beside my father's tomb.

PYLADES: My friend how could you think I would want to live if you were dead?

ORESTES: Pylades.
> You have your country, your father's house and wealth.
> Marry and have heirs. The bonds which bound us once are broken now. Goodbye my only friend.

PYLADES: I murdered with you. I helped plan the crime for which you suffer and now I should die with you and Electra. It is my duty. *(Pause.)*
> Wait! But since we have to die, is there not some way to make Menelaus suffer. He did not one thing to help his brother's children.

ORESTES: How could he be avenged?

PYLADES: Listen: we will avenge him by murdering Helen.

ORESTES: There is no way we could do this.

PYLADES: Yes there is. We'll go inside the palace pretending that we are about to kill ourselves.

ORESTES: And then?

PYLADES: We will weep and tell her how much we suffer.
> Then she will pretend to weep.
> We'll carry the swords hidden in our robes and while she pretends this grief we'll lock her slaves in different rooms.

ORESTES: Then death to Helen.

PYLADES: Not only do we avenge her for ourselves, but we avenge her in the name of all Hellas, whose fathers and sons she murdered.

There will be celebrations in Argos.

Men will bless our heads and sing songs of glory to us for doing away with her.

Should we fail we'll burn this house around us as we die.

Orestes you shall not be cheated of honor.

(ELECTRA, *who has been sitting, joins in.*)

ELECTRA: Listen Orestes: you too Pylades. Do you remember Helen's daughter, Hermione?

ORESTES: The little girl our mother took care of?

ELECTRA: Yes. Well she has now gone to Clytemnestra's grave to pour libations there.

ORESTES: What has this to do with our escape?

ELECTRA: When she comes back we will seize her.

ORESTES: How will that help us?

ELECTRA: We must have a plan. Once Helen is dead Menelaus may attempt to capture one of us. And if he tries, we will set our sword at Hermione's throat and warn him, we will kill her. If then seeing Helen lying in a pool of blood, he decides he wants his daughter's life, and agrees to spare us, we will let Hermione go. But if he tries to kill one of us in a mad rage then we will slit her throat.

He is a coward as we have seen. I believe he will not fight.

And there you have my plan for making our escape.

ORESTES: I like this plan.

How soon do you think Hermione will return?

ELECTRA: Any moment now.

ORESTES: Then Electra you stay here and wait for her return. Make certain that no one and no friend of her father's enters the palace. But if someone does beat your fist on the door and raise the cry. But let us know. Pylades and I will go inside now to Helen. Have your sword ready.

(*He raises his arms in prayer and invokes the ghost of* AGAMEMNON.)

ORESTES: O my father, ghost who walks the black house of Atreus, your son Orestes calls upon your help in his hour of need.

It is for you father I suffer.
For you I was condemned to death unfairly.
And your own brother has betrayed me though what I did was right. Come father, help me to capture Helen.
Help me kill her.
O Father help us now.

ELECTRA: O father if you can hear our prayers beneath the earth know that we die for you.

PYLADES: O Agamemnon kinsman of my father.
Hear my prayers.
Save your children.

ORESTES: I murdered my mother.

PYLADES: I held the sword that killed.

ELECTRA: I was their spirit.

I made them brave.

ORESTES: I offer my tears to you.

ELECTRA: And I my grief.

PYLADES: Enough. If prayers can penetrate this earth he hears.
We must go about this business now.
Three friends together. One common cause. Together we shall live or die.

ELECTRA: Women of Argos, a word with you please.

CHORUS: What is it Princess Electra?

ELECTRA: I want half of you to watch the road and the rest will stand guard here.

(Women divide.)

CHORUS: I'll watch the road to the east.

And I'll watch here on the westward side.

All's well here. Not an Argive in sight.

Nor here either. Not a soldier in sight.

ELECTRA: Then wait. *(She calls inside the palace to* ORESTES *and* PYLADES.*)*

Why are you so quiet?

They don't answer. Not a sound. O Zeus. Has her beauty blinded them too?

(Suddenly from within the palace.)

HELEN: Help me Argos.
    They're murdering me.
    They're murdering me.

ELECTRA: O Zeus send us strength.
    Help us now.

HELEN: Help me I'm dying . . .
    vo i thia pe the no

ELECTRA: Run the traitoress through.
    Kill the whore who killed so many brave men.

CHORUS: Electra we hear the sound of footsteps. Someone is coming.

ELECTRA: It must be Hermione. Yes it is Hermione herself.
    Quiet, not a sound. Appear natural as though nothing has happened here. *(Enter* HERMIONE.*)*

Hermione have you returned from Clytemnestra's grave and did you circle it with flowers and pour libations?

HERMIONE: Yes I paid her the dues of the dead. *(Pause.)*
    But what has happened here? I thought I heard a scream in the distance.

ELECTRA: A scream?

HERMIONE: What has happened?

ELECTRA: Orestes and I have been sentenced to death.

HERMIONE: Zeus, Zeus.

ELECTRA: And he went and fell at Helen's knees.

HERMIONE: I don't understand.

ELECTRA: Orestes went to implore Helen to save our lives.

HERMIONE: Then that was the cry I heard?

ELECTRA: Yes and if you love us go now, fall at your mother's feet and beg her.

Implore her to intercede with Menelaus on our behalf.
You are our very last hope.

HERMIONE: Oh yes. I will go now. If it lies in my power you are saved.

(HERMIONE *enters the palace.*)

Ach Mi ter a mu

ORESTES: *(From inside the palace.)* Silence Hermione. You are here to save us.

ELECTRA: Seize her and stop her screaming. Let Menelaus learn what it is to fight with men, not cowards from Troy. Make him suffer for his indifference to us.

(ELECTRA *enters the palace closing the doors behind her. From inside are cries and muffled screams.*)

CHORUS: Quick raise a shout, a cry to drown the sound of murder in the palace before the Argives hear.

Be still. Be still.
It is a Trojan slave. He will tell us what has happened. Be still.

(*A* TROJAN SLAVE *incoherent from terror bursts from the palace.*)

TROJAN SLAVE: Trojan scared and run,
clamber over the roof.
O
Ilium,
Ilium Troy
hear the dirge I cry ai ai.
Out of hiding
Out of purple cloaks
they drew their swords and eyes of them. O going
round to
see if danger anywhere and then they came.
They were yes shouting and screaming
die die die for traitor husband coward who
betrayed his brother's son
who left him to die in Argos.
Lady Helen screamed white arms flailing
flailing beating bosom beating breast
hair she tore in sandals leaped to run

but after after came Orestes.
Caught her O winding fingers in her hair
and neck forced back
down down
against her shoulder and lifted
the sword to strike.

CHORUS: Where were the servants?

TROJAN SLAVE: We batter doors with iron bars break down panels.
Then run some with stones.
Pylades came on brave Hectorlike or Ajax.
Steel on steel together meet but soon we see
Trojan men, ai ai one run dead
wounding this and begging that
near the dirge I cry ai ai
falling some dying others
staggering is one with wounds.
And then Hermione came in as mother Helen sank to
die.
O Earth O Night.
What then happen I do not know.

CHORUS: Now retribution follows sin.
Through the fated house more winds blow.
And through the rooms round the stone cornice
Ring out new death cries.
Grief has come down once more
On the house of Atreus.

(Enter MENELAUS *with armed men.)*

MENELAUS: I have heard this tale of brutal and mad crimes committed
by Electra and Orestes.
Men break down the door so that I can rescue my dear daughter
from these murderers and bring out Helen's body.
In revenge for her I shall put them to death.

(Suddenly from the roof comes billowing smoke.)

CHORUS: Look on the roof of the palace. *(Slowly smoke rises. They watch.)*

They are burning the ancestral house.

MENELAUS: Madness has consumed them.

(The door opens; behind it ORESTES *is holding a knife to* HERMIONE'*s throat.)*

MENELAUS: mi och i tin(z) ko ri mo
Why are you holding my daughter?
Wasn't it enough that you murdered her mother?

ORESTES: And now I will kill your daughter.

MENELAUS: But why?

ORESTES: You betrayed us Menelaus.

MENELAUS: Wasn't Clytemnestra's death enough?

ORESTES: Helen and Clytemnestra were whores.

MENELAUS: But Hermione?

ORESTES: Hermione's death will be to avenge my father.

And now we'll burn this doomed palace.

MENELAUS: Burn the house of Atreus?

ORESTES: To keep it from you Menelaus. But first the sword at Hermione's throat.

(Among the armed men and women there is great commotion and cries in Greek: ti ka non ti ji ne te.)

MENELAUS: Could you kill my child?
What is it that you want?

(Cries in Greek: prepi na skoto thun.)

ORESTES: Persuade the people.

MENELAUS: Persuade them of what?

ORESTES: To let us live traitor.

MENELAUS: Or you kill my child?

ORESTES: Yes.

MENELAUS: Then I am trapped.

ORESTES: Yes trapped by your own mercilessness.
Electra burn the parapet
Pylades set the roof to blazes.

MENELAUS: Vo i thi a
Strati ote tu argo
Vo i thia

(Chaos ensues. Suddenly APOLLO *appears in the palace doorway.)*

APOLLO: Cease Menelaus. It is I Phoebus Apollo.
Helen is here with me. Orestes did not kill her.
Helen, being born of Zeus, could not die
and now will sit enthroned forever, a star for sailors.
It is Orestes' destiny to leave Argos and journey to the city of
Athena and give justice for his mother's murder. The gods on the
hill of Ares shall be his judges and acquit him in a sacred verdict.
Then Orestes will marry Hermione.
Electra shall marry Pylades as promised.
Happiness awaits him.
Menelaus will be king in Sparta and I shall give Argos to Orestes . . .
for it was I who commanded his mother's murder. I compelled him
to kill.

ORESTES: Hail Apollo for your oracles. And yet sometimes when I heard
you speak to me it seemed the whispers of a monster. But all is well
now and I obey. See I release Hermione and we shall marry if her father gives his blessing.

MENELAUS: I envy your happiness with the gods. Orestes I betroth
Hermione to you as Apollo commands.

APOLLO: *(Dismissing them.)* Go and honor peace now. Helen I now
lead to the halls of Zeus among the blazing stars, there with Hera
she shall sit a goddess forever and reign the seas, a light to sailors.

(The palace door closes.)

CURTAIN

An Evening with Dead Essex

An Evening with Dead Essex was first performed in November 1973 at the American Place Theatre in New York. The production was directed by Gaby Rodgers, with a cast that included Mary Alice, Bill Cobbs, Sid Morgan Jr., Andre Mtumi, Fred Seagraves, and Karma Stanley.

The play was subsequently directed by Andre Mtumi at the Yale Repertory Theatre in March 1974.

This play is dedicated to Mark Essex . . . and his family.

CHARACTERS

DIRECTOR-ACTOR	Forties or older
TWO ACTORS	Early twenties (like a young actor in Negro Ensemble)
ACTRESS	Thirties (a character actress)
PROJECTIONIST	Twenties
ASSISTANT DIRECTOR	Twenties

All are black *except* the projectionist who is white.

All preparations for scenes take a long time.

Then there are voices of people down the hall and in the outer office (they are taped).

The ACTORS use their real names and the DIRECTOR should get the ACTORS to play themselves.

SCENE:

I

LATE AFTERNOON

Studio in a film company on West 47th Street
Screening room

Screen, projector
Posters, rolled and stacked in shelves
Tape recorder
A phone table with a typewriter, chairs on the table, piles of newspaper
clippings, photographs.
The area is made to look enclosed and dim except for one center glaring
ceiling light.
To the rear with his back to the audience is the PROJECTIONIST *(the*
only white character) at the projector.
He is the one who flashes the pictures on the screen.
The floor should be black or very dark, all the furniture should be dark
except for glaring silver film cans and white rolled-up posters.
There is a door to the right. EVERYONE *is dressed in light colors except*
the PROJECTIONIST *who is dressed in black jeans and black turtleneck*
shirt.
The screen on which the pictures are projected is slightly bigger in scale
than everything else. The pictures projected are razor sharp and as stated in
the text vary in focus. These are people under pressure. It is the last night of
rehearsal (the DIRECTOR *is running some film looking for something). He's*
sitting at the table and at the same time is going through a pile of photo-
graphs—attractive, black, late thirties, weary-looking, casually dressed—
light shirt, vest, some kind of jeans—when he speaks it's to the PROJECTION-
IST *who's running the film.*
Muffled sounds of Aretha Franklin or Isaac Hayes from next studio.
Throughout the PROJECTIONIST *never replies but just runs film—he's*
twenty, white, and wears dark turtleneck shirt, dark jeans.
The film continues to run. The DIRECTOR *watches it intently.*

DIRECTOR: Stop on Essex's mother. *(The footage is stopped on Mark Es-*
sex's Mother)
DIRECTOR: Closer—no a little further away—bring it back a little—
O.K. *(The photo is finally focused on Essex's mother's eyes.)*
DIRECTOR: O.K., now let's have the whole face again. *(*DIRECTOR *stares*
at photo a while, lights a cigarette and smokes.

   The photo on the screen remains. HE *goes on smoking and goes*
   through photos, clippings on the table.
   The PROJECTIONIST *is looking through cans of film and boxes*
   of slides.
   A young ACTOR *comes in carrying Army and Navy gear, puts it*
   down, looks up at the screen at Essex's mother. When he opens the

door we hear louder sounds of music and people talking from down the hall [muffled]. The ACTOR *stares at Essex's mother. He is in his twenties, dark skin, afro, looks very tired. [They've been rehearsing a long time.])*

ACTOR: Are —— here?

DIRECTOR: They haven't come back from lunch yet, —— is getting a better flag, and —— is working on the twenty-third psalm—

ACTOR: Are we going to rehearse tomorrow—

DIRECTOR: No, just be at the theater at six. *(Going on with the sorting.)*

—While we're waiting I want you to do the ex-serviceman again—

ACTOR: O.K.

DIRECTOR: It's not down enough—remember you've been in a war and you're back in the streets, broke without a job—

ACTOR: O.K. (ACTOR *sorts through clothing, the gear he has, comes up with an old G.I. jacket, walks around, preparing [preparing takes long] himself, stares at slide of Essex's mother, stares into her eyes, takes a long time getting the jacket right, then pulls a chair out from the table, sits in it as if he is alone in a room)*

DIRECTOR: *(Reads Headlines)* Headlines . . . Dead Essex Background suggests he acted alone . . .

Essex's Roommate Questioned by F.B.I. and Released . . .

Ex-American Sailor Shoots from atop Howard Johnson Motor Lodge, New Orleans— *(Reads)*

Three policemen, two hotel guests and a hotel employee were killed and 10 policemen and two firemen were wounded by ex-American sailor shooting from the Downtown Howard Johnson's Motor Lodge last Sunday. Essex was shot and killed on the hotel roof by policemen riding in a helicopter. *(Silence)*

DIRECTOR: *(Still reading)* He was shot to death by nearly 100 bullets. *(Silence)*

DIRECTOR: *(To* ACTOR*)* Remember all this— *(Silence)*

ACTOR: I'm ready.

(Intensely) About a year ago five of us ex G.I.s were arrested. We used to meet in the cellar of one of our homes. It was in Cleveland— they said we had a plot to kill white people.

DIRECTOR: A plot to kill all white people—

ACTOR: They said we had a plot to kill all white people. We didn't. But we did meet in that cellar almost every day and talk, just talk. We wished we had had a plot to kill white people—we had a lot to say to each other—about our confusion about the deep racial significance of the war between the U.S. and Viet Nam, white against non white—about our joblessness—we did *want* to *kill* but we had no plot—we had a lot to say and we still have a lot to say—about Mark Essex—to us he is a hero—we believe he was carrying a banner—we believe he was trying to save us—we believe he saw himself as a soldier of mercy—we have a lot to say about dead Essex.

DIRECTOR: Dead Mark Essex.

ACTOR: Dead Mark Essex. Amen. *(Long silence)*

DIRECTOR: I'm not sure that's enough—we should talk about the feelings of each soldier. *(They both ponder in silence)*

DIRECTOR: Each soldier should talk about how brutally used he felt to fight a darker brother for a country that despises him even more than his Viet Nam enemy—*(Photo of mother remains)*

ACTOR: After going over this material I do believe Essex was so deeply religious that he was torn to bits in spirit by having to serve alongside his white enemy—

DIRECTOR: Yes I'm convinced. The innocence of someone who believed in the equalness of the hearts of those in his home town. He believed in those white Kansas faces. *(Silence.)*

(Photo of mother big.
DIRECTOR gets up, goes out to the hall, sounds of Hayes, Roberta Flack, talking, etc., as always. When the door opens, he calls out.)

DIRECTOR: Is —— back yet? (ACTORS *use their own names*)

(Voices calling the ACTOR—wants you, etc.
Pause.
Footsteps coming down the hall, enters the other ACTOR, mid to late twenties and in a very subtle way can resemble Mark Essex. He nods hello. All the hellos, etc. throughout the evening are exchanged as much without words as possible. They are all very deep into the work. This is the last rehearsal)

DIRECTOR: We're going over the ex-serviceman part—*(all three are standing—the first* ACTOR *is studying Essex's mother's photo)*

DIRECTOR: I want the two of you to just sit and work out a meeting where you're talking about your feelings about being out of the service, about feeling being killed off by society—the frustration.

(The TWO ACTORS *go to one end of the table and talk while the* DIRECTOR *sits down and starts going through the clippings again, talking aloud to himself)*

DIRECTOR: I think we'll finally call it an evening . . . With Dead Essex or a documentary of Mark Essex—dead. *(To* PROJECTIONIST, *throughout the* PROJECTIONIST *is always busy taking notes, going through tapes on shelves looking through boxes of slides. In general he mutters replies)*

DIRECTOR: Flash Essex as a boy. *(Essex is flashed very small as a boy. The* DIRECTOR *studies it. A long time)*

DIRECTOR: The focus isn't right—get it bigger. *(In several minutes he and* PROJECTIONIST *experiment with getting Essex's photo right. They experiment with many angles. Then finally—)*

DIRECTOR: That's all right. *(Slightly bigger.*

Coffee. Door opens, ASSISTANT DIRECTOR—*about twenty)*

ASSISTANT DIRECTOR *(Reads. They all look up)*: Here's something in the Post—tomorrow night at —— a group of black actors will present an evening with Mark Essex—Essex as you may recall is the young black who was shot and killed in the New Orleans battle atop the roof of the Howard Johnson Motel—the evening will be presented at the —— church on 139th Street in Harlem.

(He exits.

Silence.

The ACTORS *are still talking at the other end of the table.*

The PROJECTIONIST *as throughout experiments with the photo, enlarging eyes smile, flashes mother and son together in different angles but always back to what* DIRECTOR *wants.*

Suddenly ONE *of the* ACTORS *stands)*

ACTOR: I'm going out to get the flag now. *(He exits.*

PROJECTIONIST *goes on experimenting,* ACTOR *is deep in preparing,* DIRECTOR *goes over to the tape recorder, looks through several tapes. Long time.*

ACTOR *returns with a large new-looking American flag on a pole. He stands in the doorway still for a second. Silence. They look at him)*

DIRECTOR *(Pause)*: That's just not the right flag—*(*ACTOR *remains still)*

DIRECTOR: It should be a beautiful old flag as through the eyes of a second-grade boy who believes the world is good. *(Pause)*

Get the other one—it looks more like the kind of flag that years ago was used in classrooms in public schools. A public school flag. We want a flag that's been in that classroom for years. *(Silence)*

ACTOR: I'll get the other one. *(*ACTOR *returns with a faded, dusty, slightly tattered but beautiful flag on a pole. He brings it stage center while* DIRECTOR *looks at it, stands looks at it, goes back to his table, looks at it. On the screen are Essex's eyes)*

DIRECTOR: That's it. Work out how to hold it. *(The* ACTORS *work out holding the flag, finally end up stage center holding flag together. Silence—pause. Long time preparing flag)*

DIRECTOR: O.K. Let's go through "My Country Tis of Thee." *(Pause)*
Think of your old school classroom, elementary school, scratched desks, the long windows, trees outside, a teacher you loved, the odor of chalk, your best friends.
(To PROJECTIONIST*)*
Flash Essex a boy large.

DIRECTOR *(goes to tape recorder)*: Now here's a refrain on piano. *(Refrain of "My Country Tis of Thee" on piano)*

DIRECTOR *(To the* ACTORS. *He goes and sits)*: Remember you're about to sing a song that has the utmost truth for you—you're spiritual—you're idealistic—*(Pause. The* ACTORS *sing.*
Stagelights dim and very beautiful Essex as a boy projected large.
The ACTORS *sing with a ringing spirit and idealism, as children, but not mimicking children. Accompanied by taped piano)*

ACTORS *(Sing)*: My Country Tis of Thee, Sweet Land of Liberty, of thee I sing. Land where our fathers died, land of the pilgrims' pride, from every mountain side, let freedom ring. *(Silence,* ACTORS *remain still,* DIRECTOR *turns on tape,* THEY *all listen. [Repeat]*
The PROJECTIONIST *flashes slain Essex [as if by mistake].*
Slain Essex photo.
At that moment the ACTRESS *enters—when* SHE *opens the door we again hear sounds of laughing and talking people in another studio watching a videotape—music—the* DIRECTOR *should pick current popular song by Stevie Wonder.*
The ACTRESS *is in her thirties, plain, character actress wears a plain, light-colored dress, carries a notebook, Bible, and a white choir robe.*
Hellos all around)

DIRECTOR *(To* ACTORS*)*: You can break now. I want to go over —— scene.

ACTRESS: Did you hear about—*(*THEY *discuss a real current news item, if possible, one that day, an item reflecting violence. The discussion lasts no more than a minute.*
ACTORS *exit)*

DIRECTOR *(Sits at table,* SHE *sits opposite him)*: What did you work on this morning?

ACTRESS: Twenty-third psalm.

DIRECTOR: I have some of "When I've Done the Best I Can" on tape. Do you want to hear a little? (THEY *listen to her sing a few lines from "When I've Done the Best I Can." It is very quiet*)

DIRECTOR: You haven't quite brought what it needs. Think about it. (*Silence*)

ACTRESS: Have you decided on the title?

DIRECTOR: No, I'm not sure. All I know is we want it to reflect everything that was happening, everything that preyed on his unconsciousness—not things that happened to him but all that was around him—his witnessing the loss of love—the loss of Christ—

ACTRESS: He was very sensitive. (*Very emotional*)
I have a list of titles. Is it O.K. to read them?

DIRECTOR: Sure.

ACTRESS: I thought (*Pause. Emotional*)
Christ Confusion. (*Pause*)
The Wilderness: Howard Johnson Motel.
From Luke: The Crooked Shall be Made Straight. (*Pause*)
I feel he felt he was setting things straight—(*Pause*)
Mark Essex's Dream of the Beginning: When God Created Man.
(*The* DIRECTOR *listens intent and moved, muffled sounds from hall.*
They sit silently for a long moment.
He gets up, walks around, looks at flag in the corner, looks at screen)

DIRECTOR: Alright, let's try the Twenty-third Psalm. (*Silence*)

ACTRESS (*Prepared*): The Lord Is My Shepherd I

DIRECTOR: What are you working for?

ACTRESS: I'm in Sunday School. I'm nine. I'm in Sunday School Class with my sister. My sister is sitting next to me. After Sunday School we're going to go home to have a big dinner fried chicken.... I have one of those beautiful Sunday School cards in my pocket... or in my hands... my Sunday School teacher is sitting in front of me, she asks us to say the twenty-third Psalm—

DIRECTOR: You're young and you're very happy.

ACTRESS (*Very lyrically. Slowly*): The Lord is My Shepherd. I Shall Not Want. He maketh me lie down... in green pastures: He leadeth me beside the still waters.

DIRECTOR: Now close your eyes, go on.

ACTRESS (*Slowly*): He restoreth my soul.

DIRECTOR: Go on.

ACTRESS: He leadeth me in the paths of righteousness for his name's sake.
Director *(To the PROJECTIONIST)*: Flash Essex Slain.

(To ACTRESS) Open your eyes look at it go on, and think of him riddled with all those bullets, think of him in Sunday School—Palm Sunday or Easter—Easter in a new suit—or on the first Sunday— the choir in white robes—go on—

ACTRESS: Yea though I walk through the valley of the shadow of death I will fear no evil for thou art with me, thy rod and staff they comfort me thou preparest a table before me in the presence of mine enemies.

(Very slow) Thou anointest my head with oil; my cup runneth over. Surely goodness and mercy shall follow me all the days of my life; and I will dwell in the house of the Lord forever—*(Silence.*

Lights dim.

They leave stage.

Lights come up slowly on PROJECTIONIST. *He is sitting at projector arranging his slides in the order* HE *will use them. He adjusts the screen a couple of times. The projector is slightly larger than reality and very black.*

He starts with slides and projects at average speed at least a half dozen slides that we have not seen. They are the faces [white] of the people in Essex's town and one of Essex's house. He goes back and refocuses them enlarging certain aspects, numbering them, putting them in box.

*VERY
SLOWLY*

Midwestern face.
Midwestern face.
Midwestern face.
Essex's hours.
Kissinger.
Essex as a sailor.
He ends with the photo of Essex as a sailor.

Lights brighter. Door opens, ACTORS *come back with more coffee, cigarettes, food, etc. The table progressively becomes more in disarray, the* ACTORS *seem more tired. For the first time when the door opens we don't hear music.*

The ACTORS *watch the screen, as the* PROJECTIONIST *goes on.* ACTRESS *comes in, she watches.*

Flash photos again)

ACTRESS: Do we have enough of the midwestern faces.

ACTOR: They seem open enough.

OTHER ACTOR: I don't know about trust but he didn't distrust those faces—it's that open American look—I guess innocence is the word—for Essex's vision. *(THEY watch—as photos are flashed.*

Essex's room in New Orleans. A teacher of Essex looking at his year book. Two wounded policemen in New Orleans.

Sign—Howard Johnson Downtown)

DIRECTOR *(Enters. Closes door ready to really work)*: Let's sit. *(THEY all return to table.*

Light focus on DIRECTOR.

Screen dark)

DIRECTOR: Alright now I think there should be the reading about the war in Viet Nam and then . . . about Essex being ripped apart . . . because they continue into each other. *(Slowly. Thinking. Thinking)*

Now I'm going to read this.

(To PROJECTIONIST*)* Flash Essex as a boy. *(Essex as boy flashed, perhaps focused on his smile.*

PROJECTIONIST *goes out)*

DIRECTOR: Here are the items. *(Reads from clippings slowly.)*

1972—B-52 bombers made their biggest raid on the Vietnam war demilitarized zone to date dropping nearly 200 tons of bombs.

1973—at 9:25 p.m. the helicopter lumbered past again. *(Pause)*

When the sharpshooters opened fire, a slight figure, rifle in hand, bolted into the open. Trapped in a withering crossfire between the helicopter overhead and marksmen in two adjacent buildings, Jimmy Essex was literally ripped apart by at least a hundred bullets. The police kept firing even after he went down, his body twitching with the impact of each slug and his rifle shattered beside him.

DIRECTOR: They very much continue into each other—they are one and the same. *(Silence.*

Momentum picks up now.

They work as a group)

DIRECTOR: Will someone find the Peace Is At Hand Speech.

(THEY look through clippings)

DIRECTOR: I want the repetition of the coming of peace, the coming of peace, peace coming of peace. In all that repetition is deception—and Essex was a man sensitive to deception. I believe it preyed on him—peace he was delivering peace unto himself and unto us. I believe that.

(Silence. They look through clippings)

ACTRESS: Have we finally found the right Bible passage—

ACTOR: Can't find the Peace Is At Hand speech but we do have that picture of Kissinger entering the peace talks again and again. Smiling.

DIRECTOR: Yes we want that picture over and over entering and leaving, entering and leaving the peace talkings with peace at hand— smiling—all this happening around Essex—all appearing deception to him.

ACTRESS: Do you think he was in that room then, the one in New Orleans. *(She goes to projector, finds slide—flashes Room In New Orleans.*
Focus on many angles of the room—closeup of the bed, writing on the wall, etc. in great detail.
Slow)

DIRECTOR: I don't know where he was . . . I'd say many places—he too was entering and leaving many places.

ACTOR: Searching for peace.

DIRECTOR: Yes.

*(*THEY *all study the room on the screen.*
All angles.
They seem tired.
Focus on "Africa—Black—My destiny lies in the Bloody Death of Racist Pigs—Blood Black Justice—BATA."
DIRECTOR *speaks)*

DIRECTOR: Black
My Destiny Lies In the Death of Racist Pigs
Blood
Black Justice
BATA
WAYU
SAVONA
LABAO
Shoot to Kill
America
(All focused very sharply on screen. They sit silent—concentrating long time)

DIRECTOR *(Quietly)*: Let's hear the tape of "When I've Done the Best I Can."

*(*ACTRESS *puts on tape.*
Then—they all wander about the room in their own thoughts listening to tape of ACTRESS *singing "When I've Done the Best I Can."*

Silence. They wander about the room.
ASSISTANT DIRECTOR *enters)*
ASSISTANT DIRECTOR: Here are some more tapes. I think the posters
are almost all ready. *(Hands tape to* DIRECTOR. HE *exits.*
PROJECTIONIST *comes back in.*
There are no sounds now when door opens.
All are subdued.
The PROJECTIONIST *looks through shelves for film)*
DIRECTOR: Let's have this tape of The Revolution is Here and the shoot-
ing—*(Looks through tape.*
They listen.
While tape is playing)
DIRECTOR: Remember let's not get away from the idea of recounting
what people said about Essex.
ACTOR: What is it the minister said?
DIRECTOR: Yes the minister...what is it the minister said about Essex?
ACTRESS: Christianity...is a white man's religion.
DIRECTOR: Yes...Christianity is a white man's religion.
(They are silent.
Still on screen
NEW ORLEANS ROOM
BATA
BLACK JUSTICE)
DIRECTOR *(To* ACTOR*):* —would you do that?
ACTOR: Essex and his minister?
DIRECTOR: Yes.
ACTOR *(Reading very slowly, strong)*: And when interviewed his minister
who had known him as a boy remarked how he had changed when
he came out of the Navy. I asked him why hadn't he come to church
since he had been home and he said—Christianity is a
(Very slowly) white man's religion.
DIRECTOR *(Absently)*: The deception again—he had been deceived...
as a boy in Sunday School.
ACTOR *(Very moved)*: I've decided on the right Bible passage. I'm going
to use Luke 3.
*(Quiet projection on room in New Orleans, quietly on tape sounds
of shooting atop the model and Essex's voice The Revolution Is
Here)*
DIRECTOR *(Quietly)*: Let's take a break.
(Darkness)

II

EVENING

Evening: Studio empty—clutter on table—chairs disarray—flag in corner—screen empty.

ASSISTANT DIRECTOR *enters carrying a pile of blown-up posters—he exits and comes back in a minute with another pile. He sets them against the table. The top poster is one of a B-52. The posters, like the slides are stark and clear. (Large)*

He goes out, when the door is open now—the hallway is dark and quiet—and brings back a notebook.

He clears a place at the cluttered table, sits down. He opens note book, goes over aloud a check list of clippings—

ASSISTANT DIRECTOR *(Slowly)*: Returning Home
>   Unbalanced, drug addicts
>   All the Peace Is At Hand speeches
>   More war headlines
>   More photographs of the Essex town
>   The tranquility
>   More church songs
>   Leaning on the Everlasting Vine
>   In the Garden
>   Blessed Fellowship
>   Jesus Loves Me
>   *(Affecting him)*
>   Items: Death at the Olympics
>
>   Items: As a Young Man
>
>   Death of President Kennedy
>   Death of Malcolm
>   Death of Robert Kennedy
>   Death of Martin Luther King
>   Kent State Killings
>   Death at Southern University
>   (HE *checks them off.*
>   *Sound of footsteps.*
>   *The* DIRECTOR *enters)*

DIRECTOR: The hall's too dark.
>   (ASSISTANT DIRECTOR *goes to turn on light.*

DIRECTOR *looks at list, goes over pages—slowly then turns to posters—*ASSISTANT DIRECTOR *comes back—he holds up the check list)*

ASSISTANT DIRECTOR *(sits at table. To himself. Going over his projects: Aloud)*: Items: War dead photos and figures McGovern and Eagleton Affair—loss of hope in McG.

Nixon's speeches without conviction

Interviews with G.I.s—Black and White G.I. Drug use rising *(Slow)*

News Items:

Resuming the Bombing
Mining the Harbor
Photos of G.I.s Black and White
(Posters—the DIRECTOR *goes through them, looking at each one rather quickly)*

DIRECTOR: We'll put them around the room. I want to see them from a distance.

(He sits down at table, puts a bottle of liquor on it—takes a drink from cup)

I see you've got the list. Let's go over it once more—put it on the tape—

*(*ASSISTANT DIRECTOR *turns on tape)*

ASSISTANT DIRECTOR *(Reading to* DIRECTOR. *Slowly)*: This is what surrounded him—

War Dead Photos and Figures
McGovern and Eagleton Affair—loss of hope in McGovern.
Nixon's speeches without conviction.
Interviews with G.I.s—Black and White G.I. Drug use Rising
Resuming the Bombing
Mining the Harbor

Photos—G.I.s—Black and White returning home
Unbalanced drug addicts
All the Peace Is At Hand speeches

More war headlines

More photographs of Essex's town—the outward tranquility
More church songs
Leaning on the Everlasting Vine

In the Garden
Blessed Fellowship
Jesus Loves Me

Items:
    Death at the Olympics

Items: As a young man:
    Death of President Kennedy

Death of Malcolm
Death of Robert Kennedy
Death of Martin Luther King
Kent State Killings
Death at Southern
(DIRECTOR *doesn't say anything. Puts up posters around room.*
    Poster 1—B-52
    Poster 2—Vietnamese Children
    Puts up Poster 3—Bombs)
ASSISTANT DIRECTOR *(Absently)*: . . . surrounded by war and killing . . .
DIRECTOR *(Absently)*: . . . he saw his battlefield. *(Silence.*
    ASSISTANT DIRECTOR *sits at table—casually picks up clipping,*
    laughs bitterly)
ASSISTANT DIRECTOR: Get this . . . cheerful newscaster
    (As a cheerful newscaster) G.I. DRUG USE SEEN RISING IN
    EUROPE—TWO CONGRESSMEN REPORT ALARMING IN-
    CREASE.—BONN, January 6—The use of hard drugs by young
    American soldiers stationed in Europe is increasing at an alarming
    rate according to two United States Congressmen who have been
    investigating the problem here.
    (They laugh)
ASSISTANT DIRECTOR: Here's another, about the same time as Essex.
    (Cheerful newscaster again) NIXON'S BIRTHDAY HOPE
    (They laugh. Sardonically)
    WASHINGTON (AP)—President Nixon, observing his 60th
    birthday today, says he "hopes to do great things" in the first four
    years of his seventh decade.
    He doesn't feel old, he says. And to keep thinking young he sug-
    gests looking to the future, not the past, and staying in contact with
    younger people.
    Nixon granted a birthday-eve interview to two wire-service re-
    porters, but limited the discussion solely to his birthday reflections.

He outlined what he called his 10-year milestones, starting at age 20, when he was "a junior in college, majoring in history and English, going out for football—but I never made the team."

At 30, he was in Bougainville in the South Pacific in World War II.

At 40, he had just been elected vice president. At 50, he had just been defeated for the governorship of California—and at 60, just re-elected for a second Presidential term.

(They laugh)

ASSISTANT DIRECTOR: Here's another, from Art Buchwald:

WASHINGTON—President Nixon has announced that he is supporting the Washington Redskins in their battle with the Miami Dolphins in the Super Bowl January 14.

He is sending Henry Kissinger to Miami to negotiate with Coach Don Shula of the Dolphins an honorable settlement to the hostilities.

More cheerful news—

(As a cheerful newscaster)

SAIGON—Air raid sirens scream day and night. The earth trembles with the violence of an earthquake, and whole sections of the city crumble in a roar of flames and flying jagged steel. For the first time in the war the people seem afraid.

(THEY sit at the table laughing bitterly—exhaustedly.

PROJECTIONIST enters, exchanges hellos, goes to projector and starts to go through his slides one by one at average pace.

The ASSISTANT DIRECTOR and DIRECTOR put up a couple more posters simultaneously.

Fur Poster

Viet Vet Poster

Slides are:

Mother

Essex as a boy

Teacher

Midwestern faces

Essex's hours

The ASSISTANT DIRECTOR and DIRECTOR look at all the posters and arrange and rearrange them.

The PROJECTIONIST flashes slain photo—moves to close up of Essex's face.

They look up.

Silence)

DIRECTOR *(Very quietly)*: Show him as a boy again.
  (Flash Essex as a Boy.
  Lights dim)

III
NIGHT

Night: Table cluttered—all posters about—flags in a corner—screen
*empty—*DIRECTOR *is sitting at table—*ACTORS *return—it is clear they*
are exhausted—they don't talk but just sit around table all absorbed in
their own thoughts—tasks—

DIRECTOR *(Very quietly)*: O.K. this is it. We're there now. We're with
  him.
  (Screen empty)
  However...
  ...to New Orleans to see a Navy buddy, and he stayed to find
  his destiny in welling black rage. The hour... in the hotel, his mother
  in Emporia was standing up in St. James Baptist Church, asking the
  congregation to pray for her son Jimmy who "doesn't want to go
  along with the Lord." After Essex died, investigators visited his shabby
  rented shack in the black slums along Dryades Street. They found a
  cheap waterbed, some clothing—and four walls scribbled over with
  anti-white graffiti. "The quest for freedom is death," said one slo-
  gan. "Then by death I shall escape to freedom."
  We're there with him now!
DIRECTOR *(Reads from clipping)*: A little after 5:30, a big green H-46
  Sea Knight helicopter from Marine Helicopter Transport, Squadron
  767 arrived from nearby Belle Chasse Naval Air Station.
  For about a dozen flights that night and the next day, Lieutenant
  Colonel C. H. Pitman brought the craft, bearing usually five police
  marksmen, hovering over the center of the city, circling only about
  25 feet off the roof while the riflemen blasted away at the concrete
  enclosures.
  At about 9:15 Sunday night, a phosphorus grenade or flare from
  the helicopter arched a red path into one of the enclosures.
  A lone figure, carrying a carbine, burst into the open, hunched
  over, crouching low, he began to cut a zigzag running path across the
  roof.
  A torrent of bullets—red tracers, armor-piercing shells, shotgun
  pellets, ammunition from AR-16 carbines, pistols and private rifles—

literally ripped him apart. Even after he fell to the roof, the gunfire continued, until police commanders screamed for a halt.

GUTS AND POTATO SALAD

Even then, at intervals, an angry, cursing, frustrated policeman would fire another burst at the body. The coroner's office said it had been struck by more than a hundred bullets.

The body was identified as that of "Jimmy" Essex, a quiet black youth from a middle-class family in Emporia, Kan., who was said to have developed a hatred for whites while serving in the Navy. In the baggy cargo pockets of his fatigue pants, the police said, were found cherry bombs, and firecrackers, along with spare ammunition.

Friends here said that on the night before his death he had enjoyed a dinner of grits and potato salad and said that it might be his last big meal.

Five days after his death, the police found the last of his four addresses here, a $40 a month flat whose walls were covered with black and red painted slogans: "Shoot a devil like you shoot a dog pig." "My destiny lies in the bloody death of all racist pigs," and, scribbled in pencil, "The quest for freedom is death—then by death I shall escape to freedom."

The weapon he carried was broken in four pieces by the gunfire; the police put it together for display later with Scotch tape. It was identified as a .44-caliber magnum Ruger carbine purchased by Essex from Montgomery Ward in Emporia on April 11, 1972.

(Screen empty.
All are very silent)

DIRECTOR: Get the flag again. (ACTOR *gets flag—brings it forward)*
Now we'll want the tape of Allegiance to the Flag
America the Beautiful
Battle Hymn of the Republic
Star Spangled Banner
all of them.
(To ACTOR*)*
Can you do one of them.
(ACTOR *very simply sings "America the Beautiful."*
He puts the flag back.
Screen empty)
DIRECTOR: Now the church music all of it.
Just How Much He Cares

Blessed Fellowship
Leaning on the Everlasting Vine
Jesus Loves Me
He Comes to the Garden
Nobody Knows the Trouble I've Seen
Precious Lord Take My Hand
Were You There When They Crucified My Lord
all of it. He could be taking communion. He could be looking at the cross. He could be holding palms. He could be looking at a Sunday School card with Jesus on it, tending the flock.

(The ACTRESS *has put on the choir robe.*
Silence)

DIRECTOR: We're there now.

(One ACTOR *is looking through Bible, the* OTHER *is deep in thought.*
₁ Screen empty)

ACTRESS: I'm there now. I'm going to do "In the Garden." *(She prepares)*
The first indication that something was going to happen came last spring when I purchased a .44 Magnum hunting rifle—that gun was found next to my body when I was shot that Sunday from a Marine helicopter. *(A long silence. She puts her head down)*

ACTRESS: I'm ready! (ACTRESS *starts to sing very beautifully—"In The Garden")*
I come to the garden alone while the dew is still on the roses ... and the joy we share as we tarry there none other has ever known ...
Oh he walks with me and he talks with me and he tells me I am his own and the joy we share as we tarry there none other has ever known ...

(Slain Essex on Screen.
Silence—a long, long silence.
They sit.
Slain Essex on Screen)

ACTOR: I think I want to end with a Bible passage—

OTHER ACTOR: I want to sing Jesus Loves Me, as a kid he gave his part-time earnings to the church. *(HE sings "Jesus Loves Me."*
Flash—Bloodied Policemen.
Silence)

ACTRESS: I definitely want to end with a Bible passage—maybe as his mother read it to him.

(Empty screen.
Then Essex as a Sailor, small.
Lights very dim)
DIRECTOR: *(Barely audible)* I think we should all read Luke. *(Silence.*
Long.
Then they all very slowly, very falteringly read St. Luke)
ALL *(very slowly, falteringly)*: St. Luke 3: 3-6

And he came into all the country about Jordan preaching the Baptism of repentance for the remission of sins...

the voice of one crying in the wilderness—Prepare ye the way of the Lord make his paths straight... every valley shall be filled and every mountain and hill shall be brought low and the crooked place shall be made straight and the rough ways shall be made smooth and all flesh shall see the salvation of God—

(Lights dimmer)
Luke (5)

you know the spirit of the Lord is upon me because he hath annointed me to preach the gospel to the poor he hath sent me to heal the broken hearted—to preach deliverance to the captives and recovering of sight to the blind to set at liberty them that are bruised.

To heal the brokenhearted.

(Flash Essex—American sailor—large)
DARKNESS

CURTAIN

The Alexander Plays

She Talks to Beethoven

The Ohio State Murders

The Film Club (A Monologue by Suzanne
    Alexander)

The Dramatic Circle

For my sons, Adam and Joe,
without whose encouragement I could not continue to write

She Talks to Beethoven

First produced by River Arts in Woodstock, New York, and directed by
Clinton Turner Davis in June 1989.

CHARACTERS

LUDWIG VAN BEETHOVEN
SUZANNE ALEXANDER A Writer

AUTHOR'S NOTE

The music in the piece should equal in length the text. Anonymous diary entries are from actual sources.

SCENE: *Accra, Ghana, in 1961, soon after independence. It is early evening.*
*Interior of a bedroom at house on the campus at Legon, a shuttered
room, a ceiling fan, a bed covered with mosquito netting, a shelf of books
over a small writing table, and a delicate blue phonograph. All windows
except one are shuttered. That window overlooks a winding road. The side
of the room that is shuttered is dim.* SUZANNE ALEXANDER *listens to a
small radio. She is American, black, a pretty woman in her thirties. Part of
her arm and shoulder are wrapped or bandaged in gauze. Placed on a shelf
opposite her bed are a group of x-ray slides, the kind doctors use to analyze
a patient's illness. She studies them, watches the road, and listlessly writes a
line or so in a notebook. On the shelf is a photograph of Kwame Nkrumah,
a book on Ludwig van Beethoven, a wedding photo of* SUZANNE *and her
husband, David, and a mural displaying various scenes of Ghana's independence.* SUZANNE *is dressed in a robe of kinte cloth.*
*From outside Ghanaians play stringed musical instruments as they walk
in an evening procession.*

SUZANNE: *(Reads over notes from published diaries.)* "The production of *Fidelio* was anticipated by months of increasing tension as the war with Napoleon escalated. Soldiers were quartered in all suburbs. At nine o'clock houses were locked and all inns cleared out. At Ulm on 20 October the Russians conceded defeat to the French. Ten days later, Bernadotte and the French army entered Salzburg. One saw baggage and travel-carriages passing. In the afternoon I went with Therese to the Danube. We saw the possessions of the Court being shipped off. The Court is sending everything away, even bedwarmers and shoetrees. It looks as if they have no intention of ever coming back to Vienna.

After lunch Eppinger came with the devastating news that the Russians have retreated as far as Saint Polten. Vienna is in great danger of being swept over by marauding Chasseurs."

(SUZANNE suddenly turns to the radio.)

VOICE ON RADIO: I came into this world with the desire to give order to things: my one great hope was to be of the world and I discovered I was only an object among other objects. Sealed into that crushing objecthood I turned beseechingly to others. Their attention was a liberation endowing me once more with an agility that I had thought lost. But just as I reached the other side I stumbled and the movements, the attitudes, the glances of the others fixed me there. I burst apart. Now the fragments have been put together by another self.

ANOTHER VOICE ON THE RADIO: And that was David Alexander, the American professor of African poetry, here at the University... reading from Frantz Fanon. Mr. Alexander is still missing. Alexander traveled with Fanon in Blida. His wife, also American, the writer Suzanne Alexander, is recovering from an unspecified illness. It is known that she was writing a play about Ludwig van Beethoven when she was stricken. Alexander was by her side at the hospital when he suddenly vanished two nights ago. Mrs. Alexander has returned to their home on the campus at Legon near Accra.

(Musical passage of African stringed instruments.)

SUZANNE: *(Reading from published diaries.)* "The final rehearsal was on 22 May but the promised new overture was still in the pen of the creator. The orchestra was called to rehearsal in the morning of the performance. Beethoven did not come. After waiting a long time we drove to his lodgings to bring him but he lay in bed sleeping soundly. Beside him stood a goblet with wine and a biscuit in it. The sheets of the overture were scattered on the floor and bed. A burnt out candle showed he had worked far into the night."

(The room appears out of the darkness. SUZANNE *rises and crosses to* BEETHOVEN *and stands staring at him.)*

RADIO: Although the couple are American they have lived in West Africa for a number of years and together started a newspaper that was a forerunner to *Black Orpheus* bringing together poems, stories, and novels by African writers as well as Afro-Americans, some in exile in England. It is known that often Alexander jests with his wife about her continued deep love for European artists such as Sibelius, Chopin, and Beethoven and indeed if anyone in Accra wants to hear these composers one has only to pass the windows of the delightful white stucco house among the fragrant flowers on the campus at Legon.

*(*SUZANNE *stares at* BEETHOVEN.*)*

SUZANNE: *(Reading published notes from the diary of———.)* "Beethoven was the the most celebrated of the living composers living in Vienna. The neglect of his person which he exhibited gave him a somewhat wild appearance. His features were strong and prominent; his eye was full of rude energy; his hair, which neither comb nor scissors seemed to have visited for years, overshadowed his broad brow in a quantity and confusion to which only the snakes round a Gorgon's head offer a parallel."

You worked into the night.

BEETHOVEN: Yes. Tonight is the opening of *Fidelio.*

SUZANNE: Did I awaken you?

BEETHOVEN: I was dreaming of my mother and how every year on Saint Magdalen's day, her name and birthdate, we would celebrate. The music stands would be brought out. And chairs would be placed everywhere and a canopy set up in the room where the portrait of my grandfather hung. We decorated the canopy with flowers, laurel branches, and foliage. Early in the evening my mother retired. And by ten o'clock everyone would be ready. The tuning up would begin and my mother would be awakened. She would then dress and be led in and seated in a beautifully decorated chair under the canopy. At that very moment magnificent music would strike up resounding throughout the neighborhood. And when the music ended, a meal was served and company ate and drank and danced until the celebration came to an end.

(Loud voices from outside.)

BEETHOVEN: That must be the directors of the theater for the new overture. It's not finished.

(BEETHOVEN *starts toward the door and vanishes.*)

SUZANNE: Wait. I want to talk to you. Before David disappeared he questioned me on passages I wrote about you in Vienna. We argued.

(*She looks at drawings* BEETHOVEN *has in his room and sheet music on the floor. Suddenly she runs back to the open window watching the road for her husband. A long passage of the African stringed music from the procession on the road.* BEETHOVEN *returns and sits at the piano composing. He seems to have forgotten* SUZANNE. *She continues looking out of the window, listening to the African stringed music, watching the road for her husband, David. The music now changes into the overture* BEETHOVEN *is composing.*)

RADIO: Has Alexander been murdered?

SUZANNE: I've been unable to work. David helps me with all the scenes about you.

BEETHOVEN: Perhaps you might seek a retreat in the woods, Suzanne. It makes me happy to wander among herbs and trees.

(*He continues composing music.*)

SUZANNE: Tell me about your summers in Vienna . . . I have read life in Vienna during the hot months was not pleasant.

BEETHOVEN: Yes, like tonight here in Accra it was not pleasant. There were over a thousand horse-drawn cabs and over three hundred coaches of hire traveling across granite cobbles. They raised a terrible dust which hovered in the air the whole summer and even during part of the winter. It was like a dirty fog. I went to Baden and worked on a symphony.

SUZANNE: And your fame? I must ask you, are you happy with your fame?

BEETHOVEN: I do not like or have anything to do with people who refused to believe in me when I had not yet achieved fame. My three string quartets were all finished before fame came.

(*He composes. She returns to the window. He composes music.*)

SUZANNE: (*From diary of ———.*) "While he was working, he would stand at the washbasin and pour great pitchersful of water over his hands, at the same time howling the whole gamut of the scale, ascending and descending; then pace the room, his eyes fixed in a stare, jot down a few notes and again return to his water pouring and howling."

(Music from Fidelio*)*

BEETHOVEN: You've argued about me?

SUZANNE: Yes. David says many scenes of you are too romantic—and that I must read more diaries about you. He gave me one by a Baron about this very room.

SUZANNE: *(Reads to* BEETHOVEN.*)* "I wended my way to the unapproachable composer's home, and at the door it struck me that I had chosen the day ill, for, having to make an official visit thereafter, I was wearing the everyday habiliments of the Council of State. To make matters worse, his lodging was next to the city wall, and as Napoleon had ordered its destruction, blasts had just been set off under his windows."

RADIO: Has David Alexander been murdered? The outspoken professor at the University of Legon is still missing. As we have reported, Alexander worked with Fanon in Blida and was friends with the late Patrice Lumumba. Now that Fanon may be dying of cancer, Alexander has become highly vocal in keeping Fanon's words alive. We've played you his rendering of Fanon's essays and now we listen to David Alexander's poetry. It has never been clear, Alexander has said on many occasions, who the enemies of Fanon are and even though Ghana has won its independence, as Osegefo also continues to remind us: there are still enemies. Alexander was hated by many for his writing on the clinics and Fanon, and for his statements on the mental condition of the colonized patients. At first it was thought that when Alexander disappeared he was writing about one of the patients at the hospital at Legon, but now it has been revealed he was there waiting to hear the results of his wife's undisclosed surgery. And was indeed by her bedside and disappeared while she slept after surgery.

The Alexanders, an inseparable couple, often read their works together and have written a series of poems and essays jointly. It has been learned that at the hospital while sitting at his wife's side Alexander made sketches of his wife's illness and explained the progress and surgery procedures to her.

(Music. Passage that BEETHOVEN *is composing.)*

(From outside voices are heard shouting "Karl, Karl, Karl!" BEETHOVEN *rushes from the room.* SUZANNE *stands at the window. Music from the road blends with voices shouting, "Karl!"* BEETHOVEN *enters.)*

BEETHOVEN: My nephew Karl has tried to shoot himself. He's wounded. He's been taken to his mother's house.

SUZANNE: We'll go there.

BEETHOVEN: No. I can't. He told the police he was tormented by me and that is why he tried to kill himself and he does not want to see me. He says he's miserable and he's grown worse because I want him to live his life according to my expectation of him.

SUZANNE: *(Writes in her manuscript.)* Beethoven's nephew Karl tried to shoot himself. The tension between the two had reached a crisis. The incident left Beethoven in a shocked state. He was the only person Beethoven really loved to the point of idolatry.

RADIO: And again... Alexander... reading Fanon... still missing... where... has he been murdered?

SUZANNE: We could still walk to Karl's house near the Danube and look into his window. Perhaps you can call to him.

(Light in room fades. Now they are walking near the Danube.
They look up at what could be Karl's windows.)

BEETHOVEN: *(Shouts.)* Karl, Karl, Karl!

BEETHOVEN: *(Calls again.)* Karl!

(Long silence.)

BEETHOVEN: We've come far, Suzanne. We won't get back to Dobling until nearly four now.

SUZANNE: *(Writing.)* His nephew refused to see him. We did not get back to Dobling where Beethoven lived until seven. As we walked he started humming, sometimes howling, singing indefinite notes. "A theme for the last part of the overture has occurred to me," he said.

(Room appears again. BEETHOVEN *enters, running to the*
pianoforte. Music.)

RADIO: *(David's voice reads an excerpt from Fanon.)* Yesterday awakening to the world I saw the sky utterly and wholly. I wanted to rise but fell paralyzed. Without responsibility, nothingness, and infinitely I began to weep.

(Music. BEETHOVEN *composes.)*

SUZANNE: *(Reads from the diary of ——.)* "Beethoven misunderstood me very often, and had to use the utmost concentration when I was speaking, to get my meaning. That, of course, embarrassed and disturbed me very much. It disturbed him, too, and this led him to speak more himself and very loudly. He told me a lot about his life and about Vienna. He was venomous and embittered. He raged about everything, and was dissatisfied with everything. He cursed Austria and Vienna in particular. He spoke quickly and with great vivacity. He often banged his fist on the piano and made such a noise that it echoed around the room."

(SUZANNE *writes while talking to* BEETHOVEN.)

SUZANNE: You must dress now for the concert.

BEETHOVEN: Please go to the theater with me.

SUZANNE: I must watch the road for David.

BEETHOVEN: We'll stay together until David arrives. We'll watch the road and go to the theater together.

RADIO: An hour ago there was an accident near Kumasi that seemed to have some connection to Alexander but now that has been discounted.

RADIO: It is now believed that David Alexander, learning of a plot against his life while he sat at his wife's bedside, chose to vanish to protect her, his colleague and fellow writer. Professor Alexander still continues to speak about attaining true independence. So now it is believed he is alive and waiting for the time when he can return home. Included in the next selection are two poems read by the couple together from their recording. The first selection is by Diop.

(*Radio fades.*)

BEETHOVEN: Is it true that David made drawings of your surgery as he sat by your side so that you would not be frightened?

SUZANNE: Yes.

BEETHOVEN: How very romantic. And do you believe that he vanished to protect you?

SUZANNE: Yes.

BEETHOVEN: And you compose poems and read together?

SUZANNE: Yes.

BEETHOVEN: What scenes did you fight over?

SUZANNE: He wanted a scene where you read your contracts, a scene where you talk about money.

(BEETHOVEN *laughs.*)

BEETHOVEN: Do you disagree a great deal about your work together?

SUZANNE: No, only over this play. We set out to write it together years ago, then it became mine. Even on the morning of the surgery we argued about it.

(BEETHOVEN *laughs.*)

BEETHOVEN: I feel David will return by morning, perhaps on the road with the musicians, perhaps even in disguise.

SUZANNE: Disguise.

BEETHOVEN: Yes.

RADIO: A body has been found in a swamp in Abijan. Is it Alexander? Has he been murdered?

(SUZANNE *begins to unwrap her bandages.*)

BEETHOVEN: Why do you unwrap the gauze?

SUZANNE: The bandage is wrapped on my wound. I'm to unwrap it tonight and if the wound is pale white I'm still sick.

(BEETHOVEN *starts to help her slowly unwrap the gauze. She does not look at her surgical wound as he unwraps the gauze.*)

SUZANNE: What color?

BEETHOVEN: The color is pale white.

(*Silence.*)

BEETHOVEN: How long have you been sick?

SUZANNE: Two and one half years?

BEETHOVEN: You mustn't worry. I've foreseen my death many times. It will be in winter. In Vienna. My friends will come from Graz. *(He embraces her.)*

(SUZANNE *sits at* BEETHOVEN*'s piano. He walks to the window.*)

SUZANNE: (*Reads from the diary of ——.*) "Before Beethoven's death I found him greatly disturbed and jaundiced all over his body. A frightful choleric attack had threatened his life the preceding night. Trembling and shivering he bent double because of the pains which raged in his liver and intestines; and his feet, hitherto moderately inflamed, were tremendously swollen. From this time on dropsy developed, the liver showed plain indication of hard nodules, there was an increase of jaundice. The disease moved onward with gigantic strides. Already in the third week there came incidents of nocturnal suffocation."

(*Radio.*)

VOICE ON RADIO: A recording of Alexander reading David Diop:

Listen comrades of the struggling centuries
To the keen clamour of the Negro from Africa to the
Americas they have killed Mamba
As they killed the seven of Martinsville
or the Madagascan down there in the pale light of
the prisons....

(*Room fades. They are backstage.* BEETHOVEN *is dressed formally for the theater. Music from stage. Orchestra rehearsing Fidelio. They both watch the road.*)

SUZANNE: You must be happy tonight about *Fidelio.*
> *(He does not speak.)*

BEETHOVEN: Suzanne, because of your anguish I want to share a secret with you. For the last six years I have been afflicted with an incurable complaint. From year to year my hopes of being cured have gradually been shattered and finally I have been forced to accept the prospect of permanent infirmity. I am obliged to live in solitude. If I try to ignore my infirmity I am cruelly reminded of it. Yet I cannot bring myself to say to people, "Speak up, shout, for I am deaf."
> *(Music from stage, orchestra rehearsing* Fidelio.*)*

In the theater I have to place myself quite close to the orchestra in order to understand what the actor is saying, and at a distance I cannot hear the high notes of instruments or voices. As for the spoken voice it is surprising that some people have never noticed my deafness; but since I have always been liable to fits of absentmindedness, they attribute my hardness of hearing to that. Sometimes, too, I can scarcely hear a person who speaks softly; I can hear sounds, it is true, but cannot make out the words. But if anyone shouts, I can't bear it. I beg you not to say anything about my condition to anyone. I am only telling you this as a secret. Suzanne, if my trouble persists may I visit you next spring?

SUZANNE: I had no idea you were going deaf.

BEETHOVEN: Yes, in fact you must write any further questions in this little conversation book. I've been trying to hide them from you.
> *(He gives her the conversation books.)*

BEETHOVEN: You must write what you want to say to me in them. I cannot hear you.

SUZANNE: Ludwig! *(She embraces him.)*

RADIO: *(SUZANNE's voice reads from Fanon.)* At the level of individuals violence is a cleansing force, it frees a man from despair and inaction.

RADIO: It has been learned that the group who plotted to kill David Alexander has been discovered near Kumasi and has been arrested. It is safe for Alexander to return to Accra. And it is reported that Nkrumah himself met with the revolutionary poet a few hours ago and reported to him the details of his would-be assassins' capture.

SUZANNE: *(Suddenly.)* Ludwig, why is David's handwriting in your conversation books? This poem is in David's own handwriting.
> *(BEETHOVEN does not answer.)*
> *(SUZANNE studies the conversation books.)*

SUZANNE: Ludwig! There is a message from David, a love poem of Senghor's. Whenever David wants to send me a message he puts a poem inside my papers, in a book he knows I will read.

(She writes in conversation book and reads.)

SUZANNE: Be not astonished, my love, if at times my song grows dark

If I change my melodious reed for the khalam and the tama's beat

And the green smell of the rice fields for galloping rumble of the tabalas.

Listen to the threats of old sorcerers, to the thundering wrath of God!

Ah, maybe tomorrow the purple voice of your songmaker will be silent forever.

That's why today my song is so urgent and my fingers bleed on my khalam.

(She opens another conversation book. Music from the stage.)

SUZANNE: *(Reads David's words.)* Suzanne, please continue writing scenes. Please continue writing scenes we talked about.

(Lights fade backstage and come up on concert hall. BEETHOVEN *now stands before the orchestra, stage center. He waves baton wildly. It is obvious he does not hear. Music stops. He starts again. He waves wildly, throwing the singers and orchestra off beat and into confusion. Silence. He calls* SUZANNE *to his side. She writes in the book.* BEETHOVEN *buries his face and rushes to the wings leaving the orchestra.* SUZANNE *writes.)*

SUZANNE: Ludwig was still desperately trying to conduct in public and insisted upon conducting rehearsals even though by now during the concert the orchestra knew to ignore his beat and to follow instead the Kapellmeister who stood behind him.

*(*BEETHOVEN *returns stage center. As she speaks* BEETHOVEN *conducts. Music.)*

SUZANNE: At *Fidelio* Ludwig waved his baton back and forth with violent motions, not hearing a note. If he thought it should be piano he crouched down almost under the podium and if he wanted faster he jumped up with strange gestures uttering strange sounds. Yet the evening was a triumph.

*(*SUZANNE *stands at window writing. A shadow appears on the road.)*

SUZANNE: David!

(The deaf BEETHOVEN *turns to her, smiles, conducting violently. Music.)*

SUZANNE: *(Reads from the diary of———.)* "As for the musical success of this memorable evening, it could be favorably compared to any event ever presented in that venerable theatre. Alas, the man to whom all this honor was addressed could hear none of it, for when at the end of the performance the audience broke into enthusiastic applause, he remained standing with his back to them. Then the contralto soloist had the presence of mind to turn the master toward the proscenium and show him the cheering throng throwing their hats into the air and waving their handkerchiefs. He acknowledged his gratitude with a bow. This set off an almost unprecedented volley of jubilant applause that went on and on as the joyful listeners sought to express their thanks for the pleasure they had just been granted."

(Concert scene fades to BEETHOVEN*'s room.* SUZANNE *stands in the center staring at* BEETHOVEN*'s grand piano, his chair, manuscript paper.)*

SUZANNE: *(Reads from the diary of———.)* "Monday, the 26th of March 1827 was a freezing day. From Silesia and the Sudeten peaks, a north wind blew across the Wienerwald. Everywhere the ground lay under a soft blanket of fresh, silent snow. The long winter had been raw, damp, cold, and frosty; on that day it showed no sign of releasing its grip on the land.

By four o'clock the lights of Vienna, the street lamps, the candles of myriad rooms, began to pierce the overcast gloom. On the second floor of the Schwarzspanierhaus, the House of the Black Spaniard, to the west of the old city walls, lay a man who had all but run his course. In a large, sparsely furnished room of 'sad appearance,' amid squalor and books and manuscript paper and within sight of his prized mahogany Broadwood grand, Beethoven lost hold of life. On a roughly made bed, unconscious, he was at that moment as broken and finished as his piano. The elements continued to rage. Flurries of snow drifted against the window. Then, there was suddenly a loud clap of thunder accompanied by a bolt of lightning... Beethoven opened his eyes, raised his right hand, and, his fist clenched, looked upward for several seconds... As he let his hand sink down onto the bed again, his eyes half closed... There was no more breathing, no more heartbeat! The great composer's spirit fled from this world."

So remembered Anselm Huttenbrenner, who recorded Beethoven's end even more poignantly in the terseness of a diary entry: "Ludwig van Beethoven's death, in the evening, toward six o'clock of dropsy in his fifty-seventh year. He is no longer!"

(She cries. Music from the road, of African stringed instruments.
SUZANNE *rushes to the door.)*

SUZANNE: David. You sent Beethoven until you returned. Didn't you?

DAVID'S VOICE: *(Not unlike* BEETHOVEN'S.*)* I knew he would console you while I was absent.

END

Ohio State Murders

Ohio State Murders was commissioned by the Great Lakes Theater Festival (Gerald Freedman, artistic director; Mary Bill, managing director) through a grant from the New Works Program of the Ohio Arts Council. The play received its world premiere at the Great Lakes Theater Festival on March 7, 1992, with the following cast:

Suzanne Alexander	*Ruby Dee*
Suzanne	*Bellary Darden*
David Alexander	*Michael Early*
Robert Hampshire	*Allan Byrne*
Aunt Louise	*Irma Hall*
Val	*Rick Williams*
Iris Ann	*Leslie Holland*
Suzanne's Father	*Michael Early*

Directed by Gerald Freedman; set design conceived by Gerald Freedman and executed by John Ezell; projections by Kurt Sharp and Jesse Epstein; costumes coordinated by Al Kohout; lighting designed by Cynthia Stillings; sound design by Stanley J. M. Kozak.

CHARACTERS

SUZANNE ALEXANDER (1949–1952)   The young writer as a student attending Ohio State from 1949 to 1950

SUZANNE ALEXANDER (Present)   A well-known black writer visiting Ohio State to give a talk on the imagery in her work

DAVID ALEXANDER   A law student she will marry

ROBERT HAMPSHIRE   An English professor at Ohio State

MRS. TYLER   Suzanne's landlady
VAL   A friend
IRIS ANN   Suzanne's roommate
MISS DAWSON   Head of the dorm

TIME: Present.
SETTING: Night.
   Stacks: hundreds of books on "O" level beneath the library at Ohio State.
   A window high in the distance from which can be seen University Hall, a vast dark structure and falling snow. The snow falls throughout the play. Sections of the stacks become places on campus during the play.

>   SUZANNE *enters the stacks, wanders, gazes at the distant window and snow. She takes out a paper, studies it, gazes about her, reads from paper rehearsing a talk.*

SUZANNE (Present): I was asked to talk about the violent imagery in my work; bloodied heads, severed limbs, dead father, dead Nazis, dying Jesus. The chairman said, we do want to hear about your brief years here at Ohio State but we also want you to talk about violent imagery in your stories and plays. When I visited Ohio State last year it struck me as a series of disparate dark landscapes just as it had in 1949, the autumn of my freshman year.

   I used to write down locations in order to learn the campus: the oval, behind the green, the golf hut, behind Zoology, the tennis courts beyond the golf hut, the Olitangy River, the stadium off to the right, the main library at the head of the Oval, the old union across from the dorm, High Street at the end of the path, downtown Columbus, the Deschler Wallach, Lazarus, the train station. The geography made me anxious.

   The zigzagged streets beyond the Oval were regions of Law, Medicine, Mirror Lake, the Greek theater, the lawn behind the dorm where the white girls sunned.

   The ravine that would be the scene of the murder and Mrs. Tyler's boarding house in the Negro district.

   The music I remembered most was a song called "Don't Go Away Mad," and the music from *A Place in the Sun,* that movie with Elizabeth Taylor and Montgomery Clift based on Theodore Dreiser's *American Tragedy.*

(SUZANNE *takes out a picture of* DAVID *running the 100-yard dash at Ohio State.*

DAVID *is an extraordinarily handsome young black man. He looks like Frantz Fanon, whose biography he will one day write.*)

SUZANNE (Present): This is a picture of my husband, David, who, as you know, is a writer, political activist, and biographer of Frantz Fanon. Most people don't know David started out as a lawyer.

Although we were both at Ohio State in the winter of 1950 I had not met David. But I had seen this photograph of him running the 100-yard dash at Ohio State's spring track meet.

I knew he was a state champion and now he was in law school. David had lived in the boarding house that was to become my home. Mrs. Tyler hung this picture in her hallway. She loved David Alexander. That was later.

But first I started my freshman year in the fall of '49.

I took a required English survey course although I was not an English major. I had declared no major course of study. We read Thomas Hardy.

SCENE: *Quonset hut.* HAMPSHIRE *enters.* SUZANNE (1949) *watches him. As a student she wears pale skirt, sweater (powder blue), saddle shoes, and socks.*

SUZANNE (Present): The professor was a young man. His name was Hampshire. He was small and dressed rather formally in a tweed suit with a vest. He always walked straight to the lectern and without any introduction started his lectures.

(HAMPSHIRE *looks at his notes.* SUZANNE [1949] *watches him intently. She is fragile, pale.*)

The class was held in a quonset hut, a temporary barrack-like structure that had room for fifty to sixty students. These huts were built to house the overflow of students after the war. Professor Hampshire read from *Tess of the D'Urbervilles.*

HAMPSHIRE: "In spite of the unpleasant initiation of the day before, Tess inclined to the freedom and novelty of her new position in the morning when the sun shone, now that she was once installed there; and she was curious to test her powers in the unexpected direction asked of her, so as to ascertain her chance of retaining her post. As soon as she was alone within the walled garden she sat herself down on a coop, and seriously screwed up her mouth for the long-neglected practice. She found her former ability to have degenerated to the production of a hollow rush of wind through the lips and no clear note at all."

(HAMPSHIRE *draws a map.*)

SUZANNE: On a makeshift blackboard he drew a map of Wessex.

HAMPSHIRE: Blackmore Vale, Marlott, Edgdon Heath, New Forest, Chalk Newton, Casterbridge.

(SUZANNE *continues to watch him intently.*)

SCENE ENDS.

SUZANNE (Present): *(Stands in stacks.)* These places in Wessex, Marlott, New Forest, Chalk Newton intrigued me as did *Tess of the D'Urbervilles.*

One afternoon late, almost early evening, I walked over behind the Oval to the English Department and inquired about the catalog for English majors. A secretary said, "Come back any morning around ten. A Miss Smith will give you the information about becoming an English major. What is your major now?" she asked.

I told her I was undeclared.

I didn't know there were no "Negro" students in the English Department. It was thought that we were not able to master the program. They would allow you to take no more than two required freshman courses. After that you had to apply to the English Department to take courses that were all said to be for majors.

In my dorm across from the Old Union there were six hundred girls. Twelve of us were blacks. We occupied six places, rooming together two in a room.

The other dorms, Canfield and Neil, each also housed a few black girls.

The schools I had attended in Cleveland were an even mixture of immigrant and black. You were judged on grades. But here race was foremost.

Very few Negroes walked on High Street above the university. It wasn't that you were not allowed but you were discouraged from doing so. Above the university was a residential district encompassed by a steep ravine. I never saw this ravine until the two days I visited Bobby at his house (the ravine was where the faculty lived).

A year and a half later one of my baby twin daughters would be found dead there. That was later.

But in my freshman year the continuing happiness was Professor Hampshire's discussion of the Victorian novel.

When he lectured, his small pale face was expressionless. Only his blue eyes conveyed anger, joy, vitality.

SCENE: *Quonset hut, 1949. As* SUZANNE *watches* HAMPSHIRE *lecture she becomes excited, leaning forward listening to him more intently than ever.*

HAMPSHIRE: The idea of Chance only reminds the reader of the sphere of ideal possibilities of what ought to be happening but is not. The illusion of freedom diminishes in the course of Hardy's novels. The net narrows and finally closes.

Inherent in almost all Hardy's characters are those natural instincts which become destructive because social convention suppresses them, attempting to make the human spirit conform to the "letter."

Hardy absorbs Tess's personal situation into a vast system of causation.

SCENE ENDS.

SUZANNE (PRESENT): For a long time no one knew who the killer was. She was the one I had called Cathi. But that was later.

Before Christmas of my freshman quarter, Professor Hampshire wrote on my paper, "Make appointment to see me."

SCENE: *English office.* SUZANNE *and* HAMPSHIRE, *1949.*

SUZANNE: His office in the English Department was along a path beyond the Oval. I seldom walked there and once I left the Oval I got lost on the streets on that side of the campus and was almost late for my four o'clock appointment.

It was dark.

He was sitting in a greyish office with several empty desks.

SCENE: *English office.* SUZANNE *enters in saddle oxfords, skirt, matching sweater, cloth woolen coat. Again she wears powder blue, a popular color in 1949.*

SUZANNE (PRESENT): I was quite nervous. It was the first time a professor at Ohio State had asked to see me.

(In the office SUZANNE *sits opposite* HAMPSHIRE.*)*

SUZANNE (Present): He was crouched over his desk writing and seemed smaller than in class, very pale, glasses, the same grayish woolen suit.

SUZANNE: *(In office.)* Professor Hampshire, you wrote on my paper you wanted to see me.

HAMPSHIRE: Oh yes, Suzanne, sit down, please. Did you bring your paper?

SUZANNE: Yes.

HAMPSHIRE: Let me see it.

SUZANNE (Present): For a moment he seemed to forget me and read the brief paper in its entirety. For a moment watching him I realized he was a man of about thirty. I later was to discover he was a lecturer and this was his first year at Ohio State.

HAMPSHIRE: What is your major?

SUZANNE: I am undeclared. But if I do well this quarter I want to apply to take another English course in the spring, but I know I have to have special permission for further English courses.

SUZANNE (Present): He didn't seem to hear me.

HAMPSHIRE: *(In his office.)* Did you write this paper yourself?

SUZANNE: Yes, Professor Hampshire.

HAMPSHIRE: What reference books did you use?

SUZANNE: I used no reference books. I wrote this paper late one night in the dorm, the night before it was due.

SUZANNE (Present): He returned the paper to me, staring at the desk top. Suddenly he looked up.

HAMPSHIRE: Have you read Hardy before?

SUZANNE (Present): He didn't seem to want to continue speaking. I tried to tell him that I wanted to study more English courses, how much I loved literature. But he stood up interrupting me. He didn't speak but gathered his books together. And stared at me, then nodded. I saw the conference was over.

> *(*SUZANNE *stands in office, moves away staring back at* HAMPSHIRE.*)*
>
> OFFICE SCENE ENDS.

SCENE: *Stacks. From the window snow is falling.* SUZANNE (Present) *studies her paper.*

SUZANNE (1949) *walks across the Oval in darkness.*

SUZANNE (Present): I got lost again between two buildings behind University Hall.

Walking back in the darkness I remembered passages of my paper. And I remembered the comments Professor Hampshire had written on the margins.

SUZANNE (1949): *(Stands on Oval.)*

"Paper conveys a profound feeling for the material."

"Paper has unusual empathy for Tess."

"The language of the paper seems an extension of Hardy's own language."

(She hears HAMPSHIRE'*s voice.)*

HAMPSHIRE: It's brilliant. It's brilliant.

SCENE ENDS.

SCENE: *Dorm. Lights on dark corridors and a dim small room lit by a single lamp.*

IRIS ANN *is lying across the bed crying. Like* SUZANNE *she wears a pale skirt and sweater (possibly pink) and like* SUZANNE *her hair is in a soft page boy.*

From the corridors we hear sounds of muffled laughing and talking.

SUZANNE *enters room.*

SUZANNE (Present): At the dorm my roommate, Iris Ann, was waiting for me to eat. Iris was lying on the bed crying. Her boyfriend had broken their engagement. We went down to the dining room and ate as usual at one of the tables where the Negro girls sat.

(Scene in dorm ends with SUZANNE *looking at* IRIS ANN.*)*

SUZANNE (Present): After dinner we walked across the wet grass up to High Street. The path wound around a new structure half finished. We chattered. All except Iris Ann. After dinner it was not uncommon for us to go to Tomaine Tommy's and bring back cheeseburgers to be eaten later that night. On the way back to the dorm Iris started sobbing. It had begun to snow.

And often music came from the corridors. A song called "Don't Go Away Mad" was popular.

(Sound of music in the corridors.)

SUZANNE (Present): In class the next week Professor Hampshire read again from Hardy.

SCENE: *Quonset hut.* SUZANNE *stares up at* HAMPSHIRE.

HAMPSHIRE: *(Reads.)* " . . . It was not until she was quite close that he could believe her to be Tess.

'I saw you—turn away from the station—just before I got there—and I have been following you all this way!'

She was so pale, so breathless, so quivering in every muscle, that he did not ask her a single question, but seizing her hand, and pulling it within his arm, he led her along. To avoid meeting any possible wayfarers he left the high road, and took a footpath under some fir trees. When they were deep among the moaning boughs he stopped and looked at her inquiringly.

'Angel,' she said, as if waiting for this, 'Do you know what I have been running after you for? To tell you that I have killed him!' A pitiful white smile lit her face as she spoke.

'What!' said he, thinking from the strangeness of her manner that she was in some delirium.

'I have done it—I don't know how,' she continued. 'Still, I owed it to you, and to myself Angel. I feared long ago, when I struck him on the mouth with my glove, that I might do it some day for the trap he set for me in my simple youth, and his wrong to you through me. He has come between us and ruined us, and now he can never do it any more. I never loved him at all, Angel, as I loved you. You know it, don't you? You believe it? You didn't come back to me, and I was obliged to go back to him. Why did you go away—why did you—when I loved you so? I can't think why you did it. But I don't blame you; only, Angel, will you forgive me my sin against you, now I have killed him? I thought as I ran along that you would be sure to forgive me now I have done that. It came to me as a shining light that I should get you back that way. I could not bear the loss of you any longer—you don't know how entirely I was unable to bear your not loving me! Say you do now, dear, dear husband; say you do, now I have killed him!'

'I do love you, Tess—O, I do—it is all come back!' he said, tightening his arms round her with fervid pressure. 'But how do you mean—you have killed him?'

'I mean that I have,' she murmured in a reverie.

'What, bodily? Is he dead?'

'Yes. He heard me crying about you, and he bitterly taunted me; and called you by a foul name; and then I did it. My heart could not bear it.' "

(SUZANNE *cries.*

HAMPSHIRE *glances at her.*
He leaves quonset hut.
She remains in her seat.)
SCENE ENDS.

(Dorm music.)
SUZANNE (Present): One by one the white girls went to live on The Row. Their pattern was to live in the dorm their freshman year and

then go live in The House. Although we had sororities, Alpha Kappa Alpha and Delta Sigma Theta, we did not have "houses." We met in rooms on campus or in private homes. So we remained in the dorm.

(Dorm music. SUZANNE [1950] *sitting in dorm room.)*

SUZANNE: Sorority Row right off High Street seemed a city in itself: the cluster of streets with the columned mansions sitting on top of the lawn appeared like a citadel.

SUZANNE: *(Reads her book of symbols.)* "A city should have a sacred geography never arbitrary but planned in strict accord with the dictates of a doctrine that the society upholds."

SCENE ENDS.

SUZANNE (Present): I never walked on those blocks and saw them only from Mrs. Tyler's coupe. There was no reason for Negroes to walk in those blocks.

SCENE: *University Hall, 1950.* IRIS ANN *and* SUZANNE *watch vivid footage of film* Potemkin.

SUZANNE (Present): Before she dropped out of Ohio State, Iris Ann wanted to be a music major. She had been first violinist in her high school orchestra. She told me some of the music students went to University Hall to a film society. We went a few times, walking across the Oval in the rain and saw a movie called *The Battleship Potemkin.* The movie was shown on the ground level of the hall. Down the massive stairwells with iron flowered balustrades we walked to a small auditorium.

I had never seen a movie as old as that. There were two showings. We went back to see the other half.

SUZANNE: *(At* Potemkin.*)* Who is Eisenstein?

SUZANNE (Present): Iris Ann said she would ask one of the music students, Sonia. Sonia gave Iris Ann a typed paragraph on a small piece of paper describing the movie.

*(*SUZANNE [1950] *and* IRIS ANN *continue watching* Potemkin.*)*

SUZANNE (Present): *(Reads paper.)* "*Battleship Potemkin* concentrates on the mutiny on a battleship of the Black Sea Fleet during the 1905 Revolution with the massacre on the Odessa steps. Down a seemingly endless flight of steps march soldiers advancing on the fleeing citizens."

SUZANNE (Present): There was more on the scenes I had been drawn to.

*(*SUZANNE *and* IRIS ANN *continue watching film.)*

SUZANNE (Present): *(Reads paper.)* "The storming of the Winter Palace, the dismemberment of the Tsar's Statue and a dead horse caught at the top of an opening drawbridge."

When we went back to see the second half I tried to remember what I had read. I asked Iris Ann were any of her music students there. She said she had seen one down front of the auditorium. I went to the library and tried to find out more about "this Eisenstein."

For some reason the crumpled bit of paper Sonia had given Iris Ann about *Potemkin* became important to me. I kept it in the top desk drawer in my room and would unfold it and read it over.

SUZANNE: *(At* Potemkin, SUZANNE *studies film.) Battleship Potemkin* concentrates on the mutiny on a battleship of the Black Sea Fleet during the 1905 Revolution with the massacre on the Odessa Steps... the storming of the Winter Palace... the dismemberment of the Tsar's statue...

SCENE ENDS.

SUZANNE (Present): Iris Ann could play the violin beautifully. And sometimes she'd go into the study room at the end of the corridor and practice. I asked her about the courses she was taking. They're all theory, she said. Sue, I just like to play. I've studied since I was eight at the Institute. But here courses are all theory. She studied the theory books often on Saturday and Sunday.

Her uncle, a well-known doctor from Akron, came to visit us one Sunday. He made Iris Ann come out of the study room. That department is putting you under too much pressure, he said. I don't think they want you.

I became pregnant the following Christmas, 1950. My parents thought I spent the last day of my break with Iris in Akron but I had come back to Columbus and spent two days with Bobby above the ravine.

SCENE: *Path near quonset hut, 1950s.*

SUZANNE (Present): I had not seen him after the spring quarter ended. In fact, I did not see him until the next fall in 1950. I had applied to be an English major but had been denied. They let me take a trial course on Shaw, Wilde, Molière. I had seen Professor Hampshire on his way to the quonset hut.

SUZANNE: I am taking a trial course.

HAMPSHIRE: It's a shame.

SUZANNE (Present): The previous quarter I had taken his course on *Beowulf.* Again he had liked my papers.

HAMPSHIRE: *(On path.)* It's not necessary for you to take a trial course. It's a shame.

SCENE ENDS.

SUZANNE (Present): He hurried on.

On that same path in one year we would meet.

It was February 1951 when I told him I was pregnant. He was on the same walkway that led to the hut. Within the quonset I could see students gathering. I had not seen him since December, when I had gone to his house above the ravine.

On that cold morning I stopped him as he came toward me. I had been waiting for him as he came up the steps of University Hall and onto the Oval. The immense circle of buildings was majestic amid dark trees and snow.

I told him I was pregnant.

SCENE: *Path near quonset hut.*

SUZANNE: *(Hardly audible.)* I am pregnant.

SUZANNE (Present): He stopped an instant.

HAMPSHIRE: *(On path.)* That's not possible. We were only together twice. You surely must have other relationships. It's not possible.

SUZANNE (Present): He walked past me.

HAMPSHIRE: I don't have time to talk to you, Sue. I'm giving a talk in University Hall Thursday at eight o'clock. Wait for me afterward, perhaps we can talk.

SUZANNE (Present): He left me standing at the edge of the Oval.

SCENE ENDS.

SUZANNE (Present): I remained in the dorm until March when I was expelled. The head of the dorm, Miss Dawson, read my diaries to the dormitory committee and decided I was unsuitable. I did not fit into campus life. And after the baby was born I would not be allowed to return to the campus.

Miss D. had gone into my room and found my poems, my Judy Garland records, my essay on loneliness and race at Ohio State and the maps I had made likening my stay here to that of Tess's life at the Vale of Blackmoor.

She called me to her office at the top of the stairs. She was a spinster and walked with a cane.

SCENE: SUZANNE *talking to* MISS DAWSON *in her office.*
(MISS DAWSON *is a thin, white-haired woman wearing a dark
coat sweater. She carries a cane.)*
MISS DAWSON: I have observed you sitting alone behind the dorm. The
committee read your notes on T. S. Eliot and Richard Wright. You
will not be allowed to re-enter.
SCENE ENDS.

SUZANNE (Present): March 17, 1951, was my last day in the dorm. I
was three months pregnant.
My parents were humiliated. My father was a well-known Cleve-
land minister. They sent me to New York. I stayed with my aunt,
my father's sister. She was a music teacher who had never married.
She lived in Harlem. Those were the saddest months of my life.
My babies were born the beginning of September in Harlem
Hospital, September 2, 1951.
My aunt begged me to stay in New York. I didn't know why but
I wanted to return to Columbus. Finally Aunt Louise remembered a
friend she had known when she went to Spelman who lived in Colum-
bus. Her friend was Mrs. Tyler, a widow who boarded students in
her large house near Long Street.
I took my baby daughters and boarded the train.
Aunt Louise came to Grand Central. She cried.
AUNT LOU'S VOICE: Sue, please stay here.
SUZANNE (Present): But I wanted to return. My parents hadn't spoken
to me. But they gave me money. I settled in with Mrs. Tyler. It was
agreed I would care for my daughters in the daytime and in the afternoon from four o'clock to nine o'clock I got a job as a department
store stock girl. Mrs. Tyler asked me no questions. She knew.
Louise Carter was my aunt. Before my aunt became a music
teacher she had had a short career as a singer. She sang in local
churches as well as at concerts of Negro groups.
SCENE: SUZANNE *sitting in dimly lit sewing room, holding twins.*
SUZANNE (Present): My twins were three months old when I returned
to Columbus.
It had been a year since I had gone to Bobby's home. I remembered his wall of recordings. He talked about Mozart, one of his fa-
vorite books was *Elizabethan World Picture.* He had given me a copy.
Often I would meditate on repetitive phrases:
SUZANNE: *(In sewing room.)*

Chain of being
Sin
the Links in the Chain
the Cosmic Dance

SUZANNE (Present): I had learned he was from New York. I had also
learned he had gone to Fordham, and had been married briefly to
an Indian woman. It was his first year at Ohio State when I entered
his freshman class. He was twenty-nine.

The days were long caring for the babies. Sometimes Mrs. Tyler's
neighbors shunned me.

SEWING ROOM SCENE ENDS.

SUZANNE (Present): Iris Ann dropped out of school and went back to
Akron. I remembered the early days of my pregnancy and how she
had gone to the health center with me. The fall of my sophomore
year my major became elementary education. After I received a "C"
in the trial course on Wilde and Shaw I was told by the secretary in
the English Department that I could take no further English courses.
My professor had been a man called Hodgson, a tall man in his
fifties. He was accompanied often by his assistant. He smiled a great
deal but seldom talked to anyone. He gave me "C's" on every paper.
When I told the secretary I'd like to talk to him, she said Professor
Hodgson was not able to see any more students that quarter but I
could make an appointment with his assistant.

So in the fall I declared elementary education and began taking
courses on teaching children. How I missed the imagery, the marvel,
the narratives, the language of the English courses.

The new courses made me depressed. I hated them.

I ran into Professor Hampshire at the bookstore on High Street.
I told him how hard I had worked on my papers on Shaw. He suggested I leave one at his office. I went to his office twice before I went
to his house after Christmas.

SCENE: *Dorm room*

IRIS ANN *lying across bed.*

SUZANNE (1950) *standing by doorway listening to music from
corridor.*

SUZANNE (Present): Iris Ann had been the only person who knew I was
pregnant. She was still sad over Artie and often we cried at night.
The white girls gave parties in the dorm.

(Dorm music, OKLAHOMA.)

SUZANNE (Present): But we were never invited. Often they played music from Broadway musicals, *Oklahoma, Carousel.* Iris Ann and I went to the movies.

SCENE ENDS.

SUZANNE (Present): Easter was when I told my father that I had been dismissed from the dorm. He was sitting in the office at his church. Tears came into his eyes.

SCENE: SUZANNE *in the coupe in the stadium holding the twins.*

Now sometimes on Sunday when I thought the campus was empty, I'd put the twins in Mrs. Tyler's coupe and drive to the river or the stadium. Sometimes I'd sit in the stadium inside the car and try to figure out what I was going to do with my life. The twins were in blankets on the seat next to me. I'd hold their fingers and, exhausted, fall asleep.

SCENE ENDS.

SUZANNE (Present): I continued my routine of working as a stock girl.

Finally one February evening I went to one of Bobby's lectures sitting far in the back of the auditorium. It was on King Arthur's death. Bobby read at length in the dimly lit auditorium.

SCENE: *Auditorium.* SUZANNE *watches* HAMPSHIRE. *Her appearance has changed. She is thinner and dressed in darker clothes.*

HAMPSHIRE: Arthur Vows Revenge

"Till the blood bespattered his stately beard.
As if he had been battering beasts to death.
Had not Sir Ewain and other great lords come up,
His brave heart would have burst then in bitter woe:
'Stop!' these stern men said, 'You are bloodying yourself!'
Your cause of grief is cureless and cannot be remedied.
You reap no respect when you wring your hands:
To weep like a woman is not judged wise.
Be manly in demeanor, as a monarch should,
and leave off your clamour, for love of Christ in Heaven!
'Because of blood,' said the bold King, 'abate my grief
Before brain or breast burst, I never shall!
Sorrow so searing never sank to my heart;
It is close kin to me, which increases my grief.
So sorrowful a sight my eyes never saw.

Spotless, he is destroyed by sins of my doing!'
Down knelt the King, great care at his heart,
Caught up the blood carefully with his clean hands,
Cast it into a kettle-hat and covered it neatly,
Then brought the body to the birthplace of Gawain.
'I pledge my promise,' then prayed the King,
'To the Messiah and to Mary, merciful Queen of Heaven,
I shall never hunt again or unleash hounds
At roe or reindeer ranging on earth,
Never let greyhound glid or goshawk fly.'"
Arthur's only expression of sin in the poem is touched off by his grief over Gawain. But perhaps it was a battle-sin of caution, in that but for being "loth to make land across the low water" Arthur would have been at Gawain's side in the battle.

SUZANNE (Present): I didn't know whether Bobby knew anything of what had happened to me. And I had no way of knowing that he was often following me.

AUDITORIUM SCENE ENDS.

AUNT LOU'S VOICE: Forget about that white man.

SUZANNE (Present): Aunt Lou always said:

AUNT LOU'S VOICE: And forget about your parents. I don't know how my brother can ignore his own daughter. But, Sue, I have a little money saved. I'm going to help you go back to school.

SUZANNE: (Present) Seeing Bobby read made me brood over how he had dismissed me. Why?

I often thought of the second course I took with him the winter quarter of my freshman year.

We read *Beowulf.*

He spoke so eloquently of *Beowulf,* then read from it in old English.

Then it happened. Near the beginning of March, Robert Hampshire kidnapped and murdered our daughter. She was the one called Cathi. He drowned her in the ravine.

For a year detectives questioned me. Did I have enemies? Had I ever observed anyone following me?

At that time they didn't ask me about Cathi's father.

Aunt Lou said if they ever did she had a former student who lived in Mt. Vernon, New York, and she had already discussed it with him. He would be glad to say he was the twins' father.

He was a young man Aunt Lou had helped a great deal and had even loaned him money to start his own cleaners. He was devoted to her.

For a while they seemed to think I knew who the murderer was.

I told him the only odd thing I remembered. Once I had been sitting in the car with my daughters by the river, had for a moment closed my eyes and fallen asleep, and awoke to the sound of someone running away from the car, someone who may have been looking in the window. And I did not drive to the river again.

Then:

SCENE: *Outside the doctor's office. Snow.* SUZANNE *is dressed in a dark coat. The babies lie in white bassinets. She takes the baby through a doorway. The baby coughs violently. She reappears in the falling snow and reaches into the car for the other twin.*

The twin is gone.

SUZANNE (Present): Then there had been a snowstorm. I was worried because Carol had a bad cough and I drove the babies to the doctor's office on Long Street. I pulled the coupe up into a side entrance. The offices were in a large, old-fashioned house. In the heavy snow I pulled the car as close to the door as possible. The babies were in white bassinets. Mrs. Tyler had offered to go with me. But she wasn't feeling well herself. It was snowing hard.

I took Carol into the lobby first and just as I laid her down on the chair she started to cough violently. I held her close. And then laid her back into the bassinet. I told the receptionist I had to get Cathi. I left both the lobby door and the car door open for those seconds. I turned and stepped outside into the falling snow and the few feet to the car. The car door was open, the white bassinet lay on the seat. But Cathi was gone.

SCENE ENDS.

SUZANNE (Present): The detectives felt positive they knew who the murderer was.

Aunt Lou came to Columbus to be with us. I asked her did she think I should get Professor Hampshire to help. "No," she said, "that would serve no purpose." She was the only person who knew Bobby was the father of my girls.

And as far as I know she never told anyone, not even my parents.

For weeks Aunt Lou sat with me in the cold house.

The police would say little but my aunt finally was able to find out that a man called Thurman, who had been in the penitentiary and often walked on campus posing as a student, was suspected. The police told my aunt they felt I knew more than I said and what did she really know about the life I led.

AUNT LOU'S VOICE (1951): You don't understand. My niece is a sweet girl. A very sweet girl. All you white people are alike. You think because we're Negroes that my niece is mixed up in something shady. My niece knows no Thurman.

SUZANNE (Present): She later told me she'd discovered this Thurman had been involved in several petty crimes on campus and in the campus area but also appeared to know many students and told the police he had seen me.

My aunt would not leave me, so in the summer we went back to New York. In the fall I returned to Columbus. I felt my baby's murderer was someone I knew.

(Brief past image of BUNNY *and her friends coming along dark corridors giggling.)*

SCENE: SUZANNE *alone in her dorm room reading Thomas Hardy. From time to time* BUNNY *and her friends are heard in the next room singing.*

SUZANNE (Present): Why I thought they were capable of murder I don't know but sometimes I suspected a group of girls who lived at the end of the corridor in the dorm. They had been headed by an overweight, dark-haired girl called Patricia "Bunny" Manley. She and her group refused to speak to Iris and me and accused us of stealing her watch from the women's lavatory. If they saw us coming down the corridor they would giggle and close their door. I hated them. Their way of laughing when they saw us coming into the lounge, then refusal to speak was a powerful language. It had devastated me.

And then there had been the watch incident, an incident so disturbing, especially since I myself owned beautiful possessions and jewelry that my parents had given me on going away to school. Both my parents were college graduates (my father, Morehouse, my mother, Atlanta University). I hid in the room and read Thomas Hardy. I loved the language of the landscape.

SUZANNE: *(Still in dorm room.)* "Behind him the hills are open, the sun blazes down upon the fields so large as to give an unenclosed char-

acter to the landscape. The lanes are white, hedges low and plashed the atmosphere colorless. Here in the valley the world seems to be constructed upon a smaller, more delicate scale."
SCENE ENDS.

SUZANNE (Present): I remember how I had grown to dread the blocks bound by the stadium, the High Street, the vast, modern, ugly buildings behind the Oval, the dark old Union that was abandoned by all except the Negro students. And too, we were spied upon by the headmistress. She made no secret of the fact that she examined our belongings. "That's our general practice," she said.

Bunny and her friends bragged often to the maids that Iris and I had nothing in common with them, that there was nothing to talk about with us. I felt such danger from them. Had they somehow sought out me and my babies? Of course I told no one this. But I knew whites had killed Negroes, although I had not witnessed it. Thoughts of secret white groups murdering singed the edge of the mind.

I was often so tense that I wound the plastic pink curlers in my hair so tightly that my head bled. When I went to the university health center the white intern tried to examine my head and at the same time not touch my scalp or hair.

"You're probably putting curlers in your hair too tightly," he said, looking away.

Now I remembered my father's sermons on lynching and the photographic exhibits we often had in our church of Negroes hanging from trees.

Then I met David. He would come by and say hello to Mrs. Tyler. When he discovered Carol was my child he made every effort to talk to me. He sensed my sorrow. When he found out that Cathi had been tragically killed he started to come by every evening after he left the law library. He asked no questions but only treated me with such great tenderness.

Finally I told him of everything. My pregnancy, my expulsion, the murder, and how I had returned to Columbus to see if I could find the murderer of my daughter.

I did not tell him yet of Bobby.

In the next months David and I spent many happy hours talking.

The police now referred to Cathi's drowning as the Ravine Murder.

Aunt Lou wrote and still encouraged me to leave Columbus.
By this time David had proposed to me. He was from Washington.

SCENE: DAVID *and* SUZANNE *sitting in* MRS. TYLER's *parlor.*
SUZANNE (Present): He told me how much I would love his family,
   particularly his younger sister, Alice, who he said was so much like
   me. She was studying literature at Howard (read several books at a
   time) and was also absolutely in love with the movies. He laughingly
   told me how she wrote brief plays as a hobby and how she'd come
   home from a movie and get members of her family to act out scenes
   from them.

   He said her favorite movie star was Bette Davis, who she could
   not only imitate but also had made herself copies of Davis's dresses
   from *Dark Victory, Now Voyager,* and *The Letter.*

   He said she also knew a great deal of poetry and would recite
   Edgar Allan Poe, Shelley, and Langston Hughes.

   He had told her about Carol. And she had already crocheted a
   white bib for her and was sending it along with butter cookies for
   us.

   PARLOR SCENE ENDS.

SUZANNE (Present): My aunt said I was very lucky.
   She encouraged me to look to the future now.
SCENE: *Auditorium, past.*
SUZANNE (Present): I had seen Robert Hampshire. In the bookstore there
   was a notice that he was again reading from King Arthur. I went.

   He seemed far paler and smaller than I remembered. He didn't
   seem like anyone I had known. He read as usual without looking up
   from the page. It was clear he felt disdain for the audience. And it
   was clear he was very agitated.

   After he read he spoke of King Arthur and the abyss.
HAMPSHIRE: The abyss in any form has a fascinating dual significance.
   On one hand it is a symbol of depth in general; on the other a symbol of inferiority. The attraction of the abyss lies in the fact that
   these two aspects are inextricably linked together. Most ancient or
   primitive peoples have at one time or another identified certain breaks
   in the earth's surface or marine depth with the abyss. The abyss is
   usually identified with the land of the dead, the underworld, and is
   hence though not always associated with the Great Mother and earth

god cults. The association between the netherworld and the bottom of seas or lakes explains many aspects of legends in which palaces or beings emerge from an abyss of water. After King Arthur's death his sword thrown into the lake by his command is caught as it falls and before being drawn to the bottom flourished by a hand which emerges from the waters.

SCENE ENDS.

SUZANNE (Present): David and I had begun plans to marry. He bought me a ring at Hoensteins.

Many people at Ohio State assumed that Val was the father of my twins. But Val and I never had an intimate relationship. When he discovered I was pregnant he just stopped calling. "I'm surprised," he told Iris Ann. "I really am surprised."

Like my parents he just could not believe this had happened to me. He didn't, like them, really want to know anything further. With my preference for Peter Pan blouses and precise straightened curls I had been almost a cliché of the ultimate virgin. I had totally believed sex was a sin before marriage.

SCENE: MRS. TYLER's *parlor*

SUZANNE *and* VAL.

SUZANNE *holds* CAROL *in her arms.*

SUZANNE (Present): When Cathi was murdered he came to Mrs. Tyler's.

VAL: *(In* MRS. TYLER'S PARLOR.*)* Is it true it was your child that was murdered?

SUZANNE: Yes.

VAL: It's all so difficult to believe.

SUZANNE (Present): He had brought me a box of chocolates.

For when we had gone out to the freshman parties he often gave me a box of Whitman or Fanny Farmer chocolates.

VAL: Why don't you leave Columbus, Sue?

SUZANNE: I think I can eventually find out who killed my baby if I stay.

VAL: If I were you I'd leave. Most people at State think you left after you got pregnant, they think you went to New York.

SUZANNE (Present): I saw how uncomfortable he was sitting on Mrs. Tyler's stiff couch. I held Carol in my arms.

He seemed afraid to look at her.

SUZANNE (1951): *(In* MRS. TYLER's *parlor.)* Thank you, Val, for coming by.

SUZANNE (Present): He stood and went to the door. Finally he glanced at Carol, frowned, and left.

VAL: *(In the parlor.)* Good bye, Sue.

SCENE ENDS.

SUZANNE (Present): I often remembered Bunny and her friends had given the illusion of withholding secrets.

I had found a book about symbols on the bottom shelf of the bookstore on High Street. Often on a bottom shelf near the door there were assorted books and portfolios for sale. It was there I discovered several out-of-print soft-cover books on the French Impressionists. I bought one on Cézanne. And hung a print in my room. It was of the port of Marseilles. I studied the blues, reds, and yellows. It was the brightest color in the dorm with its dark furniture.

SCENE: SUZANNE, *past, in dorm room reading book of symbols.*

SUZANNE (Present): Bunny and her friends in the closed room next door had become something I thought of a great deal. Their refusal to talk to me made me feel that they knew something about me that was not apparent to myself.

SUZANNE: *(Still in dorm room.)* "Secrets," my book on symbols said, "symbolize the power of the supernatural and this explains their disquieting effect upon most human beings."

SUZANNE (Present): My little book of symbols that I had bought on sale became precious to me.

I remembered again that during the quarter that I had taken the trial course I became very quiet.

SCENE ENDS.

SUZANNE (Present): The police also suspected a neighbor of Mrs. Tyler's, but David, Aunt Louise, and Mrs. Tyler all said it had to be a stranger.

Alice, his sister, David said, was crocheting another bib; this one was pale yellow.

It was spring. Two years had passed since I lived in the dorm.

David and Mrs. Tyler told me every day that all this would be resolved and that one day the police would discover who had followed me in the snow.

Right after Easter Mrs. Tyler told me a grad student from Ohio State was coming that evening. He was doing a study of Negroes in the Columbus area and had heard from campus housing that she kept students and was also a native of Columbus and knew a great deal about the depression years there and the development of the neighborhoods.

When I left she was expecting him for an interview and had made cocoa.

David had gotten me a job in the law library in the stacks. The hours were 6:00 to 9:30. By 10:00 P.M. I was home. We saved money. David worked on two part-time jobs. Aunt Lou gave us something. That evening we pulled the car out of the drive at 5:20 to go to the law library. When we returned at 10:05 the Ohio State murders had occurred.

Robert Hampshire (posing as a researcher) had killed Carol, our twin, and himself. It seems that once inside Mrs. Tyler's living room he told her he was the father of the twins, that he had never been able to forget their existence. They ruined his life. He said he knew that one day I would reveal this, that he would be investigated, there would be tests and his whole career would fail.

He admitted he had waited for me outside the doctor's office and had taken Cathi. He told her he tried to follow the advice of his father who lived near London who had told him to just ignore me but he had been unable to do that. He was quite mad, she said, and had pushed her into the hallway and down the cellar stairs. When her son returned at 8:55 he found her crying and injured on the dark stairwell. Upstairs in the small sewing room where Carol and I slept Robert had killed Carol and himself (with a knife he had taken from the kitchen sink).

SCENE: *Law library, past.*

SUZANNE (Present): David found me here in the stacks of the law library on level zero sorting definitions of words.

He remembers . . .

SUZANNE: *(In the law library, past)* Abyss, bespattered, cureless, misfortune, enemy, alien host, battle groups fated to fall on the field today.

SCENE ENDS.

SUZANNE (Present): For many months I made drawings of the corridors in the dorm with the doors of each room outlined in red ink and muttered definitions of rooms, stains, color, skin.

I wrote long passages about my scalp and how it had bled and how I had examined my pores in a magnifying glass. And how the spots on the pillow cases had frightened me so that I had hidden my pillow cases even from Iris Ann.

But it seems the maid in the dorm corridor had told Miss D. that my pillow cases were stained. And they had examined the cloth together.

I thought I would die. David told me years later that he believed I was unable to go on. His parents and sister prepared a room for me in their house in Washington on 16th Street. It overlooked a part of Rock Creek Park. It was Alice's room. She gave it to me. It was a large, pale, cream-colored room with an arch and lovely windows. I didn't leave that room for months.

David and I were married the following year.

I remained in Washington living with his family in the big old house on 16th Street. His father was a lawyer with the NAACP. In a year David finished law school at Ohio State.

The university protected Robert Hampshire for a long time. Nothing of the story came out in the papers. There were stories that a white professor had wandered into the Negro section of Columbus and was killed.

But years later I heard Robert Hampshire's father had come from London at the time. My father, who knew the state politicians, had also put pressure on the papers to bury the tragedy. He convinced them it was best for me.

Mrs. Tyler and her son stuck to the story that a researcher had come to the house, had gone into a fit of insanity, and that was all they knew. Within days the stories were confused.

David, Aunt Lou, and David's family told me nothing. Not even that my mother had been hospitalized.

Before today I've never been able to speak publicly of my dead daughters.

Good-bye, Carol and Cathi.

Good-bye . . .

(Pause.)

And that is the main source of the violent imagery in my work. Thank you.

(Lights bright on hundreds of books in stacks and on the window, falling snow.)

END

The Film Club

(A Monologue by Suzanne Alexander)

Often when I'm despondent, I watch Bette Davis's movies. Yesterday I started to make a list of them. While I wrote I found myself remembering when my husband, David, was detained in West Africa the winter of 1961. He was missing for fifteen months. Often evenings in Accra David read to me about methods of torture during imprisonment. It was from Fanon:

"The brutal methods which are directed toward getting prisoners to speak rather than to actual torture. There is a mass attack . . ."

In that winter of 1961, David's and my life changed. As did Alice's, my sister-in-law's.

Alice and I waited for David in London. I had flown from Accra, she from Washington. We expected David to arrive in London in a week.

I looked at one of Alice's movies today. In remembrance. I call them Alice's movies because it was Alice who formed our film club, in 1959, typed our scripts, directed, and filmed scenes with all of us playing parts. She chose Bette Davis movies. And "adapted" them. She referred to them as "my films." She even sent one to Kazan.

That was also the summer we went to Birdland. Dizzy was there.

I'm sure you know Alice Alexander's poetry and her collections of slave narratives. She died last week of an asthmatic attack in Washington, D.C.

In 1961 we were staying in a room in London at 9 Bolton Gardens, waiting. We had no word from David. I became so distraught that one

night I tried to climb into the closed garden to sleep. I developed ail-
ments, nausea, breathlessness. My doctor tried to involve Alice and me
in a theatrical reading he was working on with patients. They were doing
excerpts from Bram Stoker's *Dracula*. My doctor's name was Freudenberger. He said, "The readings will distract you while you are waiting
for your husband."

I read the role of Lucy and Alice read Mina. The doctor lived in the
Little Boltons in a dark, damp dwelling. We didn't know it but David
was in trouble. Alice filmed our readings as well as us walking on Old
Brompton Road.

David and I have written several poems together. We record together
and perhaps some of you have seen my most famous play, *She Talks to
Beethoven,* a play set in Ghana during David's first disappearance. I also
teach the essays of Alice Walker, the poetry of Borges, Lorca, Ishmael
Reed, and the plays of Wole Soyinka. Students at New York University
are doing an early play of mine. The first line is: "Everyone is reading
Catcher in the Rye."

In those early days Alice often told me plots of Bette Davis movies. She
knew them by heart, as well as the stories of Davis's life. She'd say: In
1930 Bette Davis stepped off a transcontinental train in Hollywood
with a six-month contract in hand, a dream of stardom in her head . . .
dreams that soon began to fade.

She'd read from a book she'd bought at Marboro's. She'd say: "Kate
Bosworth, a young artist, meets a handsome lighthouse inspector, Bill
(Glenn Ford), while spending the summer on Martha's Vineyard as the
houseguest of her guardian, Mr. Lindley (Charles Ruggles). Kate believes
she is in love with Bill and he with her when her identical twin sister,
Patricia, shows up and becomes enchanted by Bill.

Patricia and Bill marry. Determined to forget her painting and studies with a cruel but brilliant artist, Kate hears that Bill and Patricia will
leave for Chile to live. She decides to give up studying and retreat to
the Vineyard house. When she returns to the Vineyard, she discovers
Patricia did not go with Bill . . .

. . . For a while Kate pretends to be her twin, Patricia, hoping to gain
Bill's love. But one day she decides she cannot go on. And for the final
time returns to the Vineyard. But Bill follows Kate to the Island, knowing now she is the sister he should have married . . ."

That winter of 1961 every day we went to the American Embassy for word of David. After we left the Embassy we'd go to Windsor in the rain. Queen Victoria had grieved for Albert there. My husband, where was he? Alice clutched her *Blue Guide* and we went to see the Roman wall in the City.

I remembered in our garden in Accra how David read me the love poems of Senghor.

Now I was expecting our child, Rachel.

Evenings in Accra David had often told me of soldiers who were prisoners. Generally speaking they had a noise phobia and a thirst for peace and affection. Their disorders took various forms, as states of agitation, rages, immobility, many attempted suicides, tears, lamentations, and appeals for mercy.

Alice continued to write David at the American Embassy in Ghana. But we didn't know where he was. She wrote:

"Suzanne wants to return to Africa and search for you. The doctor says she cannot travel back to West Africa. It might kill the baby."

In the rain we take the 30 bus down Old Brompton Road, past the South Kensington station, take another bus and walk into the Haymarket and wait for letters at American Express. And in the afternoon again we go to Windsor.

Suzanne is drawn to the painting of the tiny, sad figure of Victoria dressed in black mourning her husband's death. We walk in Windsor Park until it is dark and we have to take the train back to London. Suzanne's doctor phones. His theatrical group is waiting for us. We read from Stoker:

> '. . . *All at once the wolves began to howl as though the moonlight had had some peculiar effect on them. The horses jumped about and reared and looked helplessly round with eyes that rolled in a way painful to see; but the living ring of terror encompassed them on every side—*'

Dr. Freudenberger gave me the part of Lucy. These readings were for our amusement and I don't think the others realized how strongly I was affected by the passages I read on Lucy.

I began to utter them in my sleep.

Lucy sleepwalks to the
suicide seat on the East
cliff.
Dracula drinks her blood
for the first time.
She receives a blood
transfusion.
The wolf Berserker escapes
from the zoo, breaks
a window providing
Dracula with passage to
Lucy
again.
Lucy dies.
She is buried in a church
yard near Hampstead
Heath.

Dr. Freudenberger sat behind his desk as we read. His nervous German wife, Heike, served tea, sat aside, and studied *Steppenwolf.*

Alice wrote David:

"On the Thames going to Greenwich Suzanne recites one of your favorite poems from Diop. She carries notebooks of your records of slave ships, slave quarters, slaves crouching below the stern on the ship. My husband, she told a stranger, gives lectures on slave ships crossing the Atlantic. We reach Greenwich and see the place where Elizabeth I was born.

"She recites Diop as we cross the grounds up to the observatory. Her breathlessness is worse. And my asthma is bad. Yet she quotes the poem:

The Vultures
Way back then with their civilizing edicts
with their holy water
splashing on domesticated brows
the vultures in the shadows
of their claws were setting up
the bloody monument of the
guardian era
way back then
laughter gasped its last . . .

"Suzanne must leave London, Dr. Freudenberger says, by the beginning of March. Often nauseated, she is in the Haymarket at American Express mornings when the offices are still closed. She doesn't want to leave Europe without word of you. Afternoons she sits by the gas fire and cries. 'Do you trust Dr. F.?' she asks.

"Freudenberger walks us back from the reading along the dark curved street to No. 9, staring at Suzanne.

"In three nights we plan to leave London. Our theatrical group reads sequences that Freudenberger loves.

> *Jonathan Harker arriving*
> *at Klausenberg stays the*
> *night, leaves by coach for*
> *Castle Dracula . . .*
> *realizes he is a prisoner,*
> *watches Dracula crawl*
> *face down over the castle*
> *wall . . .*
> *enters the forbidden*
> *room . . .*
> *Dracula makes Harker*
> *write three misleading*
> *letters to England . . .*
> *Harker discovers his*
> *personal effects are gone . . .*
> *Dracula leaves the castle*
> *dressed in Harker's*
> *clothes and returns with a*
> *child for the three*
> *vampire women . . .*
> *the bereft mother is killed*
> *by wolves . . .*
> *Harker climbs along the*
> *castle wall to the cellar*
> *where he finds Dracula in*
> *a box.*

"These sequences we read sitting in a circle. Sometimes it makes Suzanne cry. We have to leave London with no word from you. Our

last day we sailed again on the Thames to Greenwich, returned and
went to a movie in Leicester Square."

In three weeks we knew David had disappeared. I went back to
Washington and lived with his family. Our daughter, Rachel, was born.
David's family says I lapsed into sleeplessness, hysteria. I began to exhibit signs of the prisoners David had described to me, states of agitation, rages, immobility, tears, attempted suicides, lamentations, appeals
for mercy.

We heard from the Ghanaian Embassy there was a doctor in Algeria
who had once tried to kill Fanon. And this Sottan was behind the plot
against my husband. We later learned this Sottan has us followed through
the villages in Africa. We remembered an incident at our cottage behind the Ambassador Hotel, a man who said he was the gardener. And
earlier on our voyage on the *Elizabeth* there had been a man in the
ship's orchestra who had befriended us.

On the last morning in London Dr. Freudenberger and Alice found
me wandering along the Embankment near More's Gardens. I thought
we were at one of our readings and began to cry the words of Stoker:

> *"When I saw again the
> driver was climbing into
> the calèche and the
> wolves had disappeared,
> this was all so strange
> and uncanny that a
> dreadful fear came upon
> me and I was afraid to
> speak or move. The time
> seemed interminable as
> we swept on our way
> now in almost complete
> darkness . . ."*

My husband, where is he?

Alice wrote that I was delirious and had started to speak of branches
of trees cracking together wild roses, mountain ash, lines from Stoker.
It was after the birth of our daughter, Rachel.

We read in the *Washington Post*:

"It is believed that Professor David Alexander, a native of Washington and a graduate of Ohio State University, was taken to dinner by a Swiss journalist in Geneva last winter, a journalist who was working for the French Secret Service. Alexander, who worked with Fanon, had been trying to uncover a plot against the revolutionary writer's life. During the dinner observers say Alexander became violently ill after having an aperitif and was admitted to the hospital.

Nothing more is known but it is suspected he was poisoned with fil-icin. His family has been unable to determine his whereabouts.

As you may recall, Fanon died here in Washington last year.

The Alexanders of 16th Street, N.W. here in the city have endured great sorrow this year. Two months ago the baby daughter, Rachel, of Alexander and his wife, Suzanne, was involved in an accidental death. Circumstances are not known."

After David returned sometimes we walked at night in Rock Creek Park. I reread *Wretched of the Earth* to try to understand what you had been through. Your symptoms:

idiopathic tremors

hair turning white

paroxysmal tachycardias

muscular stiffness

anxiety and feeling of imminent death

heavy sweating fits.

We never got to see Frantz. Alice and I went to the hospital in Washington where we thought he was. We were not admitted.

I still read from his life and search for the cause of his illnesses and death.

My romantic sister-in-law, up until her death we all lived on 16th Street. I see her writing scripts, arranging us all for the camera.

We never had a film club again. After David's imprisonment Alice didn't make films much.

Several years ago at Thanksgiving we looked for Alice's favorite scene of *Now Voyager;* it was missing. She believed she lost it that winter in London.

I continue to read long passages from Fanon, but for now a brief segment:

*"But the war goes on:
and we will have to bind
up for years to come the
many sometimes
ineffaceable wounds that
the colonialist onslaught
has inflicted on our
people."*

END

Dramatic Circle

A radio play commissioned by WNYC, New York City. *Dramatic Circle* is a dramatization of the events in the monologue *The Film Club*.

PLACE   London, 1961

CHARACTERS

ALICE ALEXANDER	Narrator, a writer and college teacher
SUZANNE ALEXANDER	Her sister-in-law, a writer
DAVID ALEXANDER	A writer and college teacher, Suzanne's husband
DR. FREUDENBERGER	An English doctor
THE DRAMATIC CIRCLE	Dr. Freudenberger's patients
THE AMBASSADOR	

ALICE ALEXANDER: London, 1961. We were staying in Old Brompton Road waiting for David to come from Ghana.
   (Sound of clock striking.)
   Suzanne had been delirious the night before, sleepwalking, speaking lines from the historical letters of Napoleon and Josephine. Her breathlessness had become worse.
SUZANNE ALEXANDER: "I can only write you a word at five o'clock in the morning. I have beaten the Russians and taken two cannons and their baggage train and six thousand prisoners. It was raining and we were in mud up to our knees ... I was worried, the road ..."
   (Sound of footsteps under.)

ALICE ALEXANDER: In the past my brother had written me when he had been traveling with Frantz Fanon, the famous psychiatrist and revolutionary from Martinique. He'd written about the psychiatric cases they had encountered in Algeria. I realized now some of the symptoms of Fanon's patients were like Suzanne's symptoms. She had always missed David when he traveled to do research.

His first trip to Russia had been the summer she found a worn paperback of Napoleon's letters when he was away in battle. I had never seen her as sad as she was that summer that David traveled to Russia and then to France to meet Fanon. David and Suzanne had always traveled together, but now his research on Fanon, the trips the research required, were trips he forbade her to take. He said there was danger surrounding Fanon.

SUZANNE ALEXANDER: "I would like as much to see you, to live quietly, I could do other things but fight, but duty comes before all else. All my life I have sacrificed everything, tranquillity, my own desire, my happiness, my destiny." *(Sigh.)*

ALICE ALEXANDER: Often he sent me notes on Fanon's observations, some on Goa.

DAVID ALEXANDER: Even the sky is constantly changing. Some days ago we saw a sunset that turned the robe of heaven a bright violet. Today it is a very hard red that the eye encounters. At Tessalit we cross the French military camps. We must work fast, time passes, the enemy is still stubborn, he does not believe in military defeat but I have never felt victory so possible, so within reach. We only need to march and charge. We have mobilized furious cohorts, loving combat, eager to work. We have Africa with us.

(Music.)

ALICE ALEXANDER: I decided Suzanne had to see a doctor. I found out from a chemist near the South Kensington underground station that National Health was right down the road from us. There were several doctors there. The chemist said, "Dr. Freudenberger is the one I recommend. I think you would find him most sympathetic. I believe he actually went to school in America for a while. He's very insightful. I'm sure he could help your sister-in-law."

(Rain falling.)

We went the next afternoon. It was raining heavily. Suzanne's breathlessness was worse. We sat in the outer office. Then Suzanne was called.

DR. FREUDENBERGER: Mrs. Alexander? Mrs. Alexander, yes. Would you—would you just—would you just come in for a moment?

ALICE ALEXANDER: Freudenberger came to the doorway, he was a dark-haired man, very tall, dressed in a suit. He smiled. Suzanne went inside.

DR. FREUDENBERGER: Mrs. Alexander. Mrs. Alexander, I've examined you and can find no reason in your heart or blood for your breathlessness. I recommend rest, especially since you're expecting a child. Have you been in London long? It says on this form that you're American.

SUZANNE ALEXANDER: I am from Washington, D.C., but my husband and I have been living in West Africa for the last two years.

DR. FREUDENBERGER: And why are you in London?

SUZANNE ALEXANDER: We are waiting for David. He is a writer and professor. He's still traveling. For many months he's been doing research, trying to find the source of Frantz Fanon's illness.

DR. FREUDENBERGER: Oh yes, I know his book, *Black Skin, White Masks.*

SUZANNE ALEXANDER: Yes.

DR. FREUDENBERGER: Are you friends of Fanon's?

SUZANNE ALEXANDER: David has traveled with him in Blida. He's writing Fanon's biography. Fanon is in Washington, very ill.

DR. FREUDENBERGER: You came here ahead of your husband?

SUZANNE ALEXANDER: Yes, the doctor in Accra insisted I start my journey home if I want to have the baby in Washington. My sister-in-law is with me.

DR. FREUDENBERGER: Oh, she came to join you?

SUZANNE ALEXANDER: Yes.

DR. FREUDENBERGER: I see here that you're living in Old Brompton Road.

SUZANNE ALEXANDER: We live on the top floor at Number Nine, in rooms with a green marble fireplace. It overlooks Bolton Gardens. We have not heard from my husband in two weeks.

DR. FREUDENBERGER: You are worried.

SUZANNE ALEXANDER: Every day we go to the American Embassy for word.

DR. FREUDENBERGER: That's the cause of your breathlessness.

SUZANNE ALEXANDER: He was to have arrived last week. We called Accra. They say the last they heard was that he went up country.

DR. FREUDENBERGER: Here, Mrs. Alexander, take this drink. It'll help. It's just valerian.

(African music.)

SUZANNE ALEXANDER: You see, in Blida with Fanon, David saw soldiers who were prisoners. Their disorders took various forms, states of agitation, rages, lamentations. I'm afraid David will be imprisoned. He has enemies. He insists West Africa has not yet achieved independence.

DR. FREUDENBERGER: You work together?

SUZANNE ALEXANDER: We write poems and essays, and we've been teaching at the University of Legon in Ghana. I want you to meet my sister-in-law, Alice. Alice! Alice!

ALICE ALEXANDER: Suzanne called me into the office.

SUZANNE ALEXANDER: Dr. Freudenberger, this is David's sister, Alice Alexander.

DR. FREUDENBERGER: Hello.

ALICE ALEXANDER: How do you do?

SUZANNE ALEXANDER: She came from Washington to be with me.

DR. FREUDENBERGER: Mrs. Alexander, I'd like to talk to your sister-in-law alone for a moment.

SUZANNE ALEXANDER: I'll wait outside.

DR. FREUDENBERGER: Good, good ... I'm worried about Mrs. Alexander's health.

ALICE ALEXANDER: Yes, yes. I am very worried too. We're a close family. I forced her to come to you because she seemed almost delirious last night. When I awoke she was sleepwalking. Since we've been in London she has inexplicable dreams of historical characters and speaks as the characters in her sleepwalking. I have written down what she said last night for you to read.

DR. FREUDENBERGER: Oh, thank you.

ALICE ALEXANDER: This is how she began as she walked down the hallway. "When I returned from Martinique to France at the close of 1790..."

SUZANNE ALEXANDER: *(overlapping)* "When I returned from Martinique to France at the close of 1790, I leaped from one revolution in the new world only to encounter it in the old. A November journey across the French countryside to Paris brought me to a capital where violence and terror soon were to dominate the scene. A Paris mob burst into the Bastille with the bloody head of a governor. The next night Napoleon's secret plans for a French attack on Egypt were completed. The campaign would undercut British sea power. I was to accompany my husband as far as Toulon and later join him in Egypt. My husband's fleet of ships of war was spectacular."

(Breathlessness. Sound of ocean.)

DR. FREUDENBERGER: And she does this nightly?

ALICE ALEXANDER: Almost each night since we've not been able to reach David. The characters are in different stages but the themes of separation, violence, and love are always present.

DR. FREUDENBERGER: She is greatly distressed. Are you able to stay with her until Professor Alexander arrives?

ALICE ALEXANDER: Yes. We were to meet here and return to Washington together.

DR. FREUDENBERGER: This sleepwalking and her troubled nerves are not good for her baby. Let me get her. Mrs. Alexander? Mrs. Alexander.

SUZANNE ALEXANDER: Oh, yes.

DR. FREUDENBERGER: Your sister-in-law and I have had a good talk. I was thinking, since you're both here waiting for Professor Alexander, perhaps you'd welcome a little diversion. I'd like to invite you both to my home. My wife and I have a dramatic circle. We're currently reading Bram Stoker's *Dracula*. Readings will distract you both while you're waiting for Professor Alexander. Suzanne, you could read the role of Lucy, and Alice, you might read Mina. My house is in the Little Boltons.

ALICE ALEXANDER: Very well. Thank you, we are lonely. We know no one here. We're to see a West African writer, but he's in Paris. We will be happy to come to your dramatic circle.

DR. FREUDENBERGER: Lovely. Please come this evening, you're nearby. My wife, Heike, is a translator. She makes tea. We have sherry.

ALICE ALEXANDER: Thank you.

SUZANNE ALEXANDER: Thank you. Good-bye, Dr. Freudenberger.

ALICE ALEXANDER: Good-bye, Dr. Freudenberger.

DR. FREUDENBERGER: Oh no, please, please. I'm Sebastian.

(Overlapping good-byes.)

ALICE ALEXANDER: As we left I heard Dr. Freudenberger reading the paper I'd given him.

DR. FREUDENBERGER: "My life was transformed. Violence flared savagely when mobs appeared and the courtyards of the Tuileries ran with the blood of Swiss Guards. Danger struck everywhere."

(Music—Wagner chorus. DRAMATIC CIRCLE *greetings.)*

ALICE ALEXANDER: We arrived at eight for the reading of *Dracula*. Dr. Freudenberger's parlor was small and dark with water-stained gold-and-white wallpaper. His tall wife, Heike, poured tea. Dr. Freudenberger sat behind a large desk, we read from crimson books. He had a giant handwritten script. We later discovered that all the participants were his patients. We read sitting in a circle.

(Music and voices in background.)

DR. FREUDENBERGER: Ladies and gentlemen, please, everyone. We have two new actors tonight. They're both from America. I've invited them here to join us while they're here in England. In fact, both are writers themselves. Mrs. Alexander, Suzanne, writes essays and plays and Miss Alexander, Alice, writes poetry. So, let us begin.

Dracula, Chapter 15, Dr. Stewart's diary continued: "For a while sheer anger mastered me, it was as if he had, during her life, struck Lucy on the face. I smote the table hard and rose up as I said to him, 'Dr. Helsing, are you mad?' He raised his head and looked at me. And somehow the tenderness of his face calmed me at once. 'Would that I were. My madness were easy to bear compared with truth like this. Oh, my friend, why think you did I go so far round? Why take so long to tell you so simple a thing? Was it because I hate you and have hated you all my life? Was it because I wished to give you pain? Was it that I wanted now so late revenge for that time when you saved my life and from a fearful death?'"

WOMAN: *(Reading.)* "'Oh, no. Forgive me,' said I. He went on."

WOMAN: *(Reading.)* "We found the child awake."

DR. FREUDENBERGER: "It had had a sleep and taken some food and al-together was going on well. Dr. Vincent took the bandage from its throat and showed us the punctures. There was no mistaking the similarity to those which had been on Lucy's throat. They were smaller and the edges looked fresher, that was all. We asked Vincent to what he attributed them and he replied that it must have been a bite of some animal, perhaps a rat, but for his own part he was inclined to think that it was one of the bats which are so numerous on the northern heights of London. 'Out of so many harmless ones,' he said, 'there may be some wild specimen from the south of a more malignant species. Some sailor may have brought one home and it managed to escape or even from the zoological gardens a young one may have got loose, or one he bred there from a vampire. These things do occur, you know. Only ten days ago a wolf got out, and was, I believe, traced up in this direction. For a week after the children were playing nothing but Red Ridinghood on the heath. And in every alley on the place until this bloofer lady scare came along. Since then it has been quite a gala time with them. Even this poor little mite when he woke up today asked the nurse if he might go away.'"

(Music, voices.)

ALICE ALEXANDER: After reading *Dracula* we had tea and sherry and listened to music. Dr. Freudenberger pulled his chair next to the divan.

(Piano music, Chopin.)

DR. FREUDENBERGER: Tell me about your teaching in Ghana.

SUZANNE ALEXANDER: Oh, we teach Césaire, the plays of Wole Soyinka, Chinua Achebe, and Richard Wright and many other writers.

DR. FREUDENBERGER: And do you write plays?

SUZANNE ALEXANDER: My most recent play is *She Talks to Beethoven,* a play set in Ghana about a time two years ago when David disappeared.

DR. FREUDENBERGER: He has disappeared before?

SUZANNE ALEXANDER: There were threats against his life and he disappeared to protect me from danger.

DR. FREUDENBERGER: He must love you a great deal.

SUZANNE ALEXANDER: We went to school together as children. We won the state reading contest together.

ALICE ALEXANDER: After tea we read *Dracula* again. Then we started to say good night. Sebastian was once more at Suzanne's side.

DR. FREUDENBERGER: How do you spend your days in London?

ALICE ALEXANDER: Well, we walk all over, in Primrose Hill, Regent's Park, along Charing Cross Road. After we leave American Express we take tours of Trafalgar Square. Yesterday we went to Windsor in the rain.

SUZANNE ALEXANDER: Victoria grieved for Albert there.

ALICE ALEXANDER: In the evenings we return on the tour bus to Old Brompton Road and sit by the gas fire and write David.

SUZANNE ALEXANDER: Where is he? Where's my husband?

DR. FREUDENBERGER: Suzanne, you must rest. I'll walk you both home, you're just along the road. Perhaps I can help you. I know someone at the American Embassy, I'll ring there tomorrow. Also, another patient's daughter has lived in Ghana for years. I'll talk to her, but, Suzanne, you must not think of returning to Ghana. It might kill the baby. I forbid it.

SUZANNE ALEXANDER: I understand.

DR. FREUDENBERGER: I'll go with you to talk to the American ambassador tomorrow.

(Music.)

SUZANNE ALEXANDER: *(absently.)* In our garden in Legon, David read me the love poems of Léopold Senghor, then he'd tell me of the incidents in Fanon's life that he'd written about that day. His notebooks covered Fanon's entire life but always it was Blida that haunted him. He told me, "In Blida with Fanon, I saw soldiers . . ."

(*African music.*)

DAVID ALEXANDER: (*His voice is heard.*) Generally speaking they had a noise phobia and a thirst for peace and affection. Their disorders took various forms, as states of agitated rages, immobility, and many attempted suicides, tears, lamentations, and appeals for mercy.

SUZANNE ALEXANDER: . . . appeals for mercy. (*Breathlessness.*)

DR. FREUDENBERGER: Suzanne. I'll help you up the stairs. Here, let me carry you.

(*Steps.*)

ALICE ALEXANDER: Here. Here's her room. Thank you, Doctor.

DR. FREUDENBERGER: Not at all.

ALICE ALEXANDER: Good night.

DR. FREUDENBERGER: Good night.

ALICE ALEXANDER: Suzanne, are you all right?

SUZANNE ALEXANDER: Yes . . . Alice?

ALICE ALEXANDER: Yes.

SUZANNE ALEXANDER: I feel like I've seen Sebastian somewhere before.

ALICE ALEXANDER: Where?

SUZANNE ALEXANDER: I don't know.

ALICE ALEXANDER: Before she let me leave her she began to relive those hours two years ago when she sat in the cottage in Legon and listened to the radio all day for word of David.

SUZANNE ALEXANDER: I can't forget.

ALICE ALEXANDER: As I walked down the hall to my room I heard her.

(*African music.*)

SUZANNE ALEXANDER: "Has David Alexander been murdered?"

VOICE ON RADIO: (*partly unintelligible*) . . . again, David Alexander is still missing.

SUZANNE ALEXANDER: Still missing.

(*Music.*)

ALICE ALEXANDER: I too was agitated but finally fell asleep. But just after midnight Suzanne awakened me and stood over me.

SUZANNE ALEXANDER: I want you to come with me and look down into the garden.

ALICE ALEXANDER: What do you see?

SUZANNE ALEXANDER: It's shadowy but I think it's him.

ALICE ALEXANDER: What?

SUZANNE ALEXANDER: Over there in the corner of the garden, underneath the plane tree.

ALICE ALEXANDER: I can't see anything.

SUZANNE ALEXANDER: A figure sitting on a bench. I think it's Dr. Freudenberger.

ALICE ALEXANDER: I see nothing but a shadow.

SUZANNE ALEXANDER: No, it's Dr. Freudenberger, but his hair is white.

ALICE ALEXANDER: I see a shadow.

SUZANNE ALEXANDER: I see him.

ALICE ALEXANDER: I see only the shadow of the hedge. You've got to rest. I'll make you some chamomile tea. Please, rest. I'm worried about you and the baby.

    (Clock striking.)

    I had seen a figure and it had looked like Dr. Freudenberger and his hair had been white. I wanted to think about it and I didn't want Suzanne further upset. Why would Sebastian be in our garden? What was the cause of his changed appearance? Suzanne's mind was not at rest. In the morning she was still agitated and it was raining heavily.

    (Sound of rain.)

SUZANNE ALEXANDER: "I cannot pass a day without loving you. I cannot even dream..."

ALICE ALEXANDER: I was awakened by the sound of Suzanne's voice reading aloud. She hadn't walked in her sleep that night but now was awake, reading a love letter Napoleon had written Josephine. Reading it and rereading these historical letters seemed to give her strength at a time when... there were no letters from David.

SUZANNE AND DAVID ALEXANDER: *(Together)* "Every moment takes me further from you and at every moment I find it harder to bear the separation. You are the ceaseless object of my thoughts. My imagination exhausts itself in wondering what you are doing. If I think of you as sad my heart is torn and my misery increases. Write to me and write at length. Accept a thousand kisses of my love, as tender as they are true. I cannot pass a day without loving you. I cannot even drink a cup of tea without cursing the Army which keeps me apart from the soul of my existence. If I leave you with the speed of the torrential waters of the Rhône, it is only that I may return to you sooner."

ALICE ALEXANDER: I waited a moment before I went to her doorway.

SUZANNE ALEXANDER: How did you sleep?

ALICE ALEXANDER: Well. And you?

SUZANNE ALEXANDER: Well, but I'm concerned about what Sebastian was doing in the garden last night. His hair appeared white.

ALICE ALEXANDER: Now I'm convinced that was not Sebastian but a passerby. It would make no sense. Dr. Freudenberger is a charming friend trying to help us. We're both overwrought. I'm convinced it was someone who resembled him.

SUZANNE ALEXANDER: Perhaps this morning the ambassador will have word of David.

ALICE ALEXANDER: Suzanne was anxious that morning and on the bus to American Express I could not stop her from talking repeatedly about the time David had disappeared in Ghana and how she had news only from her radio.

VOICE ON RADIO: Mr. Alexander is still missing. He traveled with Fanon to Blida. His wife is recovering from an unspecified illness. Alexander was by her side in hospital when he suddenly vanished two nights ago.

SUZANNE ALEXANDER: Vanished.

ALICE ALEXANDER: She relived those moments. I worried about her. The writer we were to meet lived in Chalcot Square. We went to see him, but his wife said he was in Paris. We read that Sylvia Plath lived nearby. One night we saw *Billy Liar* at a theater on Shaftesbury Avenue. *(Music. Voices.)*

The next night Dr. Freudenberger sat behind his desk as we read. His nervous German wife, Heike, sat aside studying Steppenwolf. *(DRAMATIC CIRCLE voices. Music.)*

Dr. Freudenberger hadn't been able to come to the embassy that day. Neither Suzanne nor I mentioned the figure in the garden. Sebastian read the part of Van Helsing.

DR. FREUDENBERGER: "Is it possible that love is all subjective or all objective?"

(Voices reading together.)

"She yet no life taken . . ."

(DR. FREUDENBERGER alone.)

"Though that is of time and to act now would be to take danger from her forever, but then we may have to warn Arthur, and how should we tell him of this? If you who saw the wounds on Lucy's throat and saw the wounds so similar on the child in the hospital. If you who saw the coffin empty last night and full today with a woman who has not changed only to be more rose and more beautiful in a whole week after she died, if you know of this and know of the white figure last night that brought the child to the churchyard, and yet of your own senses that you did not believe, how then can I expect Arthur, who knew none of those things, to believe? He doubted me when I took him from her kiss when she was dying."

ALICE ALEXANDER: Sebastian read one last passage about Lucy.

DR. FREUDENBERGER: "There lay Lucy seemingly just as we had seen her that night before her funeral. She was, if possible, more radiantly beautiful than ever and I could not believe that she was dead."

WOMAN'S VOICE: "Dead."

DR. FREUDENBERGER: *(Others read along.)* "Her lips were redder than before, and on the cheeks was a delicate bloom."

(Sound of rain.)

ALICE ALEXANDER: Sometimes I wondered if Sebastian thought Suzanne was going to die. Had he told us the truth about her breathlessness? I continued writing my brother letters even though he was missing.

"Dear David,

In the rain we take the 30 bus down Old Brompton Road past South Kensington Station, take another bus at Hyde Park Corner to American Express in hope of a letter from you. We went to Windsor Castle again. Paintings of the sad figure of Victoria seem to comfort Suzanne."

(Dog barking. Footsteps.)

The next night, in the garden, Sebastian seemed to have somewhat changed his appearance. That night his white hair was gone. He limped from one end of the garden to the other, not as the young man he was, but as an old man with a severe ailment. As he limped I felt he knew we were watching although he never looked up.

(Piano, Chopin.)

The ambassador says tomorrow there may be word of David.

(Music. DRAMATIC CIRCLE voices.)

The next reading I still did not mention to Sebastian the figure in the garden, but I did tell him of Suzanne's sleepwalking and her words from her historical letters. He had me recite to him all that I could remember.

"I move against a tragic background but it's clear I not only have a rendezvous with you but one with destiny. Wars have always colored my existence. I was born during the Seven Years' War, and was imprisoned during the French Revolution. Now we are married, my whole life is overshadowed by war. Cannons sound."

Neither of us ever mentioned the garden but I was convinced the figure was Sebastian even though I insisted to Suzanne that it was not... New patients joined our dramatic circle, a man from Budapest, a Trinidadian painter.

(*Music.* DRAMATIC CIRCLE *voices.*)

The ambassador said we must keep our bags packed, and although he could give us no concrete word, he had learned of some events but could not yet share them. Soon. Suzanne could not stop talking about David's previous disappearance.

At our dramatic circle, we read Stoker as a group.

DRAMATIC CIRCLE: (*Reading together.*) "All at once, the wolves began to howl as though the moonlight had had some peculiar effect on them. The horses jumped about, reared and looked helplessly round with eyes that rolled in a way painful to see. But the living ring of terror encompassed them on every side."

DR. FREUDENBERGER: Suzanne, I would like you to recount the sequences of Lucy's life.

SUZANNE ALEXANDER: Lucy sleepwalks to the suicide seat on the last cliff. (*She reads breathlessly.*)

DRAMATIC CIRCLE: Yes.

SUZANNE ALEXANDER: Dracula drinks her blood for the first time. She receives a blood transfusion. The wolf, Berserker, escapes from the zoo, breaks a window providing a passage to Lucy again. Lucy dies.

DRAMATIC CIRCLE: (*After each sentence*) Yes.

SUZANNE ALEXANDER: She is buried in a churchyard near Hampstead Heath. (*Sobbing*)

(*Rain.*)

ALICE ALEXANDER: The passage made me cry too. We broke the circle then and said good night... We continued going to the embassy each morning. The ambassador said we would be leaving London soon. We sailed to Greenwich on the Thames. One afternoon we saw a Bergman movie. Sebastian came again in the middle of the night. That time, just as he left through the gate he seemed to look up at our window... I wrote David.

"On the Thames to Greenwich Suzanne recites one of your favorite Diop poems. She carries notebooks of your records of slave ships. Slave quarters, slaves crouching below the stern of the ship. My husband, she told a stranger..."

(*African music.*)

SUZANNE ALEXANDER: My husband gives lectures on the slave ships that crossed the Atlantic.

ALICE ALEXANDER: We reach Greenwich and see the place where Elizabeth I was born. Suzanne recites Diop as we cross the park up to the observatory.

SUZANNE ALEXANDER: "Way back then, with their civilizing edicts, with their holy water splashed on domesticated brows, the vultures in the shadows of their claws were setting up the bloody monument of the guardian era. Way back then laughter gasped its last."

(Telephone rings.)

ALICE ALEXANDER: Finally the ambassador said there was word. We went to Grosvenor Square.

AMBASSADOR: Mrs. Alexander, sit down please. May I get you some coffee?

SUZANNE ALEXANDER: No. No, thank you. Have you heard from David?

ALICE ALEXANDER: Yes, what's the news?

AMBASSADOR: You'll see him tomorrow morning. I spoke to Alexander a few hours ago. He is fine.

ALICE ALEXANDER: Thank God.

SUZANNE ALEXANDER: Are you sure he's all right?

AMBASSADOR: Yes. Last week we knew a few details but I didn't want to talk to you until I was sure of your husband's, and your's brother's, freedom.

SUZANNE ALEXANDER: Freedom?

ALICE ALEXANDER: Freedom? He's been imprisoned?

AMBASSADOR: Yes. But please assure yourself, he is fine now. Let me explain. We have finally heard from our sources that there was a doctor in Algeria who had once tried to kill Fanon, a man named Sottan. And this same Sottan is behind a plot against your husband. We have also learned that this Sottan had you and your husband followed through the villages. There may have been a man who was your gardener at the cottage behind the Ambassador Hotel. And earlier there may have been a man with the ship's orchestra when you were on the *Queen Elizabeth*.

ALICE ALEXANDER: But is he all right?

SUZANNE ALEXANDER: How long was David detained?

ALICE ALEXANDER: How long was my brother in prison?

AMBASSADOR: I don't know. I'm afraid you should know that there has been a rumor that there may have been an attempt to poison him with a drug called filicin. There were rumors that he became violently ill after having an aperitif with a Swiss journalist and was hospitalized. It was at that time we made our connection. But I talked to David this morning and he sounds fine. And he will arrive at Gatwick in the morning at 8:10. I want to assure you, he sounded fine. You will all leave Heathrow at 2:35 in the afternoon, Pan American, he asks that you be ready. And one final note: In the morning there will be an article in the *Herald Tribune* that Frantz Fanon has died in a hospital in Washington, D.C. I'm terribly sorry.

SUZANNE ALEXANDER: No, no.

(Crying. Piano music.)

ALICE ALEXANDER: We hardly felt like going to the dramatic circle, but we went. We knew Sebastian would be disappointed. Instead of scenes, he had us read a litany of dramatic events. He seemed to have a purpose in doing this.

DR. FREUDENBERGER: "Jonathan Harker, arriving at Klausenberg, stays the night, leaves by coach for Castle Dracula."

WOMAN'S VOICE: "Realizes he is a prisoner."

DR. FREUDENBERGER: "Watches Dracula crawl, face down, over the castle wall."

WOMAN'S VOICE: "Enters the forbidden room."

WOMAN'S VOICE: "Dracula makes Harker write three misleading letters to England."

DR. FREUDENBERGER: "Harker discovers his personal effects are gone. Dracula leaves the castle dressed in Harker's clothes and returns with a child for the three vampire women."

WOMAN'S VOICE: "The bereft mother is killed by wolves."

DR. FREUDENBERGER: "Harker climbs along the castle wall to the cellar, where he finds Dracula in a box."

ALICE ALEXANDER: Then he read the last section.

DR. FREUDENBERGER: "When I looked again, the driver was climbing into the calèche and the wolves had disappeared. This was all so strange and uncanny that a dreadful fear came upon me and I was afraid to speak or move. The time seemed interminable as we swept on our way now in almost complete darkness."

ALICE ALEXANDER: He reached out and held Suzanne's hand, staring at her. We returned to our rooms for the last night at Old Brompton Road and finished packing. Even though the ambassador had said David sounded fine, of course we were very fearful. Three weeks ago we had arrived in London happy and everything had changed. I forced Suzanne to go to sleep and then I went out into the garden and waited for Sebastian's arrival. He came a little before midnight. I ran toward him.

(Steps.)

Sebastian, why have you walked in the garden at night, limping, hair white, almost as an apparition?

DR. FREUDENBERGER: I wanted to appear as an apparition.

ALICE ALEXANDER: But why?

DR. FREUDENBERGER: To prepare Suzanne's mind for the darkness I knew she must face. The moment I met Suzanne I fell in love with her. As a matter of fact, I'd seen both of you before you came to my office, in a restaurant next to the South Kensington underground station. It was a Sunday. I was struck by Suzanne's fragile beauty. I followed you along the road. I had a premonition that David, like Jonathan Harker, was going through bad times and she, like Lucy, would become the victim of an unfair, tragic plot. I'd hoped that my dramatic circle would help her and you on this difficult journey.

ALICE ALEXANDER: So, David will be changed.

DR. FREUDENBERGER: Yes. But he will recover.

ALICE ALEXANDER: Sebastian kissed me and disappeared before I could even thank him. We never saw our friend again. As the ambassador had told us, in the *Herald Tribune* was the article on Fanon's death . . . We arrived at Gatwick early and waited in the hall behind a glass partition for visitors from Africa. Suzanne had worn David's favorite dress, white silk with a kinte cloth sash. I hardly recognized David, he had changed so. He limped like an old man and his black hair had turned white. Suzanne ran toward him.

(Sounds of terminal.)

SUZANNE ALEXANDER: David!

ALICE ALEXANDER: It was hard to tell at first if he even recognized her. Finally he smiled, they kissed and embraced.

DAVID ALEXANDER: I wanted to see Frantz before he died to tell him of things I had discovered. We'll have to continue to live by his words.

"But the war goes on and we will have to bind up for years to come the many, sometimes ineffaceable, wounds that the colonialists have inflicted on our people."

(Voices in terminal.)

ALICE ALEXANDER: We helped David through the terminal. In months to come he would recover. The book on Fanon would be powerful, but for now he was lost in Blida.

(Voices increase. African music.)

END

Letter to My Students on
My Sixty-first Birthday by Suzanne Alexander

1

The only thing holding me together was Teddy's performance in *Hamlet*. And my mother singing spirituals every morning as she dressed to go to the shopping center, putting on her London Fog raincoat and driving her 1979 Chevrolet down to Superior.

That day the director of *Ohio State Murders* (a small man in enormous sweaters) said he didn't need me at rehearsals. I was relieved. It would give me a chance to watch the rehearsals of *Hamlet*. I took the bus to Dayton and then to Yellow Springs.

The theater department was on the edge of the campus, a gray structure that seemed once to have been a Victorian house. A long hallway led to the theater. Here the company sat at a table reading sections of the play. I watched them for a moment as they finished a discussion on betrayal, disillusionment, and Ophelia. The company was a mixture of black and white students. I didn't see Teddy.

Then suddenly he came through the door from the theater. Teddy was a slight young man, twenty-one, sallow skin like mine, black hair (thinning). He usually wore glasses. Ever since he'd been a child he had been described by everyone as brilliant. He always wanted to be a theater director/writer and actor. But like David, he had a scholarly side and his essays on culture, race, theater, and literature had already been published by a college journal in New York. This was his senior year at Antioch. I joined them at the table. Teddy gave me a book on *Hamlet* they were studying. The company spent two hours discussing the opening of the play.

In Cleveland, it was impossible to focus on the tribute to my work, even though parties, panel discussions, and evenings of segments of my work were all over the city. The mornings when I had to go to rehearsals were a time of exhaustion. I dreamed Teddy was accused of murdering a French king again. And while he was in jail in Virginia (after being condemned) Teddy's right hand was cut off. And his body was drawn in sunder and dismembered by five horses and his carcass and quarters cast into a fire and consumed to ashes and the ashes scattered to the wind while I yelled at the killers that I had been to Concord and read Thoreau and Emerson and my grandmother had gone to church twice a week and our family had worked hard for justice.

I held up a photograph of my father's church.

"Please believe me."

Alice said she ran out onto the lawn in her nightgown, blinded by lights, police yelling, as a gun was put to her ear and she was told to stand back. Teddy was held over the hood of the police car, handcuffed then kicked.

"Get back, get back, get back," police yelled when she tried to go to him.

In the dozen years she lived there her yellow early American clapboard house with green shutters at the end of Washington Lane seemed a place totally safe from brutality.

That morning in January Alice called me at half past five crying, explaining how they had been sleeping when the sound of police sirens awakened them. The room appeared aflame with light and then a scream. It was Teddy.

In the middle of that same night I dreamed about a documentary I saw on CBS that showed men living underneath the Westside Highway at 96th Street. One man had a white linen tablecloth spread prettily on cement. I realized that I saw these same men constantly walking to Broadway. Many were black. I realized that to go home under the highway they walked through the cross blocks 86th, 87th, 88th from Broadway to Riverside Drive. I wondered if the man with the baseball bat lived there.

Patrice and Teddy had both been in A——— at Alice's for the weekend.

It was Patrice who hid behind the door and videotaped the police running around the yard pointing guns.

"What did I do?" my son screamed. "What did I do?"

And that's what I'd wondered ever since. What did we do? What did our family ever do except try to be excellent citizens? What kind of country was this where a policeman could beat you and then you had to defend yourself with letters of character?

During these weeks, I dreamed: David and I are sitting on the small terrace outside the cottage beneath the tree. I stare at the red poison berries. Beyond, men play golf. David writes in *The Scarlet Fever List,* "Great storms will be, this day there are great storms of wind, over-turned trees, barns and houses, even forest. We live near the epicenter."

We drink cappuccino. It is the day after the 1989 earthquake. Part of the Bay Bridge has fallen.

There is another aftershock. The radio says there will be approximately three hundred aftershocks in the next two months. But if the *big one* doesn't come before Christmas then it probably won't. All around us are yellow tapes that say "Crime Scene."

A white sign on the door of the cottage says, "Do Not Enter. This property will be examined for damage October 30." I enter. In the living room amidst fallen furniture, Teddy is being kicked in the stomach by the Virginia police. His clothes are covered with mud, his face swelling from the blows of the policeman's elbow.

I offer the policeman poison.

Teddy's crying. They kick him.

"Mom, help me."

"Please, Mom, help me."

They handcuff him.

And take him away in the paddy wagon.

"Mom, help me."

Since December, David's lapse and a month later Teddy's being bru-talized by the Virginia police, my dreams were savaged by unaccount-able symbols. I dreamed often of a Garden of Health (called so by my daughter, Patrice). She writes it on a leaf for me to read. Flowers of the bugloss are growing in Riverside Park near my apartment in New York. A man who says he's homeless stands by the Soldiers and Sailors Mon-ument at 89th Street. Then he goes across the Hudson on a sailboard shouting to me that bugloss (of which I've never heard) will console my heart and memory and engender good blood, void the melancholy mad-ness and frenzy I feel. As I run down Riverside Drive away from him he shouts that briony is good for suffocation.

2

My current work was called "Collapse of I," and I couldn't stop writing it, even in the midst of rehearsals for *Ohio State Murders.*

During the time I was in Cleveland the stage manager picked me up at ten o'clock in the morning. We drove down Superior to 18th Street. The Loews Theater was next door to the old Palace. The car had to be driven down into a concrete alley—an alley bounded by a series of iron fences that led to concrete walkways and finally the walkways led to a steep fire escape. The steep, long fire escape opened onto a narrow passage with plain windows that faced the alleys. And at the end of the passage was a porter to the theater.

He sat in a booth. Inside the booth on the wall was a rehearsal schedule for two plays, *Dracula* by myself and *Ohio State Murders* by the local playwright. My version of *Dracula* was to open when *Ohio State Murders* closed in three weeks.

Ohio State Murders was not my play but a play of my life by ——, a local playwright. She had written a piece about my years at Ohio State. And today students from my old Cleveland high school were coming to the theater to a rehearsal to question me on my technique as a writer and my views on race and how Cleveland had changed since the 1930s and '40s. Their teacher had given me their journals, and I was surprised to see that many were already married and had children.

Cleveland had been a city I had loved when growing up there. The parks, Lake Erie, Dale Creek, the streets with maple trees leading to Public Square, and on the streets beyond the Square my father had an office in City Hall. Our house was blocks from the Lake and Rockefeller Gardens. From the house you could walk to a road called Herrick. That road led to a winding boulevard called East Boulevard. From East Boulevard you walked down two levels of grass into the Cultural Gardens (each dedicated to a different European country) and woods. Our family had walked in the Cultural Gardens at night. In the 1940s you could leave the house after dinner and walk toward Lake Erie across a woods through which ran a creek and find yourself on the shore of Lake Erie.

"Canada's on the other side," my best friend's mother said. Once we had actually taken a small white excursion boat, the Erie, to the distant side and gotten off for an hour.

"We're in Canada," my friend's mother said.

I bought an ashtray and ice cream. I'm eating ice cream in Canada, I thought. I was eleven.

Now in 1992 a walk down into the park would be an invitation to murder. The old mansion on East Boulevard remained the same, but the diagonal streets that led away from the park were dangerous.

I loved my son's entire performance as Hamlet, but it was his scenes with the Ghost that made me weep:

> "I am thy father's spirit
> doomed for a certain time to walk the night
> And for the day confined to fast in fires
> Till the foul crimes done in my days of nature
> Are burnt and purged away."

3

The local playwright, ——, was my age and had reached adolescence in the 1940s. Her father had worked with young blacks in the YMCA. In the lobby of the theater there was a screen with articles about her family in the 1930s and '40s. And even a letter from Congressman Louis Stokes. Her father had been one of Stokes's heroes.

My mother now had moved from our lovely house to a dim apartment on a hill. From the hill you walked down to a disorganized shopping center that appeared to serve people from several neighborhoods.

Each morning on the way to rehearsals the stage manager came to get me in a blue van. I waited in the huge lobby painted silver with plastic trees. My mother, although financially comfortable, had been frugal in choosing an apartment. The security guard stood by the door.

I ran out to the car. On the drive down Superior, I had to pass Lakewood Cemetery where both my father and brother were buried.

As we drove further downtown into the decaying neighborhoods and deserted areas where there had been clothing factories, I thought, Why had the police beat up Teddy?

Why were these areas deserted?

Where was David?

Why was I sixty?

One night two months ago my precious son, Teddy, had been beaten up by a policeman. He had a taillight out on his car.

I wrote to Governor W—— again as I waited for rehearsals to begin, sitting in the subterranean greenroom.

New York City 10024

Dear Governor W——:

My name is Suzanne Alexander. I am a black writer. I have written you once before in February. I am writing to you again about the A——, Virginia, Police Department.

We are an outstanding black American family. My husband, David Alexander, is a professor emeritus at Stanford and biographer of Frantz Fanon. My plays and stories are published and taught widely.

We are now a grieved family. Our son is being persecuted by the A—— Police Department just as surely as happened in the deep South in the 1930s or during Emmett Till's time.

On Friday night, January 11, my son, a fine citizen who has never been in any trouble whatsoever, was knocked to the ground and beaten in the face, kicked repeatedly in the chest and the stomach, and dragged in the mud by an A——, Virginia, policeman whose name is ——. This occurred in Teddy's aunt's front yard on —— Street in A——. My son was stopped because he had a taillight out on his car. There was no further provocation from him. The A—— police arrested my son, then concocted a totally false story and charges, and charged him with assault and battery.

This is the height of persecution of a black male with tactics of the deep South in the 1930s and overtones of Emmett Till. My son has never been in any trouble at all. He is a fine citizen and student at Antioch College. Please look into the A—— Police Department and its racial persecution of our son and our family. We are grieved and shocked. We want these false charges dismissed.

Suzanne Alexander
Dr. David Alexander, Professor Emeritus at Stanford
Patrice Alexander

I took the bus to Antioch that day and walked across the muddy field to the theater. The long foyer with the folding chairs was cold. It was a dress rehearsal.

The set resembled a scene from Orson Welles's *Othello:* shadows, very dark spaces, little furnishings. By now I knew Teddy's favorite scenes and I could tell how emotional he became when his father's ghost appeared on the ramparts.

After another performance he walked me back across the muddy field to my rented car. He asked what else can we do to find his father.

"Teddy, we hired the detective and every day my friend, ——, editor of the *Tribune,* is writing about David. I don't know what else we can do now until your criminal suit is over. We'll go back to California the moment it's over."

"The cast can't believe that under those circumstances I face Hamlet's father's ghost. Mom, you do believe Dad's alive, don't you?"

I murmur, yes.

My son still wore his costume, which was a kind of gray cotton pajama. The production was set in the 1930s; Hamlet had walked around stage in pajamas. I realized that Teddy didn't even have on socks.

"You've got to get in from the wind. That jacket barely covers your pajamas," I laugh.

The night after I saw *Hamlet* I dreamed of David, who had done so much to help fight for racial equality in the United States, his teaching, his books. Now at sixty-four he suffered memory lapses and often seemed forgotten by younger activists and educators. Many times he sat alone on the round stone seat near the Stanford post office. Sometimes he walked with St. Clair Drake. Few of the black students knew of his role in history with Fanon, Nkrumah. In my dream I saw my husband wandering in the Palo Alto hills when a bicyclist attempts to murder him, piercing his face with a poniard and breaking some of David's teeth. Then students appear in white tennis outfits. Behind them Patrice. They take her to the Quad where she is condemned to stand naked.

When I'm in Cleveland, I think of New York.

In the foyers of the brownstones on my street people are robbed just as darkness comes. One man carried an ax and a gun at four o'clock in the afternoon. The next morning at fifteen past eight I leave the apartment to go to my class at New York University. Waiting for me outside, sitting on the stoop, is a woman my age, searching for food in the garbage. She stops me to warn me that there is a vault underneath this street where brimstone lies and over it gunpowder. And there is a plan for the muggers on the Upper West Side to come up through a trapdoor dressed like workmen, cast holes into the vault so that it catches fire and consumes all.

She knows everyone.

The mugger with the ax and the gun told her he had a plan as well to burn all the woodstacks in London.

"My grandfather worked in war plants during World War II and built bombers that won the war and made people in the brownstones secure," he said.

As I walked toward Broadway, I looked back. The woman was drinking from a paper cup thrown onto the curb.

My lecture that morning at New York University in the Tisch School of the Arts was to be "The Construction of a Play with Aristotelian Elements."

She waved at me.

The opening night of *Hamlet* I couldn't stop crying when the ghost appeared.

In Cleveland as I watched the afternoon rehearsal, my mind wandered. I wondered about my character, Suzanne (in my journal, "Collapse of I"). Rather than watch rehearsals I sat in the back of the theater unable to stop myself from writing about my character, Suzanne.

The journals I kept on my character, Suzanne, often contradicted each other, but suppositions and fictions about this character were my lifeline. I often forget I gave "her" my own name and was surprised when people said, "Why is your character named after you?"

After rehearsals the cast and I went out with the local playwright. She took us to the high school that I had graduated from. However, it was not the same building or the same location. My high school had been torn down, and a new school had been built several blocks away. The school was given the same name.

Night came. We stopped at the Radisson for food. As we drove up St. Clair in the darkness, I wanted to turn around and flee into the night. We arrived at the building I had never seen; fences, floodlights dwarfed the square structure. It looked like a prison camp. I remembered my high school covered with ivy.

Students read sections of their papers on me and my work.

4

Even though there was a vacant lot where my old school, Glenville, used to be, and this new school was meaningless to me, I still feared looking at the photographs the sweet students had made into a display in my honor. The faces of the four people I loved the most from high school were pasted on a giant wall hanging. (They had taken the pictures from my memoir, which covered my 1947–49 high-school years.)

Their lovely faces and memories of their faces haunted me. I sought replicas of these four friends in my friendship thereafter and had a myriad of fictional characters based on variations of them: Leonard, Rachel, Joan, Arenzia.

They asked me to come to the display on stage and look at the text.

Glenville was incorporated as a village on October 4, 1870, and was annexed to the city of Cleveland on June 19, 1905. Glenville was once known as a resort for the wealthy and the "garden spot" of Cuyahoga County. Glenville was born out of an early Irish settlement on the lakeshore between East Cleveland and Collinwood in 1873. Glenville got its name because the area is full of shady, thick glens through which little streams tumbled. The first to settle in the Glenville area were early New England farmers, followed by immigrants from Scotland, Ireland and England. Over time the area grew into a secluded rural village and its lakeshore location made it a fashionable summer residence for Cleveland's affluent families. . . .

It was difficult to concentrate on the student reading. I had to fly to Washington the next morning to meet again with Teddy's lawyer. I thought of my street, West 87th in Manhattan. A man often appeared in the last two years walking from West End Avenue to Riverside Drive swinging a baseball bat. I had been so frightened one snowy morning that I ran down steps into a courtyard and fell. In subsequent dreams the man with the baseball bat is now a clerk at Food Emporium on Broadway and 90th. When I put my groceries on the counter he tells me he is being sentenced that day in a court near the White House and he will lose his ears and be branded on the forehead "Black" and be condemned to the galleys. He says his supervisor at Food Emporium says that such burnings die out in a short time and that he should be branded on the cheeks with a letter *B* by a surgeon and that an acid be poured into the brand to color it so that it would never vanish.

In Stanford Patrice was staying in David's Lagunita cottage. Although the cottage is charming it's surrounded by a red berry whose name I've forgotten; this berry is poisonous and lines the side of the cottage that faces the golf course.

"Why did they plant poisonous flowers here?" I asked the administrator of the cottages. She didn't know.

The Scarlet Fever List had been on David's desk at Christmastime. Patrice is reading.

"My father is so brilliant," she said. "My father is a genius."

On opening night of *Hamlet* I couldn't stop crying when the Ghost appeared to Teddy.

When David disappeared this time, he was working on a group of essays about race called *The Scarlet Fever List.*

I laughed when he told me the title as we sat by Lake Lagunita eating. David had for years had unexplained fevers that lasted for two or three days. The doctors were never able to explain their origin. I would put cold towels on his forehead and fret.

"Maybe it's because he had typhoid fever that time," the doctor could only say.

"All of these illnesses you both have," said Patrice, "is because you've both worked too hard. That's the problem. You've both been too dedicated to work."

When I left Stanford, I knew Patrice would care lovingly for David.

"My parents separate all the time," she told her friends.

Stanford had given her a temporary position in Afro-American studies. She taught two courses on Black Women's Literature. And no matter how busy she was she looked in on her father at six o'clock in the evening at the cottage. And that was when his door was open (right before Christmas break). But he wasn't there.

In Cleveland, I called the local playwright. She was in meetings every day. At home her answering machine was on, and when someone did pick up it was a babysitter. Children cried in the background. Whenever we met, she was effusive and talked loudly about how much she loved my work. Then she'd hurry down the aisle of the theater, seeming to be late for another appointment.

I read on the brochure about her that she received a grant to write *Ohio State Murders* because I was a former Clevelander (in fact, the productions of both *Dramatic Circle* and *Ohio State Murders* were underwritten by Ohio grants) and that she was a past professor at Cleveland State. Perhaps that's why she was always coming from receptions and State Council meetings and usually dressed in small suits.

She would wobble off in very high heels and disappear down the aisle. Minutes later I'd see her at the back of the stage talking with the set or costume designer.

I flew to Washington and met with Teddy's lawyer.

I dream Governor W—— answers my letter. Enclosed is a thesis on the force and effect of all manual weapons of the fire and another thesis on present remedies against the plague and the play *Hamlet.*

I'm sitting with the Antioch students in the snow on the Quad; beyond, some play football, and we go to Yorick's grave.

I am sleepwalking toward Yorick's grave. David enters our room in Earl's Court the autumn of 1961. We arrive in London from Southampton on the way to Ghana. There is some problem with a visa.

I ask Teddy is he still going to the group for victims of violent crime.

I asked Teddy again is he still going to the group for victims of violent crime.

"Tell me about the times Dad disappeared before," Teddy said. He called right after midnight. He was back at Antioch College in Yellow Springs.

"Mom, you say he may have gone to Ghana. Where? Where in Ghana?"

Even with his lapses it was a shock that on Thanksgiving weekend David had walked from the Stanford campus through the arch of eucalyptus trees to the bus terminal and vanished. The fact that we were separated (I lived in New York) made it worse. I left Stanford because I couldn't stand David's depressions. Now I blamed myself. I had thought coming to Cleveland, seeing a re-creation of our years at Ohio State (by the local playwright) would comfort me. And maybe David would appear at opening night. His depressions about the condition of American blacks had worsened. Sometimes he seemed in a dream and was seen sitting in the sun near the Leland Stanford chapel. Stanford offered him economic security for life yet the columns of the Quad, the golf course, the Palo Alto hills became a source of melancholy for him.

"Even though they honor me," he often said, "this is like a white country club."

The Rodney King beating further depressed him.

In the lawyer's glass offices with flowers I kept crying over and over, "How can a policeman beat up my son for no reason? Then charge him with assault?"

By now I had a list of cases where black men were beaten: athletes, college students. It was long. I read the Black Caucus was investigating the circumstances surrounding Rodney King.

I called Patrice in California.

"I'm writing too many letters. But I can't stop, Patrice."

"Mom, I know you are. Please, could you write a lecture for your students."

"My students?" I wasn't teaching that semester.

"Yes. Turn these feelings into a lecture for your students. You love them so much."

My students and I usually discussed themes, characters and times of the plays. And very often the playwright's life. But I usually avoided talking about my life. I did not teach my own plays.

She said she had to go to Tresidder to eat and she was sending me another book on blood pressure.

I didn't know she spent every evening walking and driving through the Palo Alto hills searching, in case her father had fallen ill there.

That very night I started a lecture about all of these events called "An American Writer Speaks on Her Sixty-first Birthday." The first paragraph began:

"The only thing holding me together was Teddy's performance in *Hamlet*. And my mother singing spirituals every morning as she dressed to go to the shopping center, putting on her London Fog raincoat and driving her 1979 Chevrolet down Superior."

5

On the bus from Dayton to Cleveland I dream I see Teddy in Attorney Edelstein's office on M Street in Washington. He says he's finishing up his term papers in Washington because on campus the plague is increasing and there is increasing lawlessness on the Ohio border. And none of the students are allowed to have meat during Lent.

"I want to study in Cleveland, but Cleveland is submerged in Dale Creek" (a creek that ran through my old neighborhood).

He says he's discovered that after World War II moths called Canadian soldiers covered the shores of Lake Erie one July evening and that bit by bit that section of the city sank into the creek.

"If you want to see your father and brother again all we have to do, Mom, is walk to 88th and St. Clair, descend into Rockefeller Park (now called Martin Luther King), and we will see your old neighborhood just as it was." And when Teddy was on the submerged street yesterday he said he saw my father mowing the lawn in 1943, hurrying so he wouldn't be late for the Cleveland Indians' game. My father didn't get home until late because after the game he went to a meeting of the NAACP.

Teddy said: "I saw your grandmother. Remember she took care of you and your brother the fall of 1941 because your mother worked in a war plant. She was planting petunias in the tree lawn."

In Yellow Springs, the actor who played the Ghost had a large head. I couldn't take my eyes off the large head covered with slimy and dried blood oozing from the openings in his skin. He described his murder:

"Sleeping within my orchard
My custom always of the afternoon
Upon my secure hour thy uncle stole
With juice of cursed verbena in a vial
And in the porches of my ear did pour
The leperous distillment whose effect
Holds such an enmity with blood of man."

I can tell Edelstein thinks I may jeopardize Teddy's case by writing too many letters. He told me to write two: one to the governor and one to the county manager. I have written seventeen, but I haven't told him.

I begged him to tell me about the detective he said he uses. I asked him was it possible for me to talk to the detective.

I wanted to find out where the policeman lived.

I wanted to see the policeman who dragged my son in the mud.

I could tell Edelstein had begged Teddy not to tell me too many details.

"You're too emotional, Mrs. Alexander," he said, as we walked through his glass offices.

He told Alice, "I'm afraid your sister-in-law may do something foolish."

I sensed he saw me as foolish. And it was hard to be cast in this light. He judged me for being a mother.

I dream we are sitting on the edge of Lake Lagunita after the earthquake. David tells me there is an explosion in Dublin and dogs for the French king are carried over to France. And Martin Luther King is imprisoned. There is an aftershock. We run down the steps to our cottage when the aftershock stops and open the cottage door. Our belongings lie broken.

In Stanford's daily newspaper there was an item: "Biographer, political activist, essayist disappears from campus . . .

"Last spring a documentary of Mr. Alexander's life and work was shown on KQED."

I dream David is giving a talk. He's not in class but standing in the middle of Lake Lagunita. There is no water in the lake. David has climbed into the lake's recess.

"David," I call. "Are you working on your *Scarlet Fever List* this morning? The publisher called from New York. He wants the parts you've rewritten; there is a new deadline. The book has to be in by the day of Rodney King's trial.

"And Edelstein says the district attorney wants to read your first draft."

I take him a cup of peppermint tea which he loves and a strawberry yogurt.

"David, you've got to get the first draft ready for the district attorney and chief of police."

He sips his tea.

"Three thousand trees were overturned this morning, Suzanne.

"And the minds of all men at this time are in great perturbation, our son's trial and the robberies in the vestibules on 87th Street. What has befallen us? The Queen's jewelry of silver has been sent to be guarded with crown jewels and many private persons conceal their groceries and even themselves. Many of the ministers are hated by the people," David says. He gazes at me.

"Suzanne, we've been together a long time.

"I won't let the state of Virginia harm Teddy." He kisses me.

The phone rang again. It was Teddy. If he lost the hearing, he would have to have a trial by jury. His lawyer said the judge (in Virginia) always sided with the police, and the police would be sure to have secret witnesses as a surprise. I had written to the county manager, the NAACP, the police chief, powerful friends black and white. Many friends wrote to the police chief. My friend the journalist at the *Washington Post* said I should do no more. Undue publicity would hurt Teddy's case. Between now and the hearing my son traveled back and forth between Virginia and his classes in Yellow Springs, Ohio.

"Have you listened to the tapes of my play, Mom?" Teddy was writing a play on Robert Johnson.

"Teddy, did you see the lawyer today? Who else should I write to? What does he hear from the county manager? Who else should I write to? Have you heard from the NAACP? Congressman ———? How does your head feel? Are you going to your group for battered victims? I'm sending Gov. ——— another message. I got a letter yesterday from Congresswoman ———.

"I can't talk, Mom. My head hurts. I can't think about my case tonight."

Patrice sent her television treatment about David and me. It has scenes of our giving joint lectures. I don't know if Patrice realizes she's taken the whole segment from one of my published pieces, *The Film Club*. "What do you think of my television treatment, Mom?" she says.

My daughter makes me laugh.

Teddy's trial was in five days. I reread the replies from the police chief, the senators and the county manager again. Patrice said she had a friend who grew up in A—— and she would try to find out more about the district attorney. She read me a long list of new people we should write to.

"Patrice, I need you," I scream. She didn't tell me she had several graduate students searching in the Bay area for David.

The new list said:

Mr. ——, Chairman of Supervisors

Honorable ——

Executive Director, NAACP

Senator ——

Senator ——

I carried copies of the character letters in my script. Why, why should we have to defend ourselves with character letters when we were innocent? All our lives our families had tried to fit in American society and improve our situation.

In Cleveland, the local playwright was given a reception at the producer's apartment on Shaker Boulevard. She passed out brochures about herself and gave me more journals written by Glenville High School students.

I continued writing letters to senators and called two Washington writers who I learned were connected to the governor's office. One advised me to stop writing letters, that I would hurt Teddy's case if I continued to write letters. My friend the journalist said I should call Jesse Jackson.

Teddy sent me a tape from his play on Robert Johnson that he thought he had lost:

NEXT EVENING
Depot:
White/Colored signs

Roberts gets off the train with his satchel and guitar. A Negro man selling fruit from a basket:

MAN: Someone was found murdered in the bottom.

ROBERT: Honeybunch?

MAN: At first they thought it was him. But it's an older man. Part of his face is missing. They took him to Hawkins Funeral Home. They've laid him out. Most everybody's there.

THAT NIGHT

Hawkins Funeral Home (CHARLENE clinging to ROBERT)

(ROBERT stares at man's torn face. In the background people are saying a psalm.)

LATER THAT NIGHT

ROBERT, *his mother,* CHARLENE, *walking down the road from the funeral home.*

CHARLENE: Where's Honeybunch?

LAVINIA: People just disappear in this town. Especially colored people. They'll never find that little boy.

(Robert walks on ahead.)

LAVINIA: I worry about you, Robert, when you're not running around the country you sit up in that little house by yourself.

(Silence)

I read two or three student journals. How far they were from my own high school journals about Nat King Cole, *Our Town,* Y dances. I received a reply from Senator ——.

UNITED STATES SENATE

Dear Mrs. Alexander,

Thank you for your inquiry to my office. I am sorry to learn of the circumstances that prompted this contact.

As a result of previous correspondence, I have been assured by the Chief of Police of A—— County, Virginia, that this matter is being investigated by their Internal Affairs Section. In an effort to be of assistance, I have forwarded your letter to the A—— County Police Department and the A—— County Commonwealth's Attorney.

As soon as I have received a response from the above agency, I will be in touch with you again.

Please do not hesitate to let me know if you have any additional information, questions, or comments.

Sincerely,

Senator R ——

6

I remembered Aaron Grossman. He was our friend at Columbia. And the first person to write about David and me in Ghana. He fictionalized us, called us the Crawfords:

It was right after Patrice Lumumba was killed. I remember Crawford's wife made one last appearance in the common room. It was before she went back to the States and was hospitalized. Her appearance was shocking. She came forth to me and began talking rapidly. I wanted to cry at the sight of her: her hair on her temples was gone and parted from the back of her head to conceal her bare crown. She combed a slight fringe about her forehead which only emphasized her poor baldness.

March Crawford [David] began one of his monologues and spoke tenderly of the man as an American Negro might do. I saw that she noted the tenderness and appeared to tremble.

"Do you know?" she said, "that I'm going to be bald."

"You know," she said, "Lumumba was like my husband trying to find Genesis in the midst of golden savannas. He wanted the black man to rise." Then suddenly, "Have they discovered who murdered him?"

I said, "Mobutu's men and the CIA."

I leaned toward her. She trembled, holding a poinsettia in her hand.

New York had been a city I loved. As I wrote in my memoir, I walked on the Upper West Side singing, "I like New York in June." Now a great deal of my time was spent worrying about the man with the baseball bat.

I think I'll call my thoughts, "Letter to My Students on My Sixty-first Birthday."

7

On the plane to Washington I took *The Death and Rebirth of the Seneca* by Anthony Wallace, *Language and Culture in Conflict,* and reread sections of *The Body in Pain.* Images more terrible than I could bear flashed through my mind. If Teddy lost his case would they handcuff him and carry him through that door in the courtroom to jail?

At the same time I had no idea where David was. Had he been in an accident? If he knew about Teddy he would come immediately. (He worshipped our son.) The lawyer, Edelstein, violently insisted we keep Teddy's case out of the press.

Over and over again in my mind I wondered where had David gone after he left Stanford's campus. I knew he liked to walk in the Palo Alto hills, he liked to walk around the edge of Lake Lagunita, through the paths and underbrush. Was he still in California? Stinson Beach? San Juan Bautista?

His state in the last years had been despondency, and the medications he took for the injuries he suffered when he was imprisoned briefly in Algeria in 1961 robbed him of stamina. To comfort my ill nervous feelings I drank a spoonful of valerian every day. And read an article Patrice gave me on blood pressure.

I listened to more of Teddy's tapes.

In the *Plain Dealer* on Sunday Alice wrote an article about events that occurred after the play *Ohio State Murders* "ended."

She had just published an article about me in *Theatre Magazine*. She wrote about me now more than ever.

Though Alice has returned to Virginia, her piece on my development as a writer will be in the playbill. My sister-in-law teaches my work at Howard. The publicist, William, feels (despite our antagonisms) Alice is the foremost scholar on me.

I don't understand "Collapse of I," my sometimes fictional character, Suzanne, but I keep writing it.

She has a daughter called Patrice too. But this Suzanne dies in an inn in Columbus, Ohio.

I made a list of black mothers whose sons were beaten by the police. I added a white woman to the list when I read in the *New York Daily News* that a white woman heard a commotion at night. She ran into the yard (just as Alice had). She saw a car driving off with her son in the back seat. In her panic she ran into the house and got a gun and fired the gun into the car. In the confusion she didn't realize it was a police car. She now faces five years in prison. Her son had a traffic violation: speeding.

I haven't heard from the governor yet. Teddy says the governor doesn't get involved in these cases. But I must talk to him. My friend Samuel is trying to help.

My friend Charles called (he had won the Pulitzer Prize). When he was just out of college he worked briefly as a detective. I asked him about the number of letters.

"You're supposed to write a few letters, Suzanne. I called to give you the name of a scholar on prosecuting the police as well as another lawyer I know who does legal aid as well as a public defender in Brooklyn. You must try and talk to all of them. You need all this information so you can judge what your lawyer is doing."

Other people called suggesting Al Sharpton, Edward Kennedy, Jesse Jackson.

I read the pages Patrice gave me on hysteria and herbs to help: skunk cabbage, saffron, skullcap, valerian, mistletoe, peppermint, vervain, catnip, pennyroyal, antispasmodic tincture (quick relief).

In my dream the commander held the intercepted letters, reading them aloud to show me they were in his possession. I begged him to show them to the A—— District Attorney so that she would be sympathetic to my son.

"I'm praying you will," I say.

I pray every day on my knees in my mother's guest room kneeling by the old secretary with my brother's baby shoes on the top shelf.

I miss rehearsals, rise in the night to pray. I get on my knees and pray for Teddy.

Sometimes on stage as *Hamlet* he broke down and cried. But as himself he tries to act brave. No matter what he says I see the fear in his eyes.

"Is the legal system fair?" I ask Edelstein again on the phone.

"How many cases has Edelstein won against the police?" I ask Patrice.

"I don't know how to get that information, Mom. We have to trust him."

"But he's a stranger."

"Whatever happened about the detective who was supposed to investigate the policeman and his past? He must have found something. This policeman must have beat other people. There's no place I can go and get that information?"

"I don't know."

8

I dreamed three thousand soldiers were to be sent to Broadway and 86th Street where the king of Spain was making fortifications. (I saw them when I was buying the *New York Times.*) And this week 198 persons are dying of plague in Riverside Park near the Boat Basin at 79th. And Teddy died last night in the Tower where he remained under sentence of death because I don't have the right letters of character.

The district attorney tells me that Teddy seems nice but how can she be sure.

She's a white woman with a pink ruffled blouse on. She says she lives in Georgetown. I give her a sheaf of photos of Teddy when he was president of the black students group at Riverdale and show her his speeches he made to help the cause of black students.

She says that's nice and washes her pink blouse.

I couldn't go back to sleep. I loved my daughter very much. But it seemed she had more in common with Alice as time passed. She felt herself to be more an Alexander. They were always planning trips together and had been to London, Senegal, Accra, and Cairo.

Now they were researching a book on David's journeys while he was writing about Frantz Fanon in the 1960s. They had sold the treatment to television.

I don't know why, but I remembered my birthday a few months earlier. I was sixty years old. And alone on my birthday. I had just arrived in Cambridge to teach at Harvard for the fall. The phone system had not been turned on, and the apartment was empty of my postcards and photos. In the middle of the night before my first class a tiny mouse ran into the light from a hole by the radiator. My family was unable to reach me by telephone. I placed the small birthday cards on the huge dark mantel and went to Au Bon Pain and bought a grilled chicken sandwich. I had no desire to be sixty years old, but there it was.

This winter after my sixtieth birthday I began to write about myself in the third person. I could not stop myself. It became . . . Suzanne said, Suzanne did. I'd rise at 5:00 A.M., walk to the desk in the large drawing room of my suite at Adams House, look out over the courtyard, count the lights on in Apthorp House. And start to write. I was extraordinarily happy gazing into the courtyard at early dawn.

I remembered winter afternoons walking through the Master's Gate of Adams House on Linden Street, looking up at my window anxious to get to my desk. I loved my classes.

And I didn't cease writing about myself in the third person. Why?

In the Cambridge winter I taught a course, Black Playwrights of the World. We read sections of Fanon's *Wretched of the Earth,* the pages on "Colonial Disorders." Late at night I read *The Body in Pain,* Elaine Scarry; Philip Fisher's essay on Hamlet, *Thinking About Killing Hamlet and the Paths Among the Passions*; Milosz; and *Malcolm X's Speeches at Harvard.* Adams House put on my play *She Talks to Beethoven* in the lower common room. It opened the weekend after Thanksgiving, the same weekend David walked from his cottage by Lake Lagunita (at Stanford) down Therese to Tresidder and past the old Union, took the bus to the terminal to San Francisco and vanished.

In the course Black Playwrights of the World we read Soyinka, Walcott, Cesaire. We were all still upset over the Rodney King beating. (The black and white students sat on the top floor of Warren House in the enchanting windowed room that overlooked the Harvard Faculty Club.) We read the Negritude poets and *Mulatto* by Langston Hughes. Hughes's South of the 1930s was a South I knew well as I had spent every summer with my grandparents in Georgia in the 1930s.

In Cleveland I wrote another letter to a senator. My frantic letters to the senators were identical and in each letter I enclosed a picture of Teddy on a trip to Senegal.

The publicist called at 11:30. Alice had come by her house with a gigantic portfolio of snapshots of David at OSU. "I don't know what to do with them. But she does have a rather fascinating collection of material about that time, 1950–53 at OSU. It seems that she used to visit David when he was in law school before you met. And she took a lot of pictures."

And she'd written a ten-page history of Cleveland and the decline of the neighborhoods. "And although she didn't grow up here sections of it are brilliant. She has tremendous insight into the fragmentation of American cities."

I could tell Alice had beguiled the publicist with her sweet Alice Walkerlike face and embroidered cotton dresses. She knew exactly when to say she was a doctor of English or when to say she was a professor of history of which she was both.

The publicist went on, "Did you know she has a new work called *Deserted Areas* about the abandoned areas and deserted people in Washington, Detroit and Cleveland? And that she and her husband adopted a child from right here in the old Cedar area?"

"Of course I know about Nelson. . . . He was an orphan and he's legally blind."

She hung up.

I couldn't sleep and reread Philip Fisher's essay on Hamlet and sleep:

> Killing plays the role that it does in the literature of the passions in part because it breaks off the response and counterresponse of action by means of the one act that removes the possibility of any further personal response.

I wondered where the policeman lived who beat my son. I tried to visualize him at home talking to his wife. Neither Teddy nor Patrice nor Alice would describe him to me. They'd only say he had black hair.

"You mustn't think about how he looks, Mom."

In my dream the commander shows me letters of character from my friends. He says they were intercepted at the Washington, D.C., main post office.

"Do you mean the district attorney's office never got them!"

He smiles and starts reading the precious letters I have spent the winter gathering together for my son's defense.

Now Teddy says there may not be a trial in five days. He doesn't want me to plan to come to Washington. Edelstein says the prosecution is angry about the letters and they're going to take the case directly to trial by jury.

"I don't understand.

"I don't understand."

I couldn't stop writing about myself in the third person. The pieces were fiction and fact and some ended in my death. Often I spoke as if Alice were observing me:

> By 1973 she talked more about the passages she had forgotten in *She Talks to Beethoven*. Particularly Beethoven's funeral. "How could I have left out Beethoven's funeral?" She tried to find the book but the page was lost.
>
> One thing that worried me was that she never mentioned the murder of the girls. She would talk about the songs of Dizzy Gillespie or the melodies in a 1940s Hollywood musical, *Orchestra Wives*, but not the murder of her girls by Robert Hampshire, the English professor she had been so tragically involved with.

The sleepwalking continued. David worried about her falling down the stairs in the house on 16th Street on the inner as well as the outer stairs as the house sat high on a knoll.

She still sometimes told people that she had known David since she was a child just as she told Sebastian: "We won the state reading contest together." But that was not true. They met at Ohio State after the babies' deaths.

The name of my lecture to my students is "An American Writer Speaks on her Sixty-first Birthday."

The next morning new pages were added to the script, material from Alice's article. Several of the actors embraced me as I passed the dressing rooms and came into the theater. I was surprised. "We understand this character better now," they said. They sat on the stage and read aloud:

"Remember how Sebastian read," she said.

"When I see again the driver was climbing into the caleche and the wolves had disappeared, this was all so strange and uncanny that a dreadful fear came upon me and I was afraid to speak or move. The time seemed interminable as we swept on our way now in almost complete darkness. . . ."

She taught that winter of 1972 in New Haven, a college seminar at Yale. When I asked her what she was teaching she said, "Creative writing and my own play ——."

"How will you teach your play?"

"I have pieces I wrote in Ghana, pieces I left out of the play on the savannas and drives into the Liberian Goodrich plantation. These pieces were experiments with narrative."

During her first days in Liberia she had used the narrator from her first novel, *People and Strange Progressions,* a white student called Aaron Grossman.

From New Haven she called:

"I read my students the Grossman narrative first and then the narrative I discovered in the north of Ghana . . . an American Negro woman who roamed the beaches at Accra and had falling hair." It was then she started using the first person, "I."

The play she taught was a play she seldom mentioned because it had caused her so much unhappiness when it was produced off-Broadway the year after she and David returned from Africa, 1962. This theater piece almost destroyed their marriage.

She had gone back and forth on the train to New York. David stayed home sitting in the middle of the upstairs hallway reading his notes on Fanon. Dr. Lee, our doctor, said they both were in a perilous condition. David insisted upon reading me continuous case studies of patients he had observed when he traveled with Frantz. His dead hero and compatriot occupied his mind.

I felt torn between them. Suzanne would come to my house on Sunday morning. (We all lived on 16th Street.) Sometimes David took their daughter Patrice for walks to the Capitol and Lincoln Memorial.

"Do you think I should give my students this story?" she'd ask. Then she'd take a taxi to Union Station, sometimes without even calling to say goodbye to David . . . her papers falling from an old Mexican wedding bag she had carried through the savannas of West Africa.

She taught early Monday morning at Timothy Dwight on Temple Street and stayed at the Duncan Hotel on Chapel. As soon as she got to Temple Street she'd call from the office and read me the old Ghanaian passages she'd prepared for her lecture.

I often thought of writing Sebastian. Because it was in London that the "I" narrative collapsed in her pieces and to my surprise she decided to use me as a narrator in her stories as well as my name, Alice. She didn't seem to see anything odd in this.

I had my own stories and poems and felt that she had violated a boundary, but I never spoke of it to her. Whenever Suzanne bewildered me I suppressed my anger because I would remember the murder of her babies and how she had come to our house in Washington before she and David married . . . so broken.

I asked my editor at R—— could I stop Alice from writing articles about me?

He told me to leave her alone.

But this is making me sick.

"I think if you leave her alone she will stop. I didn't want to upset you, Sue," he said, "but last week I saw parts of a manuscript she submitted to —— on you. Do you want to see it? It's down in ——'s office. I took a look at it to see if she is violating your legal rights. She's not. However, I feel this is leading to something terrible between the two of you."

The local playwright and the director decided to add parts of Alice's *Plain Dealer* article to *Ohio State Murders*.

"It enhances it," the director said. "It would be helpful to the audience to know what happens to Suzanne after she left Ohio State. We're going to try new passages today from Alice's article. She did take care of you in Washington and she has very precise notes and a wonderful memory."

I began to fear this play that was meant to be a tribute to me.

When we were sitting in the green room beneath the theater the local playwright said she'd begun to think Alice's memory of my life had an accuracy that may have been lacking in the notes I'd given her a year ago. (She had written the play from these notes I sent her.)

"Greater accuracy?"

"Sure, Sue. She seems to see the whole picture of you and David's life, especially the effect of the passing years on both your personalities, the competition between you both in work and over the children. And your weariness."

"Then you're going to use her notes?" I said quietly.

"I think so," she paused. "This isn't going to make you unhappy. Is it? I think this will make for a stronger piece. I don't want further to upset you. I've heard about your son's case."

"Who told you? Alice?"

"Yes, and we're all aware now that Professor Alexander wanders off from time to time?"

"And Alice told you that too."

"Sue, that puts a different light on the material we're presenting now."

"I'm beginning to regret this project. When you wrote me last year you said you wanted to do a brief piece on my Ohio State years. Now you're reaching into parts of all my life. It wasn't in our agreement."

Before she went up the stairs, she turned.

"Sue, I sense your disdain for me. But believe me, I just want this piece to be accurate. David's lapses of memory, his sick spells reminiscent of the prisoners he studied, your many separations are important."

She reached out for my hand. I pulled away.

Why did people have to live inside the Soldiers and Sailors Monument near my apartment house in New York?

Why was there a constant stream of people searching through the trash cans on my street?

Why had the vestibules in the houses on my street become areas of danger? Neighbors were mugged in them by gunpoint while trying to unlock the door.

Now that I was sixty sometimes I found I retreated more than ever into the romantic mythology of the fulfilled European artist. Giants. Chagall, Rodin, striding into life. In my early twenties it was stories of these men in the countless pages of the *New York Times,* the artists, the painters in particular, presented in mammoth art books . . . Skira, Abrams . . . posters at Marlboros . . . their lives, works, thought, delineated in long tables of contents . . . titles of their sketches . . . final sketch for the ceiling of the Paris opera. Paris through the window . . . the bridges of the Seine.

I dream I am coming home from Food Emporium with Frusen Gladje ice cream; the homeless man with the baseball bat is spreading the garbage from the cans on the sidewalk in front of my brownstone. Beyond at the Soldiers and Sailors Monument maimed soldiers are being examined as well as people who are waiting for the Riverside Drive bus 5. A commission is appointed to examine the people waiting for the Riverside Drive bus who claim to have been maimed during the last four years in the war in Riverside Park and on the Hudson waiting for the PATH train.

The names of the men and women are to be recorded showing the counties and cities where they were born and under what captain they served when hurt.

At that moment David comes up the path from the park. He says he's just been walking along the road to Stinson Beach in California.

He has heather.

The commander of the prison, Christopher Columbus, invited me to a banquet. After much feasting and triumph (I was forced to watch them) the commander asked me to go down to the river. When we came to the edge of the river he showed me a written command he had received from an anonymous source to execute us all—myself, Teddy, Alice, Patrice, David, my mother—and he immediately carried out this command. We were all beheaded and our bodies taken to Concord, Massachusetts, and our heads were carried with speed to a terminal that resembled Union Station in Washington. The cause for the murders the commander said was that he had intercepted the character letters for Teddy and they revealed secret intelligence with the king of Spain.

"But I have not met the king of Spain," my head replies. I can't help but think how like the Ghost in *Hamlet* we look.

"But I have not met the king of Spain," I reply over and over.

Edelstein hung up on me today. He said I must see Teddy's case realistically. Few people win cases against the police; the judge tends to side with them. And he is doing everything possible, that I must understand it is his profession to prosecute the police and he hopes I won't write too many letters. He went on about the delicacy of all the elements. I tried to listen. Alice had told me he was brilliant at prosecuting the police but all I could whisper pathetically was, "Will Teddy have to go to jail?"

"That's a possibility. Everything is a possibility."

"But what about the videotape?" I cry.

"Mrs. Alexander, the videotape is dark and it has only the very end of the incident. You must get hold of your emotions. I do think in the end it will come out fairly. But I don't know if it will come out fairly without a long process. I've prosecuted many policemen. Prepare yourself for this case going to trial by jury."

"And then the jury will be white Southerners?"

My blood pressure soared. I took medication.

9

I had not slept. It was eight o'clock in the morning. My mother's bedroom door was still closed. She seldom went to sleep before 3:00 A.M. I stared out of the window on a small park called Forest Hills and beyond the strange shopping center.

Nine years ago Alice married the well-known writer, Henderson Young, a writer more famous than David. He wrote novels and taught at Cornell. She seemed happy in her marriage and yet grew increasingly angry about my being an Alexander.

We had once been close.

My play *Dramatic Circle* was about this stage of our lives.

I'm beginning to see that the monologues the local playwright added are insightful. I think I understand what she's trying to achieve.

In *Hamlet* I remember when Teddy said:

"Not a whit, we defy augury, there is a special providence in the fall of a sparrow. If it be now, this is not to come, if it be not to come it will be now if it be not now, yet it will come. The readiness is all."

My life (as seen by the local playwright) was to open in fourteen days. The piece she invented was a long monologue. The heroine named after myself recounted racial hatred in college:

I was asked to talk about the violent imagery in my work; bloodied heads, severed limbs, dead father, dead Nazis, dying Jesus. The chairman said, we do want to hear about your brief years here at Ohio State but we also want you to talk about violent imagery in your stories and plays. When I visited Ohio State last year it struck me as a series of desperate dark landscapes just as it had in 1949, the autumn of my freshman year.

I used to write down locations in order to learn the campus: the Oval, behind the green, the golf hut, behind Zoology. The tennis courts beyond the golf hut, the Olentangy River, the stadium off to the right, the main library at the head of the Oval. The old Union across from the dorm, High Street at the end of the path, downtown Columbus, the Deshler Wallach, Lazarus, the train station. The geography made me anxious.

The zigzagged streets beyond the Oval were regions of law, medicine, Mirror Lake, the Greek theater, the lawn behind the dorm where the white girls sunned.

The ravine which would be the scene of the murder and Mrs. Tyler's boarding house in the Negro district.

The music I remembered most was a song called "Don't Go Away Mad," and the music from *A Place in the Sun,* that movie with Elizabeth Taylor and Montgomery Clift based on Theodore Dreiser's *American Tragedy.*

I dream of a summer evening in Cleveland in the 1940s. My father and his friends held the meeting of the NAACP on an old campsite I loved as a child, a place called Aurora, Ohio. I walked down a path lined with whitewashed stones. But seeing into the wooden cabin where my father and his friends sat was difficult. The Canadian soldier moths covered the screened door of the cabin. It was Cabin 17.

I write it down on my yellow pads, Cabin 17. I stand on the bottom step. And hear my father and his friends laughing and he whistles, "Let Me Call You Sweetheart." I'll come back in August when the Canadian soldiers die, I think. I want to see my father and his friends. I hoped when I returned to Cabin 17 in August I would hear my father and his friends discuss (as they always did) how to make Cleveland a better place for Negroes, how to raise money for the Quincy Library and for the cornerstone ceremony for the Central Y and as they also did, talk about *justice* for their children, and Bob Feller.

I asked Teddy was the back porch of my house with the trellis of honeysuckle submerged there on the floor of Dale Creek. Yes, he said, he saw my mother sitting on the steps stirring a cake, and I was seven and licking vanilla icing.

"Oh, Teddy, I can hardly wait. When can we go there? I want Patrice to come too. What steps do we take? The steps on East Boulevard or the steps on Herrick Road?"

"We take the steps that lead from the Czechoslovakian gardens."

I was so happy. When I was young I had wandered through Dale Creek on summer days. Then one day they built a highway over it.

Each day I passed Lakeview Cemetery where my father and brother were buried.

A magazine called *Avenues* came out with an article, "Welcome Home, Suzanne Alexander."

A student from my old high school sent me his paper on Cleveland.

Each day on the drive downtown to the theater we passed deserted and ravaged neighborhoods. My city and what happened to it since World War II was always on my mind.

I read the student paper.

The students invited me to visit one last class. It was the tenth grade.

Teddy had to go to Washington to meet with the district attorney's office today. I was shocked to discover the prosecution heard his defense and everything he will say in court yet he knows nothing about what the prosecution will say. They will probably have a surprise, Edelstein said. But he can only surmise what they will say.

"Teddy, you mean they know all your information and you know nothing of theirs?"

"Yes."

"Mom, I may have to go to jail. They want me to plea bargain."

He hung up.

Patrice called. She said Teddy told her not to tell me but the district attorney's office is angry because there have been too many letters and

Teddy will be denied the trial in four days with a judge. They say the trial will go straight to trial by jury and we will have to wait several more months and that Teddy and Edelstein shouldn't bother to come to court. For the first time Patrice cried.

Edelstein said they know we fear a trial by jury. Juries tend to side with police.

Edelstein told Teddy when he was in the D.A.'s office she threw some of the letters to the floor.

Teddy calls.

"Mom, there's no need for you to come to Washington. The prosecution wants the trial to go to trial by jury. There's not going to be any trial in three days."

The prosecution still wants Teddy to say he struck the policeman. If he does he will get three months' probation.

They want Teddy to say he struck the policeman. If he does he'll get two months' probation and the record will be wiped clean.

"I don't understand."

Teddy says he's not going to "confess" to anything he didn't do.

He's in A—— at Alice's.

"My head hurts, Mom."

"Please let me come."

"Mom, there's not going to be a trial. I'll see you this weekend in Cleveland."

"He's come back," Patrice said.

"Dad's back." She explained that in the evening as she sat in the cottage reading David's *Scarlet Fever List* she heard the latch turn and there was David. "He's dazed, Mom, but he's fine. He's sleeping now.

"A Mr. Chavez brought him in a truck."

The local playwright gave me her schedule. I was surprised to see she would be "out of town" for the next eight days. Many episodes in her version of my life were inaccurate. She told me her daughter was getting married in Boston. And they all would be going to New England (including her grandchildren by her son . . . the children who cried in the background when I phoned.) Her daughter, she said, graduated from Harvard and was marrying a Harvard business student.

"I'd like to talk to you about the production," I said. "I don't think parts are quite accurate."

"Here's my number, dear, in Boston," she said, handing me a pretty piece of ivory note paper with her name engraved at the top. "Please call me. We can talk."

The local playwright did not return from her daughter Margaret's wedding in Boston. After the wedding she took the Amtrak train from Boston to New York and went across Penn Station, down two levels to Metro North. (She was planning to visit a former college friend who lived in New Brunswick.) She caught the 6:33 A.M. train to New Brunswick. In the Metro North carriage a man started to fight with the conductor. She was sitting in front of this passenger on the window side. The passenger pulled a gun. She was shot accidentally and fatally.

Both plays in Cleveland, *Ohio State Murders* and *Dramatic Circle*, were cancelled.

I unpacked my bags that night Teddy told me there would be no trial. It was the day after —— was killed.

I sat in the old tapestry recliner my mother bought in the thirties. And looked out of the windows onto Forest Hills Park. After all this anxiety... no trial. We'd have to wait again for the trial by jury. Maybe July, maybe August. I reread the section on hysteria in *Back to Eden*.

"How can they do this?" I asked Teddy.

"It's the right of the prosecution to ask for this," he said, his voice very low.

Now ——'s funeral would be the same day that Teddy's trial was to have been.

The publicist, William, described how on that morning her body was carried from Metro North and how her daughter came from a honeymoon in New York to New Brunswick to bring her mother's body home. She was shot on the side of the face, still wearing the lavender orchid corsage from her daughter's wedding.

If this was my sixtieth year, I feared sixty-one.

Motherhood 2000

Motherhood 2000 was produced and commissioned by the McCarter Theater in Princeton, New Jersey, for Winter's Tales '94, January 12 through January 23, 1994. The staged reading was directed by Michael Kahn.

CAST

Mother/Writer	*Lynne Thigpen*
Richard Fox	*Karl Light*
Passion Play Actor	*James Morrison*
Passion Play Actor	*Stephen Lee*
Passion Play Actor	*Brendan McClain*

PRODUCTION

Assistant director	*David Herskovits*
Technical director	*Colin Hodgson*
Sound operator	*John Collins*

MOTHER/WRITER: I finally found the policeman who beat my son that January night in 1991. He ran a theater on the steps of the Soldiers and Sailors monument on Riverside Drive at 89th Street.

Homeless people who had lived in the park under the 89th Street overlook now lived on 89th Street on the sidewalks, in the hallways of apartment buildings 311 and 145 Riverside Drive, as well as in the apartments with the legal tenants.

This policeman who had haunted me for nine years performed a play nightly: it was an ancient miracle play.

How amazing that this man should appear on the very street where I lived.

Evenings I could hear the actors, from the roof of my brownstone where I went to rest. The "Soldiers" spoke to "Christ."

(Quoting actors)

"And I have gone for gear good speed. Both hammers and nails large and long, then maybe boldly do this deed."

I walked to the edge of the roof and listened.

This man who I had thought of constantly since 1991 was playing Christ.

The soldiers spoke again to him.

(Quoting actors)

"The foulest death of all shall he die for his deeds. That means cross him we shall."

It was quite by accident that I had found him. I had come out of my brownstone one morning when I saw a band of disheveled men walking up Riverside Drive in the rain. They stopped when they came to the Soldiers and Sailors monument. One stepped forward and climbed the steps to the doorway of the statue. I recognized him immediately.

I had seen Richard Fox only on videotape. The night of the beating my sister hid in the doorway of her house and photographed him: he handcuffed my son and kicked him again and again in the stomach.

I had wanted to find him. I wanted to find his house somewhere in the suburbs of Virginia, but the lawyers concealed any information about Fox from me.

"You're behaving like a mother," the lawyer said. "You could hurt your son's case. Don't interfere. We have a detective looking into this policeman's history. Anyway, we've heard he will no longer be with the force. He's going to work for the Secret Service at the White House. Mrs. Alexander, please go back to your classes. Don't interfere. You will hurt your son's case."

Now nine years later I sat on the grass at the monument and watched Fox: acting the role of the Savior. The name of the troupe was The Oliviers.

I recognized the other actors. They were the former district attorney, the county manager, the police chief, and two policemen who had been involved in my son's case. They had been at the hearing.

At that time I wrote to them as well as to the governor, congress-men, the NAACP, and friends.

"I am writing to you again. On Friday night, January 11, my son was knocked to the ground and beaten in the head and face, kicked in the chest and stomach and dragged in the mud by a policeman.

My son was stopped because he had a tail light out . . ."

I wrote again and again:

> Congressmen
> The Black Caucus
> The County Manager
> NAACP
> Chief of Police

My beloved son was also a Rhodes Scholar and traveled the coun-try giving speeches for the causes of Blacks.

Nine years had passed. It was 2000.

The sun and the ships on the Hudson were still wonderful. But I hadn't been to Broadway for more than a year. It was impossible to make my way through the men on the sidewalks fighting among themselves. Shootings occurred daily.

I remembered the lovely street fairs when I strolled and bought faded voile dresses and sweet oils in green bottles. The children and David and I gorged on ice cream and crimson ices and bought pa-perback books on trees and gardens: trees and shrubs, trees for shade and shelter on the lawn.

"Mom," the children said, "We want another ice."

Now I was often hungry. Food was at the market on Broadway and 91st, but unexpected shootings on the street kept me fearful. I saved sacks of potatoes so that in case of shootings I would always have something to eat.

It was then I daydreamed of old movies, *The Sound of Music,* Fellini's *Amarcord.* The old movie theaters, the Thalia, New Yorker, the Symphony, had closed long ago.

Refugees from New Jersey arrived every morning at the 79th Street Boat Basin where armies of people lived.

Riverside Park between 86th Street and 116th was dangerous: inhabited only by gangs.

I remembered when my baby sons and I had walked in the snow deep into this park down to the highway, across to the shore of the Hudson. The Circle Line cruise ship sailed past. We waved, then walked to 116th Street and Broadway and stopped at Prexy's for chocolate. I dreamed of the beauty of Columbia University Mall where civil unrest and chaos now never ceased.

Members of The Oliviers were all white. They seemed protected by the soldier costumes they wore. My neighbor, a casting director, Judy, said she thought The Oliviers were one of the groups who traveled from national monument to monument trying to find asylum.

Judy still delivered tapes of her clients to an agency on 47th and Sixth and said things in that area were sometimes pretty much as they had been in the past.

She said the most popular movie downtown was called *Suicide Mission*, about a group of unhappy housewives from Davis, California. Sometimes she still went shopping at Saks and once bought me a straw hat. I wore it when I sat on the roof to read. Sometimes she had to stay downtown for the night. You never knew when bombings would occur. Still she was younger than I was and less afraid.

Often people who made it across the Hudson lived in the Path Station for weeks. Civil strife had destroyed a great deal of New Jersey. Yet some suburbs remained intact.

In the brownstone I lived in it was impossible to tell friends from enemies: the five floors were occupied by Bosnians, Californians, Haitians, Neo-Nazis: all were split into subgroups and each group had their own agenda, wars, and language.

My sons were somewhere in Washington but I didn't know where.

I lived on money from the royalties of my plays, a very small but sufficient amount.

City officials were constantly drowned near the Statue of Liberty.

Nights I continued to watch the ancient miracle play from the roof.

One night I came into the park just as a scene began. The soldiers spoke.

Although my asthma was very bad due to the conditions of the dirty streets, I tried to speak along with the actors.

And I never took my eyes off Richard Fox. His costume was very shabby; soldiers closed in upon him. I realized how agonized I still was by him.

I decided to join their company. I told them I had once been a playwright and had taught at Harvard. I was relieved to see they did not remember my name from my son's case.

I became their only Black member. They said I could rewrite a section of the play.

That night as I sat on the roof writing I remembered my son screaming when the policemen kicked him in the stomach, my son who as a child laughed at his turtle and ate pop tarts and watched *Rawhide* with his cowboy hat on.

The next night I arrived at the monument early.

On that night The Oliviers allowed me to perform with them. I was to be one of the soldiers.

The play began.

(The play appears before her. Three SOLDIERS *and Jesus—* RICHARD FOX—*stand directly opposite her.)*

SOLDIER: We have them here even at our hand.

SOLDIER: Give me this wedge; I shall it in drive.

SOLDIER: Here is another yet ordand.

SOLDIER: Do take it me hither belive.

SOLDIER: Lay on them fast.

SOLDIER: Yes, I warrant
I thring them sam, so mote I thrive.
Now will this cross full stably stand;
All if he rave, they will not rive.

SOLDIER: *(to Christ)* Say, sir, how likes you now
This work that we have wrought?

SOLDIER: We pray you say us how
Ye feel, or faint ye aught.
*(*WRITER *speaks with them.)*

SOLDIER: We! Hark! he jangles like a jay.

SOLDIER: Methink he patters like a pie.

SOLDIER: He has been doing so all day,
And made great moving of mercy.

SOLDIER: Is this the same that gan us say
That he was God's Son almighty?

SOLDIER: Therefore he feels full fell affray,
And deemed this day for to die.

SOLDIER: Vah! qui destruis templum . . .

SOLDIER: His saws were so, certain.

SOLDIER: And, sirs, he said to some
He might raise it again.

SOLDIER: To muster that he had no might,
For all the cautels that he could cast;

As Pilate deemed, is done and dight;
Therefore I rede that we go rest.
SOLDIER: This race mun be rehearsed right,
Through the world both east and west.
SOLDIER: Yea, let him hang there still,
And make mows on the moon.
SOLDIER: Then may we wend at will.
SOLDIER: Nay, good sirs, not so soon.
For certes us needs another note:
This kirtle would I of you crave.
SOLDIER: Nay, nay, sir, we will look by lot
Which of us four falls it to have.
SOLDIER: I rede we draw cut for this coat—
Lo, see how soon—all sides to save.
SOLDIER: The short cut shall win, that well yet wot,
Whether it fall to knight or knave.
SOLDIER: Fellows, ye thar not flite,
For this mantle is mine.
SOLDIER: Go we then hence tite;
This travail here we tine.
WRITER: I spoke my lines coughing, wheezing... then found my place
directly before Fox and struck him in the head with a hammer.
(She does.)
(He falls.)

Secret Paragraphs about My Brother

There have been killings in Cambridge.

They want me to help them find the murderer, but I can't concentrate. The police feel there is a literary connection between the murders since all of those killed (except the nun from California) had belonged to an Upper West Side Video Club in Manhattan that had more than an ordinary number of writers as members. And at one time each had rented either *The Vanishing* or *Vertigo*.

It was the semester I dreamed of my son when he was sleepwalking. That was the winter before the summer of 1963 when my brother went for a drive in his car and was in the accident. I lay across the bed after I put my sons to sleep and suddenly painted one wall in the apartment red. My brother was in a coma for five months. When he woke, he was brain damaged and paralyzed. He died in 1972.

When I'm in Manhattan I retreat to the rooftop of my brownstone and read Russian classics—*Crime and Punishment* is my favorite. Some mornings I walk down Riverside Drive to 72nd Street. I often think about my brother.

Before he joined the Army, my brother went to Ohio State for a semester. He used to stand beneath my window in Baker Hall and practice his Spanish. Then one day he disappeared.

In Florence, July 1961, I didn't know that two summers from then there would be a terrible accident. I had given up writing plays. I had come to feel hopeless.

During that month, after I left American Express, I would often stop at the American Library and read *The New York Times*. One morning there was an exhibit in the window called *The Plays of Tennessee Williams*. It had been a long time since I had thought of Williams but now, as I stood staring at the volumes of *A Streetcar Named Desire, The Glass Menagerie, The Rose Tattoo*, I realized how much I still admired what Williams did. Perhaps I could write another play. The work on my desk that I had started in Ghana was an unclassified assortment of pages. I had no idea what form it would take but there was a character, Sarah, who was concerned about her thinning hair and another character, Clara, who spoke of her journey on an ocean liner. I had these characters speaking intensely of Queen Victoria and Patrice Lumumba. And I had a Jesus character who was speaking to my heroine. Perhaps I could write a play again, I thought as I walked back to Piazza Donatello. But no, I couldn't face that disappointment again. No matter how hard I had tried, I couldn't sustain a play in three acts like Williams and I couldn't achieve the density I so loved in Lorca.

Then one day not long after I had returned to Rome to await the birth of my son, my husband arrived from Nigeria. We lived on Via Reno in a lovely apartment with a terrace that faced Rome. One morning, again on the way to American Express, I bought *The Times*. It was a very sunny morning. There was an article about Edward Albee, about the success of his one-act plays.

I had not thought of one-acts since I'd been about twenty-three. They seemed an oddity. But at that moment I decided I would try *one* one-act play and it would be the last thing I would write. I called it *Funnyhouse of a Negro*. The accident would take place the summer after its first performance.

In 1977, I was flying from London to Budapest (on the way to a theatre conference) when I met a man who had been in Mannheim around the time of my brother's court martial (1956). He said he now worked for the American Embassy in Haiti. It was a night flight. My fellow passenger did not say why he was flying to Budapest, but he questioned me carefully on my role in the theatre conference.

In Budapest soldiers with guns surrounded us as we deplaned in the December night. During our days at Hotel Royal we were never alone. I bought my sons flutes and saw the Danube. In Berlin I went to see the Reichstag. I thought of Mannheim. Yet I was not able to go there. The conference office booked me for Hamburg but I didn't go to Hamburg either. I stayed in Berlin and walked around the Alexanderplatz. And took a tour through the Black Forest.

Sometimes I think I still want to go to Mannheim. Would I have to disguise my motives in order to get my brother's old Army records? Perhaps (I) could unearth the story behind my brother's trial. I want to prove he was treated unfairly.

When he got married, his wife, Felicia, said to me, "I don't know where your brother is half the time."

"What do you mean?" (I always knew where my husband was.)

"I don't know where he is and don't know who his friends are," she said as we sat reading *House and Garden* and drinking Lipton's iced tea.

"Where did he go and who were his friends?" I asked my mother thirty years later.

"No one knew what he was doing half the time. He'd come in at three in the morning. I don't know where he'd been. He changed so after he came back from the Army," she replied.

After he got out of the Army he sought work in the psychiatric ward of Mt. Sinai Hospital. He was seldom without his white orderly jacket.

"Was your brother's nickname Charlie?" asked the undertaker at my father's funeral.

"I never knew my brother had a nickname," I said. "We called him ——. And what made you think of my brother?" (He had been dead three years, and it was a different undertaker who had buried him.) This undertaker was a son of one of my father's oldest friends. My parents married in their house in Dayton, Ohio in 1930.

"We were talking last night about your family and someone said, didn't Mr. —— have a son called 'Charlie?' He knew it was a nickname."

I said I'd never heard that but I'd ask my mother.

When I got home from the funeral parlor I asked her. She stared at me.

"I never heard that," she said. "I don't know anything about a 'Charlie.'"

Today I still wonder if he had a life as a "Charlie" and if she knew.

This reminded me of years ago and Rosemary and our Italian neighborhood. One summer evening I was playing jacks on the steps when I saw my friends run past my house toward the vacant lot on Signet.

"Aren't you coming?" some said. "—— and Rosemary are getting married."

I knew nothing of this and arrived at the edge of the field of weeds to see Rosemary and my brother standing before a boy I'd never seen. Rosemary was in her communion dress and my brother in his playsuit.

Just as I arrived they ran deeper into the field and disappeared.

"They went on their honeymoon," someone screamed.

When my brother came home toward dark he stopped and stood in front of me at the porch steps.

"Don't tell mother and daddy I'm married," he said.

He was six and I was nine.

Cars united them. It was a car in which my brother met his disfiguration. (He was driving to see Felicia.) And it was in a car that my father's second wife was instantly killed in an accident that killed his spirit. The biggest argument my father and brother had was over a car—the silver-colored Kaiser. My brother wanted to drive it to a party. My father said he couldn't take the car.

They stood in the center of the living room yelling. I ran down the stairs from my room. My father was small. Was my brother about to knock him down? I started crying. I could see my father was afraid. I feared the worst. My mother was in Maryland on a trip. I was about to run onto the front porch and call a neighbor when suddenly they stopped yelling. My father threw the Kaiser keys on the floor at my brother's feet.

Soon after, my brother joined the Army.

It was spring when my brother left for Germany. He and Felicia arrived on the train from Ohio on the day the movie *Guys and Dolls* opened in New York. I wanted to go to 50th Street and Broadway. Brando was playing Sky Masterson and the *New York Post* said he would be at the opening.

Often I dream of my father pulling the silver-colored Kaiser into the driveway, the same silver Kaiser in which my brother came back from a drive late one night with blood on the fender. He said he'd hit a dog. It remained a mystery. There were so many mysteries surrounding my brother. During those years, he and my mother would go into the bathroom and close the door.

"Mother, I want to talk to you," he'd mumble and into the bathroom they'd go and run the water loudly. I don't know what they talked about.

My mother would emerge, minutes later, and run into her bedroom. Often I could hear her sobbing.

"What's wrong?" I'd say, trying to open her closed door.

Once, months later, she said, "Your brother may have to go to court."

"Court?"

"I don't want to talk about it." And she walked away.

"Mind your own business," my brother would say whenever I'd ask what was wrong. "Mind your own business."

He died without telling me anything.

June and Jean in Concert
(Concert of Their Lives)

A theatre piece with music from *People Who Led to My Plays* with musical score and songs by Loren Toolajian. Directed by James Houghton. Premiered at the Signature Theatre Co., the Public Theater, New York City, Fall 1995.

Additional music by:

Wings Over Jordan
Paul Robeson
Judy Garland
Frank Sinatra
Nat King Cole
Church Choir
High School Choral Club

CHARACTERS

JUNE and JEAN, twins
Their MOTHER
Their FATHER
DEAD AUNT ELLA
Their brother, JACKIE
DR. BENJAMIN MAYS, President of Morehouse College
JUNE'S GHOST
many other characters

ACT I

Easter, 1943
Christmas Eve, 1942 (four months earlier)

ACT II

December, 1941
November, 1974
Spring, 1947
(without intermission)

Music Overture
At Open:
JUNE *and* JEAN *sit at piano practicing "Für Elise."*
JUNE *takes out her autograph book, writes, and draws a willow tree. Sitting atop the "willow tree" is a pretty girl of nineteen, humming. She has on a yellow organdy dress; she is* DEAD AUNT ELLA.
*(*DEAD AUNT ELLA *is one level above stage).*
As ELLA *hums,* JUNE *writes and draws in her book.*

AUNT ELLA: Dining room. Easter morning, 1943. A stained glass window of tulips. Through a side window, falling snow. Table already set for Easter dinner with white cloth and china. On radio Wings Over Jordan sing "Mary, Don't You Weep." *(music, "Mary, Don't You Weep")*

My sister, fragile in house dress, goes in and out of the dining room. My nephew, Jackie, an angelical looking boy of six, sits at the table holding his white Easter bunny.

MOTHER: Goodbye, June and Jean. Your father's waiting for you in the car. *(sound of car)*

MOTHER *(continued)*: This is the only time I can remember it snowing in Cleveland on Easter Sunday. *(Stage becomes church. Choir sings a verse of "I Come to The Garden.")*

MINISTER: On this day, Jesus arose.

CHOIR: I come to the Garden . . .

AUNT ELLA: June and Jean hold Easter baskets, dolls, choir books and autograph books in which they write the history of their family.

JUNE: The miniature photographs and gilt-edged cards of Jesus that the church gave us in Sunday school hypnotized me. The colors, the crimsons, blues, golds . . . the black of Jesus' eyes. "Jesus loves you," Sunday school teachers repeated every Sunday, winter, spring and summer. "Jesus loves all little boys and girls." I saved the pictures of this Jesus into whose feet they had driven nails but who arose. And who loves me and my family. My book, Easter Sunday, 1943. *(She continues writing. The twins write and speak. They write in the past tense as they are writing their history. They speak almost nervously.)*

JEAN: *(Writing)* Even in church we had our Easter baskets and our other favorite things. In our purse candy cigarettes, fingernail polish, a turquoise ring, our jacks and ball. And our autograph books. We couldn't carry our green ballerina dresses. *(On this Easter Sunday, the girls wear pink cotton dresses.)*

(AUNT ELLA's voice, humming.)

JUNE and JEAN: Why do Negroes sing of sorrow? In the church in Georgia where our cousins live the songs are even sadder. They are moans.

JEAN: We also had our Sleeping Beauty books.

JUNE and JEAN: We hope no one puts us to sleep for a hundred years. When we wake up, where would our parents and brother be?

MINISTER: Christ is risen from the dead and become the first fruits of them that slept. For since by man came death by man came also the resurrection of the dead.

JEAN: *(Writing)* We were excited because that afternoon our father was going to take us to hear Paul Robeson. We had seen him once and June said, I realize one person can inspire many people to strength, courage and belief. We loved Paul Robeson. Our mother will stay at home with our brother and his bunny. His asthma was bad that spring and, besides, our mother had been sick that winter.

MOTHER: Be a good girl. *(Theme music)*

JUNE: *(Writing)* In winter I was brought to her room by a neighbor who had been in the house all morning. My parents' door had been closed. And I was told to stay in my room. Suddenly I heard a loud siren. My mother's door burst open, another neighbor had been inside her room. My father came running through the house followed by two men with a stretcher. My mother was lying in bed, her face wet, her hair limp. She looked like she was dying . . . the color of her skin was almost purple.

"Be a good girl," she said and the men lifted her onto a white stretcher and carried her to a large white ambulance.

My father disappeared with them. The siren sounded and the ambulance took my mother away. I fled to the closet in my room, closed the door and started weeping. The neighbor made me open the door. "Your mother will be all right," she said.

Jean says our mother lost a child and almost died. *(Pause)*

That Easter morning our father received an award, a civic award for helping the Negro youth of Cleveland. The *Plain Dealer* called our father a gang buster. The article said my father had vision and had changed the lives of underprivileged youth in the Cedar area of Cleveland.

MINISTER: And today one of Cleveland's finest Negro leaders . . . *(Father rises, goes to altar. He stands in light.)*

JUNE and JEAN: *(Writing as they speak)* Our father saved people. People talked of what a fine social worker he was and how many young people he had helped set in the right direction. He raised money for Y scholarships, helped the young find work and provided guidance through the Y programs.

He gave fine stirring speeches at meetings and banquets on the value of working hard for the Negro cause and helping Negro youth. He read us poetry of Negro poets and told me stories of Du Bois, Marian Anderson and Mary McCleod Bethune. He listened to us sing spirituals, which we loved and popular songs, which we also loved. *(Theme music)*

JUNE: My father took me to church with him Easter Sunday. I carried my small Easter basket and wore a round straw hat with cherries on the brim. It was wonderful to drive with my father in the car to the Lane Metropolitan Church. I was happy.

We walked down the aisle into the church, a mammoth hall that had once been a Jewish temple.

White flowers covered the altar and members of the choir wore white as well. The minister preached violently of the crucifixion, Jesus, Judas, betrayal and finally Jesus Christ arising from the dead on Easter morning. My father started sobbing. (My father who smiled, laughed, made jokes, whistled, teased me.)

Jesus had died a long time ago and he had arisen on Easter morning. Why was my father so very concerned about Jesus? I tried to hold his arm.

MINISTER: And now June and Jean will play for us.

(JUNE and JEAN go down aisle to piano. They play "Were You There?" Afterward, JUNE stands up, speaks unexpectedly.)

JUNE: And this is my sermon for the day. The Japanese: They bombed Pearl Harbor and because of the Japanese, Roosevelt declared war and my mother was no longer at home at lunchtime because she went to work at the war plant, Fisher Body. I had to make peanut butter sandwiches for Jean and Jackie and take care of him from twelve to one-fifteen when school started again. It was because of the Japanese that my mother sprained her back at the war plant. She had to stay in bed for days. She limped. I was afraid. *(She continues to speak uncontrollably.)*

At home I have a slim yellow book on the piano that contains Negro spirituals. My mother often sings when she cooks Sunday morning breakfast, "Sometimes I Feel Like a Motherless Child."

(ESTELLE, their mother, stands in her faded flower house dress and sings first lines of "Motherless Child.")

In the summer of 1942 we moved into a new house in the popular Glenville section of Cleveland, far across the city from the Mount Pleasant area with Mr. Bertiloni's grape arbor. These houses are larger. My parents even have a room with a fireplace, a room that is the length of the house.

It's a *Now Voyager* room, I think when I enter and my mother is sitting in her pink quilted bed jacket reading *Cosmopolitan* and eating Whitman's chocolates (evenings after she had completed her school work). She's teaching elementary school and is completing her bachelor's degree and has college classes at night.

In our new house there is a bookcase in the living room next to the fireplace and on the bottom shelf are some old books left by the previous tenants. One book is crimson, the same crimson color as my mother's scrapbook, a thick volume with heavy pages entitled *The Poems of Percy Shelley. (JUNE and JEAN return to their seats.)*

MINISTER: Thank you, June and Jean. Dr. Benjamin Mays, President of Morehouse College, will lead us in prayer.

(Lights on DR. MAYS)

FATHER: *(To JUNE and JEAN)* Dr. Mays is a great man.

JUNE and JEAN: What is a great man?

FATHER: He's helping to lead American Negroes out of racial strife.

(Church fades.

AUNT ELLA *appears and vanishes.*

Sound of car.

Voices of MAYS *and the* FATHER.

JUNE *and* JEAN *sing "Deep Purple".)*

FATHER: *(telling Mays about the section of Cleveland they live in. The twins sing "Deep Purple" louder.)* Glenville was incorporated as a village on October 4, 1870 and was annexed to the City of Cleveland on June 19, 1905. Glenville was once known as a resort of the wealthy and the "garden spot" of Cuyahoga County. Glenville was born out of an early Irish settlement on the lake shore between East Cleveland and Collinwood in 1893. Glenville got its name because the area is full of shady, thick glens through which little streams tumbled. The first to settle in the Glenville area were early New England farmers, followed by immigrants from Scotland, Ireland and England. Over time the area grew into a secluded rural village and its lake shore location made it a fashionable summer residence for Cleveland's affluent families . . .

(JUNE *and* JEAN *start singing "Chattanooga Choo-Choo."*)

JUNE: *(Writing)* Our family: We took drives in my father's Plymouth every Sunday (unless there was a blizzard) after dinner, which was at three o'clock . . . in the summer, fried chicken, in the winter pork roast or roast beef. We started from Mount Pleasant, where we lived, drove out Kinsman, up Lee Road to Shaker Heights, through the winding streets of Tudor mansions. Sometimes we drove downtown to Cedar Avenue, where my father had his offices at the Y.

The Y had a "ballroom," a large room painted blue where Jean would one day have her wedding reception and where, as a teenager, she saw our father give many talks at Y banquets. Down the hall from the "ballroom" were rooms where guests at the Y stayed . . . small single bedrooms with plaid bedspreads and a desk. My brother and I peeked into the rooms that were empty. How could I or any of us know that it would be in one of these rooms where my father would spend the last days of his life, sick from emphysema, divorced from my mother and bereaved of his second wife?

(JEAN *sings "I'll Never Smile Again" loudly.*)

But we didn't know that then as we peeked in the rooms, and ran down the hallway to the stairway that led to the main floor and the reception room, past the office that had a plaque on the door with my father's name.

My father would greet us, rushing out of his office, smiling, and we'd climb back into the 1937 Plymouth, where my mother was waiting. "Let's drive by Lake Erie," we'd say. And so we would drive along the lake until it got dark. "They're going to build the lake up one day," my father always said. My mother would finally announce we should go home. And when we got home, she, my brother and I had chilled Jello with bananas and vanilla wafers that my mother had carefully made the night before. My father smoked a cigar. I was excited and happy because soon Jack Benny would come on the radio, and we all loved Jack Benny and Eddie Anderson (Rochester).

JUNE and JEAN: *(For the first time, they try to address* DR. MAYS.*)* Dr. Mays, we love "Deep Purple" but the songs we love the most are camp songs. Our father is the YMCA camp director near Chagrin Falls. We love to watch him play baseball. He plays shortstop.

(Indistinct voices of FATHER *and* DR. MAYS. JUNE *and* JEAN *sing fragments of: "Let Me Call You Sweetheart," "My Darling Clementine," "And the Green Grass Grows All Around," "Fight the Team across the Field," "Show Them Ohio's Here," "Keep the Earth Reverberating with a Mighty Cheer," "Rah-rah-rah," and "God Bless America.")*

AUNT ELLA: After Easter Dinner in the dining room.

JEAN: *(Writing)* June and I had never seen a great man before. The phone rang all afternoon. We could hear our mother say...

MOTHER: Dr. Mays is here.

JEAN: *(Writing)* My father and Dr. Mays continued to talk about the Race Problem. June and I were going with them to hear Paul Robeson at 3:00. We wrote it all in our book. I sang "Jim" and June told Dr. Mays about Hitler. We wanted him to know we were prodigies.

(The voices of DR. MAYS *and* FATHER, *indistinct. From time to time they turn to laugh with the twins. The twins talk uncontrollably. Sometimes* JEAN *sings "Jim".)*

JUNE: *(To* DR. MAYS*)* Dr. Mays, sometimes people say we're a little touched in the head. We're like Aunt Ella who used to climb up in the willow trees down in Georgia and sing.

JUNE and JEAN: We can be Mrs. Miniver, Annabel Lee and Bette Davis.

MOTHER: June and Jean, leave Dr. Mays alone.

JUNE and JEAN: We know "Lines above Tintern Abbey."

FATHER: When I was at Morehouse...

*(*DR. MAYS*'s voice is indistinct)*

FATHER *(continued)*: When I was at Morehouse...

*(*JUNE *speaks uncontrollably to* DR. MAYS *about Hitler. Sometimes* JEAN *sings "Jim".)*

JUNE: Dr. Mays, Hitler is the person who caused a tower to be built in the school playground across the street from our house, a frightening orange steel structure (a white light at its pinnacle shines at night into our windows) that is surrounded by a jagged metal fence said to electrocute you if you touch it. This tower is a watch tower in case an attack from the Germans or the Japanese occurs.

Hitler causes my father to announce every evening from his armchair, as he reads the evening *Cleveland Press,* "the siege of ——, the killing of ——, the capture of ——, the bombing of ——, the worsening of the war." And in my mind, the possibility that from the tower the air raid warden will soon discover the enemy is marching into Ohio. Sometimes in the night I awake and stand at the window in my pajamas and watch the tower, bright orange and hideous in the night. Would the Germans come in the back door? In Mrs. Miniver a German came into the rear of the house. Would they hide in the garage?

My Jewish friend, Yvette, says that Hitler doesn't like Jews and she and her widowed mother are afraid. Hitler doesn't like anyone except the Aryan race ... the blond race. When I went to see the movie *Hitler's Children* with my brother and the kids from next door, we were very upset that Bonita Granville was beaten by the SS, the German officers in their strangely designed uniforms, helmets and boots. She was beaten with a whip because she didn't want to fight for Hitler. We are children. If Hitler comes to Cleveland and we resist will we be beaten and sent to a concentration camp?

My mother says she is buying war bonds, and we've given up butter and meat, we save coupons. I ask my father when he comes home at night, is that helping? I don't want the Nazis to come, I don't want to be a Hitler's Child or go to a camp. My best friend said as long as the tower is up we are in danger.

(JUNE *and* JEAN *interrupt each other. Sometimes* JEAN *sings "Jim".)*

JEAN: Dr. Mays, after Miss Eichenbaum told me of Chopin, even though I'm not advanced enough to play the pieces, I bought a book of polonaises and "struggled" with sections of them.

In the evenings after I do my homework, I sit at the kitchen table and write penny postcards to the movie stars to get their autographed photos. Toby, who sits in front of me in seventh-grade home room, gives me her list of movie studios: MGM, Universal, Twentieth Century–Fox, Warner Brothers, David O. Selznick, that she had carefully copied on notebook paper. I carry the list in my school bag at all times with my fingernail polish, cologne and natural-color Tangee lipstick that I am allowed to have but not yet wear.

I love Frank Sinatra. On the Saturday night Hit Parade. *(Frank Sinatra sings "I'll Never Smile Again.")*

Orson Welles (in the movie of Jane Eyre), he is Edward Rochester, whom Jane Eyre loved, therefore I love him.

My classmates at Empire Junior High: like the kids at Lafayette, they have parents who were born in Europe, but in our new neighborhood, it's not Italy but Poland, Hungary, Russia, Czechoslovakia.

JUNE: Dr. Mays, although I love my grandparents immensely, I hate the train ride to Georgia that my brother and I take every June, especially the ride from Cincinnati to Montezuma in the dirty Jim Crow car. When the Travelers' Aid meet us in Cincinnati station, my brother is still crying. As soon as the train pulls out of the Cleveland Terminal Tower he starts to cry and he cries with his head on my shoulder.

Once my father bought me some magazines at the Cleveland Terminal. One was a *Modern Screen* with a picture of Clark Gable in Army uniform. I tried to interest my brother in the magazine, but he kept sobbing, "I want to go home." I put my arm around my brother, looked out of the dirty double-panel windows and clutched the *Modern Screen* magazine with Gable on the cover.

(FATHER *and* DR. MAYS *talk inaudibly, perhaps repeating,* "When I was at Morehouse . . . ")

JEAN: Dr. Mays, in 1942 my mother worked at the war plant on Sundays. Everything was different. We rode the Kinsman streetcar downtown to the Palace Theatre and saw Cab Calloway, Nat King Cole, Lionel Hampton and Lena Horne. June and I in wedgies, gloves and hats; Jackie in long pants, shirt and tie. After the show our father picked us up in the Plymouth.

(DR. MAYS *and* FATHER *exit to living room.*)

JUNE: Dr. Mays, did you see our Philco radio?

(JUNE *and* JEAN *hardly notice they have exited. They continue talking to* DR. MAYS.)

JUNE and JEAN: We listen to Jack Armstrong, Tom Mix, Little Orphan Annie, I Love a Mystery and Jack Benny. And send away for maps, rings, puzzles.

FATHER: *(Laughing)* June and Jean, leave Dr. Mays alone.

JUNE and JEAN: Dr. Mays, here's a picture of our father planting petunias in the front of the lawn. *(Theme music)*

JUNE: *(Absently, to* DR. MAYS*)* People my mother dreams about: In the morning I can hardly wait to hear about them. The stories she tells of them are all as exciting as the movies of Frankenstein and Dracula that I see at the Waldorf. *(*JUNE *leaves the stage.)*

JEAN: These people my mother dreams about continue to grow in my imagination. Like the people in the red scrapbook, they often know each other and knew my parents when they were young. I list them in my mind as I sit on the front steps of our house (the steps that face the orange tower).

Her mother who died when she was three.

Her stepfather who was killed walking across an electrified railroad track.

Her Aunt Hattie who died when my mother was pregnant with me.

When my mother's making oatmeal on winter mornings as I sit waiting with my bowl at the kitchen table, I secretly yearn that she'll talk more about people she dreams about. *(Brown Derby music, "Siboney")*

JEAN: *(Writing)* June took off her Easter dress and came downstairs in my mother's long dotted Swiss dress.

JUNE: *(Returns in dotted Swiss dress)* I keep stacks of *Modern Screen* in the vanity table drawer and make a scrapbook from my favorite pictures. I especially like pictures of people at parties in evening dress. And I keep another scrapbook on Ingrid Bergman. How marvelous to have a Swedish accent and a radiant smile.

Sometimes when no one is at home, I go to the attic and get this old blue-and-white dotted Swiss evening gown and try it on and sit at my vanity table with my movie photos lined up in the mirror and daydream of being at the Brown Derby. *(JUNE might comb her hair differently.)*

MOTHER: June, go back upstairs and put on your Easter dress.

(JUNE leaves.)

JEAN: *(Writing)* Our brother had one of his asthmatic attacks and our mother rushed upstairs to get him steam and vapor.

AUNT ELLA: They gather around him and hold the towel over his head. Radio plays, "Oh, Johnny."

(Radio plays "Oh, Johnny." One actor should imitate Wee Bonnie Baker. JUNE returns with Easter dress on.)

JEAN: *(Writing)* Before we left my father and Dr. Mays looked at photographs of Morehouse and Atlanta University.

MOTHER: June and Jean, would you play a piece for Dr. Mays?

(Twins go to piano and play "Für Elise.")

JUNE: *(She stands, day dreaming)* In a few minutes we'll see Paul Robeson.

(Imagined ROBESON *enters stage center. He sings beginning of "Waterboy." Music fades. Sound of car.*
Interlude.
Theme music continues. Music can convey JUNE*'s vision of the future.)*

JUNE: *(Writing)* We drove past Lakeview Cemetery where my father and brother will be buried. And the school where my brother *will* run the fifty-yard dash and win the state championship.

AUNT ELLA: The car swerves.

JUNE: I can't stop thinking of Lakeview Cemetery where my brother and father *will* be buried.

AUNT ELLA: Car swerves again and rolls over in snow.

Voices of DR. MAYS and FATHER: *(Calling)* June and Jean. June. Jean.

JUNE: *(Barely coherent)* Before he joins the Army Jackie will go to Ohio State where he will run track. He stands beneath Jean's window in Baker Hall and practices his Spanish. It will be spring when he leaves for Germany. He leaves from Fort Dix and that's where Jean will next see him, seventeen months later.

Voices of DR. MAYS and FATHER: *(Calling them)* June and Jean.

JUNE: On his last night in New York he will go to see *Pajama Game.* When Jean is in her twenties she will secretly call herself a lyric poet. Our father will say, on a visit to New York, "The sun? You mean you're writing about the sun?" Yes, she will smile. They will be at the Greyhound bus station. He's on his way back to Atlanta where he lives after the death of his second wife, who dies in a car crash.

Voices of DR. MAYS and FATHER: *(Calling them)* June and Jean.

JUNE: My mother had always said holding her family together was the most important thing in the world. Yet they will divorce one spring in 1961. Suddenly that spring Jesus will become a character in the play Jean will write, and a surprising Jesus, a punishing Jesus, berserk, evil, sinister. She will remember how so long ago when we all took drives, when we had sat at the campfire together or listened to Jack Benny, I had seen Jesus as sweet, docile. She had believed "what a friend we have in Jesus." But that spring, sitting in the Pensione Sabrina, she will go on creating a cruel Jesus Christ.

Voices of DR. MAYS and FATHER: *(Calling)* June and Jean.

JUNE: After his second wife dies, my father will visit Jean in New York.

FATHER: Can I come live with you, Jeannie? Please let me come live with you.

JUNE: This will be the winter before Jackie goes for a drive in his car and is in the accident. He is in a coma for five months. When he awakes he *will* be brain damaged.

My grandmother, my great aunt: Their houses surrounded by petunias, hedges, sunflowers, magnolia trees, their wells, their blue-and-white dishes, the dippers and bucket, their pot-bellied stoves, the way the houses sat on the Georgia roads... the picket fences... these houses with their vistas of cornfields, vegetable gardens, fig trees, flower gardens that faced the road, the porches that wound around the house, the stone paths that led to the steps... these houses were the most beautiful houses in the world to me. Before he dies, my father will return to these places.

(Theme music has continued in this section)

Voices of DR. MAYS and FATHER: *(Calling)* June and Jean.

FATHER: The girls are trapped.

AUNT ELLA: Dining room. Evening.

FATHER: The girls were trapped inside the car twenty minutes when the car rolled over into a snow drift down Snake Hill.

JEAN: *(Writing)* My mother rushed to help us and gave us hot cocoa. She had been out in the snow searching for our brother who let his bunny run onto the porch and chased after him. Our father drove Dr. Mays back to the hotel.

(Judy Garland sings, "Easter Parade.")

JUNE: *(Holds her head. Still dazed but speaking loudly. She continues to see the future.)* What I see, Easter evening, 1943:

My father's death bed. It will be winter.

FATHER: When I was a boy... Papa... Mama... My Aunt Mary Lee... when I was a boy... Mama, Papa, I'll see them soon.

(JUNE stands speaking.)

JUNE: When I went to Georgia, I slept in his boyhood room. The window faced a small corn field, the room was exactly as it was when my father was a boy. A brass bed, a marble night stand with a blue and white pitcher and basin, a mahogany dresser, a hooked rug beside the bed.

AUNT ELLA: Then June sees my sister pushing Jackie in a wheelchair.

(JUNE cries and runs out.)

JEAN: Before we could stop June, she jumped or fell off the upstairs porch. We buried my twin sister three days after Easter.

(Interlude)

AUNT ELLA *(appears)*: Everything she saw came true. Now June's Ghost remembers Christmas eve, 1942. Five months earlier.

(JUNE'S GHOST *appears. She wears dotted Swiss dress.*
"Bing Crosby" sings "White Christmas")

AUNT ELLA *(continued)*: She remembers her frail mother wearing a flowered house dress and a Christmas apron rushing in from the kitchen with a poinsettia. And Jean, dressed in her green ballerina dress setting the table with the china plates with flowers, the same plates they will use for Easter, 1943.

June's Ghost wears her Brown Derby dotted Swiss evening gown. She writes, too.

SCENE

(JUNE'S GHOST *watches* JUNE.
Theme music.)

JUNE: *(Writing)* Sometimes after I finish my homework, I sit on the floor beside the bookcase and stare at the pretty old scarlet volume, and leaf through its thick pages. One poem caught my eye. I read it many times:

> Music, when soft voices die,
> Vibrates in the memory,
> Odors, when sweet violets sicken,
> Live within the sense they quicken.
> Rose leaves, when the rose is dead,
> Are heaped on the beloved's bed;
> And so thy thoughts, when thou art gone,
> Love itself shall slumber on.

Last Christmas my grandmother died. She died days before Christmas. On Christmas our house was sad. We returned from her funeral in Georgia, where my father had thrown himself on her flower-heaped coffin and sobbed. That Christmas day he hadn't come downstairs. It was early evening. I sat down by the bookcase, took out the crimson Shelley volume and read: "Music, when soft voices die..."

I remember how amazing and wonderful it was to stay in my father's room at my grandmother's house every summer. When I awakened each summer morning, I looked out of the same window, onto the same corn field that my father had looked at when he had awakened. In the front room were pictures of my father as a boy standing in front of this very house. The manner in which my grandmother arranged pictures made looking at them as exciting as going to the Waldorf on a Saturday afternoon.

I loved these rooms: My father's room and my grandmother's front room with its leather settees and Victrola and the parlor at my great-aunt's house that we were allowed in only one hour on Sunday, a room of settees, ferns, china cabinets and photographs of my grandmother's five sisters. *(Writing)*

My mother often told me that she had been sent away to boarding school at the age of five and remained there until she was seventeen. Her mother was dead and her father thought boarding school was the best course for her. On Christmas holidays, she said, she would get very lonely and the headmaster of the school (in Fort Valley, Georgia) would invite her to his house.

(JUNE'S GHOST watches from a distance.)

MOTHER: June and Jean, the Christmas play is in an hour. And where is your brother?

AUNT ELLA: Winston rushed in from outside with the Christmas tree.

("Nat King Cole" sings "Christmas Song.")

MOTHER: Where is your brother?

JEAN: He's upstairs sitting on the porch watching for Santa Claus.

JUNE: I hope he's not reading my secret books.

(Light on JACKIE on another level)

JACKIE: *My Secret Book,* by June.

Dracula: even though he likes blood, he is noble and even lives in a castle.

Because of his nobility he can turn into a tiny bat and kill and make people grow fangs. He is Bela Lugosi.

Sherlock Holmes: He is Basil Rathbone; he lives in a place called Baker Street in London.

Then there is *The Invisible Man, Jack the Ripper* and *The Woman in Black.*

Abe Lincoln: Although he grew up in a log cabin, he became President and freed my forbears from slavery. Yet he had a mad wife.

My mother: She tells me stories of her life in Georgia. She taught me the alphabet when I was three, and she taught me to read that same year. She encourages me to compete with my Jewish, Polish, Italian and black classmates in elementary school, and took pride in the accomplishments of my gold and silver stars. She continued to encourage me to read, and by the fifth grade I had read all the books in the school library. She shares her secret thoughts and tears over the movies she takes me to see. She collected photographs of her and my father's youth in Atlanta and keeps them in scrapbooks so that I am able to imagine my parents as they were when they were young. She instills in me the desire to excel.

AUNT ELLA: Downstairs Winston stares at a tree. Suddenly he starts to whistle. He decorates the tree with colored lights. He goes outside again. Snow blows into the hallway. *(Sound of whistling)*

Jean brings in a pink cake. Estelle presents a white cake. The dining room glows. Poinsettia, candles, mistletoe, silver, china.

MOTHER: June, it's time to get dressed.

(JUNE'S GHOST watches)

JUNE: My father spoke at his mother's funeral.

FATHER: *(Staring up at tree)* My mother was a quiet woman. She had a small, almost frail body but was endowed with a heart of gold. When she died last Thursday of her heart attack, she was preparing her annual Christmas box to send us in Cleveland.

JUNE: *(Still writing)* My parents: I envy them. To me they possess a glamour. They drink highballs and smoke cigarettes, read *Crisis* magazine and the *Pittsburgh Courier*... are members of the NAACP and the Urban League, members of the Alphas, Kappas, the AKAs, the Deltas and Sigmas, play bridge, poker, tonk. They have social clubs whose doings are reported in the *Cleveland Call* and *Post*. They love formal dances (especially at holidays), Lena, Duke, Cab; worship A. Philip Randolph, Paul Robeson, W. E. B. DuBois, Marian Anderson, Joe Louis, Sugar Ray Robinson and Mary McLeod Bethune. They are devoted to the "Negro Cause."

AUNT ELLA: Winston returns with a star for the tree.

JUNE: Miss Bell: A fourth-grade teacher. She told my mother I would have a "nervous breakdown" if I didn't stop trying to be the best in everything in class. My mother said I had to stop reading so much; I had to go outside and play. She made me sit on the front porch and refused to let me take my *Katy Did* books with me. I heard my mother tell my father what Miss Bell said as they disappeared into the kitchen. When my father came out of the kitchen he smiled at me and asked me would I like to go for a drive in the car (my favorite thing) and buy some ice cream. I could get Neapolitan (strawberry, chocolate, vanilla), my favorite kind.

MOTHER: Go get your brother so we can sing "Happy Birthday" to him.

(Lights up on JACKIE. *Family sings last lines of "Happy Birthday."*
"Judy Garland" sings "Have Yourself a Merry Little Christmas.")

AUNT ELLA: June's Ghost remembers herself and Jean in blue coats and leggings. June carrying her Virgin Mary costume and Baby Jesus doll and song: "Up on the House Top."
(Actors at music stands play finger bells, tambourines, piano,
elementary school instruments.
Sound of song, JUNE *and* JEAN.
Stage becomes scene.)
The school play. A lit stage, the manger, the starry sky, the fields, the animals, blues, gold, crimson.
(The stage has become scene. Lights almost white. From far away,
through the starry night comes JUNE *slowly in her white Virgin*
Mary costume. She falters. In the starry night they come. Slowly.
Piano music, "Away in a Manger." JUNE, *the Virgin Mary, comes*
closer. She smiles.)
(fade)

AUNT ELLA: June's Ghost remembers. *(Voices of the choir sing "When*
I've Done the Best I Can.")
Days before Christmas, 1941. Montezuma, Georgia. Within the white wooden church with stained glass windows. A door to the rear of the altar leads to the "colored" cemetery. A corn field is beyond. Birds fly throughout the church, through the rear doorway is sunlight. The dark altar encircled by a banister is covered with gladiolus and carnations. And in front of the altar is the open casket of June's and Jean's grandmother.
Winston suddenly throws himself across the casket.
(Choir voices continue.
JUNE'S GHOST *watches herself and her family.*
They wear dark coats.)

JEAN: My parents' hometown: Montezuma, Georgia looked to me like the drawings we were given in Sunday School of Jerusalem, the golden and red and white colors of the landscape, the processions of people walking on the road coming from the fields, walking to church, winding roads, view of steeples.
When I walked up the road with my grandmother to the white wooden church, I felt we were in a holy procession like the people on the Sunday school cards . . . the golden-red road, the blue sky, the neighbors walking ahead of us. One day I would see a book of Giotto prints and think of these processions on the road. And use his colors

in my stories, not realizing how I had connected the Sunday school card colors, the Georgia landscape colors and colors of Giotto.

My grandmother made biscuits and fried fish for breakfast followed by a dipper full of mineral water from the well at the foot of the road.

(Faint voices of choir.
Fade.)

AUNT ELLA *(appears)*: Cleveland, November 1974. Room in YMCA where Winston was once executive secretary. Single bed, plaid bedspread. On the wall he has a picture of himself (in 1938) digging the cornerstone of the YMCA with Cleveland ministers. On a chest is a photograph of his deceased second wife. He suffers from emphysema. He will die soon.

Enter Jean and June's Ghost. They all embrace. June's Ghost sits next to Jean. Jean cannot see June's Ghost. *(As she watches her father, Jean remembers minister's voice Easter Sunday, 1943.)*

MINISTER: And on this Easter morning, 1943, one of Cleveland's finest Negro leaders, this young man with vision, came to Cleveland nine years ago and has become Cleveland's number one Gang Buster. He has transformed Cleveland gangs into Clubs for Boys. In a section of the city noted for its police problems, he is turning delinquency into constructive activity.

JUNE: *(Remembers staring at her father)* Our family: We took drives in my father's Plymouth every Sunday (unless there was a blizzard) after dinner, which was at three o'clock . . . in summer, fried chicken, in the winter, pork roast or roast beef. We started from Mount Pleasant.

AUNT ELLA: Winston holds clippings of his work from the 1930s, 1940s *Cleveland Press,* from pages of June and Jean's autograph books and his Metropolitan Life Insurance policies.

FATHER: Every afternoon I read your and Junie's Junior High School diaries. When I left Cleveland in 1961 I found pages in the vanity table in your old room. *(Reading* JUNE'*s diaries, laughing.)*

Junior High, 1943: My father often called me good-looking when in the mirror I saw a strange-looking face. *(*JUNE'S GHOST *speaks with him. Theme music.)*

I thought I looked funny in my plaid skirts and white blouses with my straightened hair curled in tiny curls.

FATHER: Jean, here are your diaries. *(*JUNE'S GHOST *speaks with him.)*

Roosevelt and Churchill: They were meeting. I saw it in the newsreel at the Waldorf Theatre. They were meeting to stop the war, they were sitting in chairs smiling. Churchill had a cigar and President Roosevelt smoked a cigarette with a long holder. They were here, there, they were in Yalta. How, I wondered, could they, sitting in chairs smiling, stop the Germans? My father had told me that the Germans were invading all of Europe. I was very worried; then my father told me the Russians were going to help. The Russians were going to help us.

The Russians (the Russian Bear): My father was smiling, the newspaper under his arm as he strode into the house. The Russian Bear is stopping Hitler. Then Paris was liberated. We wouldn't have to use coupons to buy butter or meat. We wouldn't have to wonder whether we were eating horse meat. And most of all, I wouldn't have to worry about being taken from my parents to be a Hitler's Child. We could go peacefully back to roller skating on the sidewalk and reading comics on the front porch. Soon they would take the tower down. (FATHER *laughs. He clutches his daughter's diaries.* JUNE'S GHOST *writes.*)

AUNT ELLA: *Sun.* The play Jean is writing for her father and Malcolm X.
     (*The* FATHER *appears stage center, as we first saw him, Easter Sunday, 1943. Excerpts from* JEAN'*s plays have separate music motif.*)

FATHER (*as Jean envisions him*): My head, the head of Christ,
     The head of an apostle, head of St. Anne, head of the
     Virgin, head of Infant Jesus.
     My head dismembered.
     . . .
     No, I still dream.
     Children. The body and arms of a child.
     When a new sun appears.
     I think before I was born
     my mother dreamed she saw me in the sun
     then the sun went down.
     And at night I appear within the moon.
     I keep thinking
     flowers and water views
     of a coast of Italy
     Yet all is in imbalance.
     No, I must think of trees.
     The Star of Bethlehem.

AUNT ELLA: Jean didn't read Winston lines from another play at the Public Theatre.

(JEAN *stage center. In this period she wears dark skirt and sweater.*)

JEAN: It was the War.

Our father said everyone was getting hung and shot in Europe. America wouldn't be safe long.

. . .

Remember we lived in a holy chapel with parents.
Jesus, Joseph, Mary.

. . .

People said we were the holiest children.

. . .

Why did the War start?
I want to hang myself.

AUNT ELLA: Near Christmas, 1974, a month later. Hospital room. Winston is lying on his death bed. Jean sits by his side. A December day. June's Ghost sits too.

FATHER: Jeannie, I'm reading about your play at the Public Theatre in today's New York *Post*. I'm taking it back to Georgia. It quotes you saying, "I wrote a poem for my father and Malcolm X called *Sun*." And then you talk about your writing. And you quote from a play called *Lesson in Dead Language*.

JEAN: A Pupil raises her hand.

Pupil: I bleed, Teacher, I bleed. It started when my white dog died. It was a charming little white dog. He ran beside me in the sun when I played a game with lemons on the green grass. And it started when I became a woman. My mother says it is because I am a woman that I bleed. Why, Mother, why do I bleed?

They raise their hands.

Pupils (In unison): My mother says it is because I am a woman that I bleed. Blood comes out of me.

White Dog: Since we do not know the one that killed the sun, we will all be punished. We will all bleed, since we do not know the one, we will all be punished.

The Pupils stand in the aisle, backs to audience. Silence. They each have a great circle of blood on the back of their dresses.

NURSE: Your father is having hallucinations about his dead child June and his deceased second wife. He talks about Georgia and the day last year his childhood home burned down. He keeps talking about his son Jackie, who was in a coma and is now in a wheelchair out in Highland View Hospital. And he again and again, constantly talks about June, who jumped or fell off the upstairs porch Easter Sunday, 1943.

(Sound of FATHER *whistling, "Let Me Call You Sweetheart.")*

(Fade)

AUNT ELLA: Jean still remembers spring, 1947. Drama room, Glenville High School. A room lined with theatre books, a case of Samuel French editions, moveable desks and, at the front, a stage.

(Voices of high school choral club singing Rodgers and Hart, "Manhattan.")

Seated before the stage is Jean, dressed in a jumper, a white ruffled blouse, studying *Jane Eyre.* June's Ghost studies *Jane Eyre* too, beside Jean.

JEAN: *(Writing)* After June's death, my mother would sometimes disappear to the hallway steps outside the kitchen and close the door behind her. I could hear her crying. When she came back into the kitchen, she wouldn't speak but would dry the dishes or peel potatoes for dinner. Sometimes she went to the basement and cried.

(Distant voices of choral club, "In a Mountain Greenery.")

In our drama class we read *Our Town, Night Must Fall, The Petrified Forest* and *Street Scene.* Mr. Davis told us about his summer and holiday trips to New York where he saw Broadway plays. In the final project we had to do a ten-minute characterization from a play. I asked Mr. Davis could I read from *Jane Eyre.*

(Voices of choral club singing "Oklahoma.")

MR. DAVIS: Today we do characterizations.

JEAN: *(*JUNE'S GHOST *speaks with* JEAN*)* I wore a maroon-colored velvet jumper and a white ruffled blouse, trying to dress up like Joan Fontaine in the movie. I had read the passage over and over and memorized it (the moment when Jane leaves Rochester). It was the only time in my life I publicly had a chance to become Jane Eyre. Even I could feel the passion I evoked in the class.

MR. DAVIS: You have imagination. *(Theme music)*

AUNT ELLA: Later that night in the dark dining room. Jean sits studying *Silas Marner.* My sister enters. June's Ghost sits next to Jean.

MOTHER: Remember when June wrote a penny postcard to Orson Welles? She gave it to me to read. It said, "Dear Mr. Welles, I liked you in *Jane Eyre.* Please send me an autographed photo."

JUNE'S GHOST: It arrived one lovely June day in a white envelope, a large 5 by 7 picture, not the usual 2 by 3 size of other photos, especially those from MGM. It was signed in real looking ink, Orson Welles. I convinced myself it was original. Before I could mount it in my scrapbook Jackie got peanut butter on it. I started to cry.

MOTHER: June sat right here. *(She points to where* JUNE'S GHOST *is sitting.* JUNE'S GHOST *stares at her mother. Theme music.)*

JUNE'S GHOST: *(Writing)* I thought my mother's childhood life very strange. Everyone I knew went to a public school and I had never ever seen a boarding school, that "one was sent away to." It was very difficult for me to imagine even though my mother spoke of it often. Finally when I was eleven I took a book out of the school library that was gray with green design—a pretty book, I thought—and it was called *Jane Eyre.*

Almost before the first chapter was concluded, it was decided that the heroine, Jane Eyre, would be "sent away to boarding school." How excited I was as I sat in the small rocking chair in my room. Here was a little girl who had a life like my mother's. It was so thrilling that I read the first section about Jane Eyre at Lowood many times. I began to envy my mother's exotic upbringing. It wasn't fair that I would go every day to Lafayette Public School when she lived a life like Jane Eyre's.

As much as it was possible, I used to imagine that I had been my mother when she was a little girl. I think after *Jane Eyre,* when she told me stories, I almost believed they had happened to me: her life at boarding school, her pictures in the red scrapbook of herself in white organdy dresses standing by a Model T Ford, the people in her dreams and maybe most of all her incredibly pretty hair that everyone commented on. I think now that I often thought they were mine. They all belonged to me.

*(*JUNE'S GHOST *vanishes.)*

AUNT ELLA: Estelle went out. Her descending steps were heard. Then the sound of her crying in the basement. Suddenly, for the first time, Jean sees June's Ghost. She is atop the willow tree with me. Winston comes rushing in.

FATHER: Jeannie, your mother and I may get a divorce.

AUNT ELLA: He disappears upstairs.

*(*JUNE'S GHOST *appears from atop the "willow tree" in Georgia.* JEAN *now sees* JUNE'S GHOST*)*

JUNE'S GHOST: Jean, Aunt Ella tells me about our father.

JEAN: *(Staring at her sister)* Our Aunt Ella who's touched in the head? And sings in the willow tree in Georgia?

JUNE'S GHOST: Yes.

AUNT ELLA: When Winston was a young man at Morehouse, he felt himself to be in the midst of winged spirits. He had such poignant religious vision of himself. Such ideals.

> *(JUNE hears ELLA's voice and now for the first time sees AUNT ELLA.*
> *ELLA and JUNE's GHOST appear on upper level. JEAN stands stage center looking up at them.)*

JEAN: Aunt Ella . . . *(Theme music)*
June, three years after you died, we saw Paul Robeson at St. James Church. It was just as you imagined.

> *(ROBESON, stage center, completes "Water Boy.")*
Philippa Schuyler came the next spring.
> *(Classical piano music, Schumann played by SCHUYLER)*
I didn't go to our recital the week after you died. We never get a chance to play "Für Elise."
> *(Music fades)*

JUNE'S GHOST: Jean, if you look in the vanity table in our room in the lower left hand drawer underneath the rose colored wallpaper that lines the drawer you will find Aunt Ella's writing. She used to bring it to me in the middle of the night.

> *(AUNT ELLA sings softly, "Go Down Moses.")*

JEAN: Hello, Aunt Ella.

> *(Sound of ESTELLE crying in the basement.)*

FATHER: I want to talk to you. Your mother and I may get a divorce. I want to go back home to Georgia.

JEAN: Hello, Aunt Ella. Do you still sing in trees?

AUNT ELLA: Yes.

JUNE'S GHOST: Jackie knows about our father's future second wedding. Jackie always read the pages Aunt Ella gave me. That's why he wheezes. Aunt Ella says she talks to our father early in the mornings as he dreams of being back in his boyhood room. She says he sticks his head out of the window that faces the corn field and the corn grows so close that his head is in the middle of two stalks. Aunt Ella says sometimes she sat with us on the porch swing.

FATHER: I have a memory of Mama coming through the parlor door with a lamp in her hand.

JEAN: June, often I think of us with our decoder rings sitting by the Philco radio waiting for a message from Jack Armstrong.

AUNT ELLA: Jean, your mother suffered two miscarriages. Her aunt died in '39 and on the morning of her funeral after riding nine hundred miles on the train in Estelle's fifth month she lost a second child. It like to killed her and then the Cleveland school system wasn't hiring many Negro teachers. There was a strict quota and she couldn't get a job. She fell into a state that was so different from any state she had ever been in. Remember she took to dressing in her nightgown and lost all touch with Winston and his work.

And your father, remember at the dedication of the new Y everyone had walked about the polished rooms filled with baskets of flowers congratulating him. The press was there flashing bulbs. In the midst of the congratulations he had gone to the roof. No one had known whether he was trying to catch a bird or trying to hush their moaning or trying to commit suicide. He had fallen on the scaffold, broken his arm and been rescued.

(Silence. Room very dark. AUNT ELLA *fades.)*

JUNE'S GHOST: Jean, get the pages from the vanity table on our lives. Aunt Ella's calling me.

*(*JUNE'S GHOST *vanishes.*

AUNT ELLA *sings: "Go Down Moses," "Tell Old Pharaoh Let My People Go"—one line.)*

JUNE *(appears): (as she was Easter, 1943)* Farewell for now, my sister. Write everything down for us. Before I go Jackie knows our father will try to kill himself the night of his testimonial dinner. He read Aunt Ella's pages.

(Sound of JACKIE *wheezing loud)*

JEAN: Junie, I still have your movie star scrapbook. Please don't go. We could write away to the movie studios tonight.

JUNE: Remember how we used to sing, "Would you like to swing on a star?"

(She vanishes.

Faint melody: "Would you like to swing on a star?")

(The End)

A Letter to Flowers

Dedicated to Dr. Joseph Kennedy

1

In my mid-sixties I found myself unable to adjust to my children not being near me. I often thought of not going on. Often in this mood I was perplexed and could not understand why people many times sought my advice on their lives.

I asked myself that question.

At this time my son Joe told me he was compiling a portfolio of flowers for the children at the Arlington, Virginia school where he was substitute teaching.

"What about flowers you've seen in your travels?" I said. I reminded him of places he'd loved and visited when he was a little boy, Manhattan; Mexico City; Accra, Ghana; London, England; Madrid; Florence, Italy; Rome; Freetown, Sierra Leone. He showed me his portfolio. It was called Close to Nature.

My own past travels with him were precious. I sent him a story I had written about a trip we took to Rome when he was six. These days I had so many memories of when my sons were children. I thought often of their childhood.

"Remember Rome? Italy was so wonderful."

I sent him my story, which I had reread to myself several times.

Florence, Italy 1961
A trip from Rome to Florence.

We had lived at the pensioni Sabrina since winter. Near the middle of May when your school was ending I decided we try to see a little more of Italy. So near the end of May we took the train to Florence.

From the train the hills approaching Florence were beautiful. I'd called ahead to a rental agency in Florence for information about places to stay.

As soon as we arrived in Florence we walked along the Arno river to American Express to find out how to get to the rental agency.

The agency was in a dark stone building in the center of Florence. A very friendly young woman told us she had just the right place for us to stay in Florence, whether for a week or a month. And she could show it to us immediately. She said we could walk there. It was in Piazza Donatello, a piazza named after an Italian painter. Even though it was a May afternoon the piazza with heavy stone structures seemed dark.

The estate agent showed us into a massive stone house with a marble foyer. A gigantic old staircase led up to the next floors. She told us we were about to see something very beautiful, part of this house that belonged to two wealthy elderly Italian sisters who lived on the next street.

When she opened the door we saw a tiny foyer that opened onto a great splendid drawing room (like a room in a museum) filled with at least six seating arrangements, lamps, tables, objects of art, ceiling on a palatial scale. The far side of this splendid drawing room opened onto a terraced greenhouse filled with tables of flowering plants. The greenhouse led to a garden. The Florentine sisters lived on the other side of the garden. There were three bedrooms on the main floor. Mine had a ceiling painted with cherubs. The shuttered windows faced Piazza Donatello. A staircase led down two flights into a white tiled kitchen totally equipped with cooking utensils and a long table. From the window you could see a tiny part of the garden.

Your bedroom was small. It had bunk beds and a shelf of books in Italian. A window faced Piazza Donatello.

Mornings we ate a breakfast of fresh rolls and milk and coffee on the round green marble table that faced the greenhouse. After breakfast we planned our trips around Florence for the day. "Do you remember?"

"We had a Blue Guide."

"Do you remember?"

I was so happy when the kids were little, I tell my friend Isabel. Remember the time we took Adam and —— to the Bronx Botanical

Gardens? I think they were about four years old. They had on snow-suits.

That week I tell my children when they call about a dream I had nights before.

I was in a plane crash. The plane foundered on water, an ocean. Smoke and fire filled the cabin of the jumbo jet. I tried to fasten my seat belt in my red seat. I kept thinking I want to drown strapped to my seat. I want to drown sitting up. As the plane sank, a group of Asians ran on the plane at the front and stood by the doorway. They didn't seem to see me. A man ran past me to the exit. But I couldn't move. I tried to lift two solid heavy black trunks, my luggage, so that I could leave the plane. I couldn't lift them. The plane was sinking. I woke up.

My son Joe told me he has to go back to school and continue the flower project with the group of children called Explorers.

I called her every day and I knew it was time to call my mother. She is ninety years old. She had fallen and after visiting her in Ohio to care for her, I was too exhausted to do anything but barely finish reading my student plays from the fall semester at Harvard.

My mother started to talk.

"The nurse's aide Angela talks too much and asks me so many questions. She wants to know who all the people in the photographs are on my secretary.

I asked her to open a can of Campbell's tomato soup and she could barely open it. And she put the soup in a big pot after I explained to her that the sauce pans were right beneath the sink. Then she went over to the other bedroom and stayed a long time. I'm going to put my rings in my purse. My jewelry's in my bedroom." Then: "My back's hurting this morning."

I suggested she not give Angela her house keys for any reason. I was concerned she might duplicate them.

I tried to work on my *Narrative 2000*, about a murder.

My deadline for completing my play had passed, but I was unable to work. I reread the beginning over and over. It was called *Bronte Scenes.*

I had been enamoured of the Brontes and their romantic home in Yorkshire since I was eleven years old and read *Jane Eyre.* I placed my characters *June* and *Jean* on the moors with this great family, June as a child and Jean as an adult.

When Papa came home that night from Leeds we were in bed. So next morning Branwell came to our door with the box of soldiers. Emily and I both jumped out of bed and I cried, 'I'll call my soldier Duke of Wellington.' Mine was perfect. Anne's was a queer little thing; he was called Waiting Boy. Branwell chose Bonaparte. March 1829.

JEAN: After tea Emily read to them about the day Heathcliff came to Wuthering Heights. My sister sat next to her. She appeared to be wearing an apron like Charlotte's over her dress. They all took part reading in the late afternoon.

Almost dark.

They stand outside the cottage

Staring up at the heather.

JEAN: After tea, they walked down to the road. On the way back, Branwell became ill. When they returned to the cottage, they gathered around him in his room. Anne read from *Tenant of Wildfell Hall.*

Outside. Darkness.

JUNE *remains.*

JEAN: Anne dated her preface 'July 1849.' Branwell was at home in advanced stages of addiction. Six days later Charlotte wrote that 'his constitution is shattered, he sleeps all day, is awake all night.' Two months later on 24 September he was dead. At Branwell's funeral Emily caught a cold and three months later she too was dead. The pattern was repeated again. Anne died of tuberculosis the following May. Only Charlotte remained.

I couldn't read any more. I recognized the Bronte material was an attempt to find a lost romanticism.

My mother called. She discussed her bowels, and the death of our 1940's neighbor Louise, how she spent her last days sitting, hair uncombed, in a gown, sitting in a "great big" room of sick people. How she once had so enjoyed bridge, cooking and the dances she went to.

"Should I sell my car?" she asked. "I don't use it. But I'm sure I should sell it." Her small blue coupe was sitting in the underground garage against the concrete wall.

I suggested she keep her car until April. It was January. In the spring she could better decide.

"If I make it until then," she said.

"What were those flowers outside the Achimota Guest House in Ghana?" I asked my son Joe. They were red, large red blossoms, with a powerful sharp fragrance. They surrounded the left side of the Guest House.

I read from *Narrative 2000.*

Etta dreamed:
She went for a walk.
All she could think of as she passed Riverside Drive's Historic District at 105th Street was what the Vanishing read the night before—

In the pauses of the shower you heard the rumbling of the earth beneath and waves of tortured sea, the murmur of escaping gases. Sometimes the cloud appeared to break from its solid mass and become human shapes, striding in the gloom then vanishing into an abyss.

Vapors of trouble to come.

I read the list of flowers that illustrated a diary I often carried with me, the Spring Garden, Wild Garden, Walled Garden, Water Garden, Italian Garden, Arbor, the Orchard, Flowers for Drying, the Greenhouse. And on the border of the book I'd written five years ago:

To love to live to lose with good grace and just play the melody.
—Jackie Gleason

Then I read passages from my early unpublished novels, novels written 1957–1960, written sitting near the vase of daffodils on our kitchen table, where I read Emerson's *Self Reliance.* I see myself sitting under the Monet print of poppies dreaming of capturing life on paper.

2

Adam called. He's sending me a book on Italy. My husband Joe, Joe Jr. and Adam and I sat in the gardens surrounding Salvator Mundi hospital the days after he was born. I held him in my arms. He is sending me *The Oxford History of Italy.*

He wonders how I am today. There was a gas leak in my apartment for five days before I became aware of it. He tries to get my grandson Canaan to say hello. But Canaan is crying.

"I'm going to send you the piece I wrote about the days after we left Florence, when we returned to Rome. I just finished it. It's in my suitcase with my Cambridge papers."

When I found the Rome piece I reread the letters my students wrote to get into my class. They told me of their hopes. There was something so moving about their letters. I'd sat on my bed in Adams House and read them. They wanted to be writers. When I searched again for the Rome piece I reread them. I loved my students.

"You almost gassed yourself," my former husband Joe said when I again explained how gas had been leaking and I thought the odor was my asthma medicine.

"You have to keep going," he says when I say I feel so exhausted.

When Adam calls he asks where the imagery in my play *A Rat's Mass* comes from. He wants to submit a script to the *X Files* and has been pondering the source of imagery. I go down the list of images, most of which come from my childhood Italian immigrant neighborhood in Cleveland and the coming of adolescence in World War II. I tell him about my Italian classmates, their communion dresses, Catechism, their love of the Virgin Mary, the beginning of World War II and a loss of safety, fear, the Nazis.

J—— can't type any of my work for several weeks. She and her parents agree it would be good if she took time off from her jobs and finished her play. I asked her do her friends still have the Ibsen group.

I study the flowers in a book I've carried with me for years. Blue-bells, narcissus, gardenias, tulips, camellias, orchids, yellow roses.

In the early winter mornings I again think of the heather in Northern California and in Yorkshire England.

In my mother's apartment there are ivy, ferns, pansies, violets and 1940s lamps embossed in roses, vases embossed with rose designs.

My daughter-in-law sent me a set of cards she painted . . . all of lilies.

3

In my autumn absence my landlord had rented an apartment to a woman who smoked cigarettes constantly. All day and night my apartment above had layers of smoke. The smoke had found its path up the stairwell to my door and under it. I wrote to my landlord and told her what a friend suggested.

Dear: ——,

Heavy smoke continues to seep into my apartment. My friend suggests in both units:

- Negative ion generator:

Air ionizers enrich the air with negative ions. Ion count falls between 2,000 to 4,000 ions per cubic centimeter in nature—clean outdoor air—to a few hundred or less indoors. This is caused by the integration of the ions with pollutants such as: dust, soot, cigarette smoke, and pollen. The combined molecules are precipitated from the air by electrostatic attraction to the ground. Air ionizers can actually rebuild the ion count indoors.

Ions play a significant role in our environment and everyday life. There are two kinds of ions, positive and negative. Positive ions are produced by cars, factories, heavy machinery, smoke, dust, soot and other pollutants. These positive ions are harmful to the environment and to our health.

Negative ions, on the other hand, are created in nature by sunlight, waterfalls, raindrops, and wind. This is the reason that air is fresher, cleaner and smells good after a storm. Outdoors the negative ions (if their numbers are not overshadowed by positive ions as in cities) cancel out the positive ions for a healthier environment. Indoors these beneficial negative ions are greatly outnumbered by pollutants. In fact, studies have shown that most homes, cars and offices have fewer than 80 negative ions per cubic centimeter, compared to over 4,000 negative ions found outside in the same volume of air.

- HEPA filters
- seal doors and windows
- re-route radiator
- re-route air ducts
- caulk and seal all ceiling and floor openings, light switches, outlets, pipes, etc.

In X Unit:
- "Isolated" smoking room

She didn't answer.

"This time I don't have to keep asking you how to meet people," N—— said. "We're happy. We like New York this time." She was my childhood friend's daughter. Her husband was now a director for a famous television show. Three years earlier they had called from San Francisco. They said they were thinking of moving to New York from San Francisco and did I have any advice.

Everyone should live in New York once I *always* said. "It's so wonderful. Even though I hate it sometimes."

I went on to say how anywhere in the world you went there was always someone to talk to New York City about. The people in my brownstone. Where else would you find an Israeli soldier, an Austrian translator and a writer from Berlin. A Barrymore once lived here. Itzak Perlman once lived on the corner as did Diahann Carroll. A person who works hard can go to the top here. You can attain anything in New York. It's democratic.

In four months the phone rang. They were in New York.

"I could only go so far at the station in San Francisco, —— said. He had taken a job with a new cable company but hoped for more. In two months the cable company folded but he was assistant director on a national television show. They liked walking around Gramercy Park.

That day my ex-student called. She and her friends lived on West End Avenue in a building owned by one of their parents. They had all gone to Harvard.

"Do you think we should give our script to Joe (Chaikin)?" she asked. "We have a group that meets once a week. We've revised an Ibsen play called ——."

"I don't know that play," I said. "When I was in my twenties, I read *The Master Builder* and I've seen *A Doll House* several times." They'd met more than a year and now wanted a director to help them film the project. We decided Joe (Chaikin) would be a good person to direct the Ibsen.

"Lots of people our age like to work with young people," I said. "Could you play a part?" J—— asked.

My ex-student was typing a narration for me that I was having much trouble with. An element was missing. I had abandoned that material for the *Bronte Scenes*. I reread the *Bronte Scenes* again sitting on my old rose colored sofa.

I then reread my *Narrative 2000*. The heroine was my counterpart living in New York near the turn of the century.

All evening, Suzanne thought. Why had Etta said just as she started up the stairs that first night they talked, 'Mute ashes farewell as you glide by the Gloomy River. The spirits of the air are ferocious and violent. They hate human beings, cause storms and can make themselves visible bodies out of air. Water spirits, which are cruel and deceitful, appear. They wreck ships and drown swimmers.' What was it that she foresaw? Suzanne remembered how all the way up the stairwell in slanted shadows she kept muttering, holding her head to the right side: 'Am I the intended victim?' Then after midnight Etta had knocked on Suzanne's ground floor outside window. What is she doing outside at midnight? My cousin is crazy, she thought. It would be the same spot on the bottom walk beneath the trash bins where soon she would be killed. She knocked on Suzanne's window several times. Suzanne got up and looked through the curtain cautiously. Etta sat on the bottom step knocking but not speaking. Then suddenly she said, 'Someone in the Vanishing knows where there is a severed head.' Then: 'I want to talk to you, Suzanne, but since I can't I've carefully copied your writing on green sheets as a present and slipped them under your door.' Suzanne watched Etta through the curtains. Her cousin sat outside in the dangerous night until morning. Suzanne fell asleep for an hour. When she awoke she had dreamed about Etta and her sister Ella.

Ella, appearing from atop a plane tree, visited Suzanne. She carried a single lamp and sat beside Suzanne's bed. Its rays fell over Suzanne's face. The ghost in the plane tree said to Suzanne, 'Your countenance will change this summer. And fierce will be your struggle between reason and madness. Your strength will ebb. We are now enemies.'

I fear succumbing to darkness as my heroines do.

I can't stop thinking about Florence, Italy in the dark January New York. I know I am repeating myself when I call my son again.

"Remember the Italian barber who cut your hair in Florence?" I say. "He said he'd never cut hair like that before and was it O.K. Was I happy with how your hair looked. He was so proud. You were wearing short red cotton pants and a red and white striped tee shirt. Every morning we walked along the Arno from Piazza Donatello to American Express. Twice we walked a block away and took a bus. We passed the Duomo."

"Did we go to Tivoli before Florence?" he asks.

"We went to Tivoli on a day trip in May. We spent the month of June in Florence. On your birthday we bought a chocolate cake from Doneys and Joe sent you an illustrated book he made of pictures from magazines. He couldn't find a children's book he liked in Nigeria. Nigeria was his last stop before he came to Rome." Again I mention the green marble table overlooking the greenhouse terrace.

I write a letter to Eitra (Joe's six year old son) about Florence. It's called "For My Grandson."

4

"I certainly hope you're going to put the flowers we saw at Tivoli in your notebook," I told Joe again. "Remember how we took the tour bus to Tivoli from Rome? It was in May."

"I don't remember that," he said. "I was only six."

"I know—we celebrated your seventh birthday in Florence in that grand house on Piazza Donatello. The living room had a glass wall that led to a green house. And that led to the garden."

"Yes, I remember Piazza Donatello. And the morning we were supposed to go to Fiesole," he said, "but you didn't feel good."

"What about the cypress trees all over Rome? And the flowers in the Villa Borghese?"

"I just remembered us standing looking at the gardens, walking through the Villa."

"One Sunday we saw a soccer game. And ate red ices. I just went and looked up Villa Borghese in the Blue Guide. I miss you," I say.

I miss when the kids were little, I tell my friend ———.

"It's like a slow hemorrhage," she says, "the condition of being separated from them."

"You're an inspiration," my friend says when I tell her I think her daughter can still be a major writer even though she has two children.

I returned from caring for my mother on January second, the day before the anniversary of my father's death in 1975. An invitation to a Knopf book party for Toni Morrison was in my mail. I went. I took my student Scott. She has the Nobel Prize and is wealthy, I brooded. My small apartment after more than four months at Harvard seemed dark, faded.

At the party at Balthazar I saw the glamourous Mehtas, Charlie Rose, Diane Sawyer, Carl Bernstein, and I returned to my faded apartment. I should leave New York, I thought.

At the Balthazar party I asked Sam Shepard where he now lived. We had both lived in the Bay Area in the early 80's. He mentioned a far away state. And I envisioned a splendid country farm.

Adam called. He's sending me a book on Italy. It's a belated Christmas gift since at Christmas time I was in Ohio. When Adam was born in Rome August 1, 1961 at Salvator Mundi Hospital my husband Joe, Joe Jr. and I sat in the gardens surrounding the hospital. I held the baby in my arms (I think again).

Adam sent me *The Oxford History of Italy.* And he wonders how I am. There was a gas leak in my apartment for five days before I became aware of the gas. Adam tries to get my grandson Canaan to say hello. But Canaan is crying.

Bernard called. We met at an Adams House cocktail party. He teaches Chaucer. He's decided he's going to write about being both Black and white, Christian and Moslem. Until now, his fictional stories underscored his affluent Southern Californian upbringing.

"You write about being Black," he asked, "don't you?" when we had coffee at Pamplona.

I see again that "jealousy" runs through my dark narratives. Where are my jealousies leading me?

Again I looked at some of my children's childhood books. I'd saved *William the Conqueror, Chess for Children, Babar, Winnie the Pooh.*

"Remember we saw *The Sound of Music*?" I'd say to Adam and Joe.

"Ginger and a little piece of garlic will heal your depression," I'd told my friend at the *Times* a couple of years ago.

We'd always talked about the complexity of being Black, and the Black and White literary world of New York.

"What do you think I should write next?" I'd asked her.

We often asked each other's opinion in projects but were seldom able to take each other's advice. I take ginger and garlic.

My former husband Joe called. He knew my job at Harvard had ended and wondered what I was going to do.

He listened to my stories of caring for my mother during the Christmas holidays. He had known her forty-eight years.

"She talks about her body all the time," I said. "She never asked me one word about Harvard, my semester, my students."

Every meal I prepared for her made her angry. The toast didn't have enough butter, the rice wasn't quite right, the orange juice made her sick. The coffee was too strong, there was too much sugar in it. I got the wrong pajamas from the drawers. I told Joe how frail and almost bald and tearful and breathless she was, taking a breath after each syllable. How we went on the transit for the sick, RTA to Cleveland Clinic.

"It was raining and snowing and each of the other passengers had walkers. At the clinic we were first seen by a young white female aide who asked my mother questions it seemed she should already know the answers to.

"Tell me about your fall, where did you fall, why do you think you fell," then, "What happened when you were admitted to the hospital? When did they release you? What medication are you taking? How much do you take?" Then a young male intern comes in with another clipboard. He and the female intern disagree on the amounts of medication my mother should be taking.

But Dr. —— doesn't appear. "Where is the doctor?" my mother and I ask.

The male intern said, soon.

"When is soon?"

After a very long wait the "Doctor" came in without speaking, glanced at the notes the male intern had written and asked my ailing, exhausted mother the same questions.

"Why didn't you address my mother?" I said. "Why didn't you say hello to her and address her?"

He and the intern laughed.

My mother sent me down to the lobby to beg RTA transit to please wait for her so she wouldn't have to wait for the next bus. It was snowing.

When we got back to the apartment my mother asked for Campbell's cream of mushroom soup and that was perfect but she had other troubles: the mailman had put her mail in the wrong box. I cleared up the Christmas presents from the floor by the mahogany table and took the Christmas wreath off the front door.

"Put the wreath back on the door" she said.

"But it's January 2."

"Please put it back." It was time for her Tylenol.

I wrote more of Italy for my grandson.

Joedy (my son's nickname) was the most enchanting traveling companion. We spent from March 15 to September 30, 1961 in Rome, Italy. We lived in a pensioni right off Via Veneto, three blocks from the Villa Borghese. Within this park was a famous Villa: the floors inside were marble and the rooms were constructed like an early Roman house.

Our room in the pensioni Sabrina had a balcony that overlooked the street. You could look down the street and see Via Veneto, and up the street you saw Piazza di Spagna in the distance. The pensioni was run by an Italian couple and their maid Maria; they loved your father and called him Guiseppe. Italian for Joseph.

For breakfast Maria brought espresso, croissants and milk. "Bon

Giorno," she said. Joedy's bed was next to the balcony. The floor was filled with toy cars, books and his school papers. Next to our room was the dining room. Our dinners and lunches were usually a pasta soup, veal, salad, and ice cream for dessert. Sabrina and Maria prepared the meals.

Every morning Joedy put on his school uniform. It was gray flannel short pants, a white shirt, navy blue tie and a navy blue sweater which said Parioli Day School. Mornings we walked from Via Veneto down two blocks to the American Embassy. The walk was a most exquisite sight. The beautiful sidewalk cafes were setting up for the day. It was seven-thirty in the morning. And the waiters were putting fresh flowers and tablecloths on the tables. Across the street was Doneys, where afternoons we bought chocolate napoleons. After the cafes we passed Hotel Excelsior. The bus to the Parioli Day School was waiting in front of the Embassy. A little after three in the afternoon he returned. Since it was spring we always went for a walk before returning to Pensioni Sabrina.

We walked towards Piazza Barbarini. On the way sometimes we'd go into the American Library and look at books and newspapers. Piazza Barbarini had a cafe, always crowded with people standing at counters drinking espresso. Once we bought a deviled egg. After that we ate those often. Romans wanted to talk to Joedy. They asked us were we from South America. The Italians looked at him and said "bello," meaning beautiful.

Rome was a significant city for us all.

—— called. She feels despondent that she finished a TV adaptation that aired last week and it gave her no joy. Even though it was on ABC, she was surprised at the lack of feeling of achievement she felt.

"I want to do my own work," she said. She's already published a popular book of essays but wonders why younger women (she's in her 30s) are getting book contracts that she can't get. The money from her adaptations isn't enough to give her time to work on her own books.

She wonders if I can help her with a writing schedule that will help her in doing both kinds of writing.

"How did you continue to do your own work over the years?" she asked.

"No matter what my life is like," I say, "I've tried to do at least a page or two on my own work early in the morning whether I've been raising children or teaching."

I re-read my passage on ion generators.

I dream of the plane crash again and re-read my narrative. I read from *Narrative 2000* again.

> Etta dreamed:
> She went for a walk.
> All she could think of as she passed Riverside Drive's Historic District at 105th Street was what Vanishing read the night before.

> In the pauses of the shower you heard the rumbling of the earth beneath and waves of tortured sea, the murmur of escaping gases, sometimes the cloud appeared to break from its solid mass and become human shapes, striding in the gloom then vanishing into an abyss.

> Vapors of trouble to come.

I read the list of flowers that illustrated a diary I often carried with me, the Spring Garden, Wild Garden, Walled Garden, Water Garden, Italian Garden, Arbor, the Orchard, Flowers for Drying, the Greenhouse; and on the border of the book I'd written five years ago:

> "To love to live to lose with good grace and just play the melody."
> —Jackie Gleason

Then I read passages from my early unpublished novels, novels written 1957–1960, written sitting near the vase of daffodils on our kitchen table, where I read Emerson's *Self Reliance*. I see myself sitting under the Monet print of poppies dreaming of capturing life on paper.

5

When I got up it was dark. I found a book I've had for twenty years called *Botanical Illustrations*.

I write down the names and descriptions on its pages: wreath of roses, hand colored engravings of irises, water color drawings of carnations and forget-me-nots.

"Remember London," I tell Adam when Canaan's not crying. "Remember the Cinderella pantomime at the Palladium and the auto show at Olympia, the house in Primrose Hill filled with toy soldiers from Selfridges and painted train cars and games, one called Bezique, and the miniature Roulette wheel, the big Christmas tree in you and Joe's room downstairs. We played endless Christmas songs on the red and blue plastic record player and ate hovis bread and butter and drank hot chocolate.

In this January I remember another January. One of the most beautiful drives I ever took was a drive with Erskine through Marin County, the hills and heather, and down to Stinson Beach. Erskine always felt the collards he grows in his backyard, first in Berkeley now in Indiana, keep him healthy. He wrote a book on meditations, and one winter in Berkeley when rains were violent for weeks and my body ached he came to see me at the Faculty Club and brought me a sweet potato pie.

"When these rains let up we'll drive in the heather again," he said when he brought the sweet potato pie. In Stinson Beach I bought a book called *California Wild Flowers*. I wish I could remember the flowers in San Juan Baptista. But I do remember the redwood trees outside my window at the Faculty Club in Berkeley.

"Remember the chocolate ice cream on Via Frattina, walks to Piazza Barbarini sitting on top of the Spanish Steps in the sun?" I tell Joe again.

Adam called. He wonders if I think he should change the main character C.W. in his novel. When his agent sent his book, the editors were indifferent to his political story line. The story takes place in the 1960's Congo.

He wonders should he have a Black character at all? We talk a lot about the content of his political thriller and about being a Black writer.

I reread *Bronte Scenes*.

"Where do I go from here?" my student Monica writes (now that she's finished a play). "And will I ever be able to write any thing again?"

"These questions go on forever," I said.

In the beautiful autumn afternoon in Cambridge we had read her lyrical passages.

6

Joe came. We saw *Titanic*. He's finished his flower project with the Arlington school children. But he did bring me a book on garden writing. He said he has another book called *Famous Gardens of the World* he will send me. We discuss going to London in June. He stared at the drawing over the fireplace I have of Primrose Hill. We look at the three remaining black and white photographs I have of 35 Chalcot Crescent. He's standing amid the hydrangeas. I remember now they were blue.

"It is always early evening or night, twilight or dusk," is a line from Monica's play, "never morning or summer."

Roses and Chestnut trees were what Ann mentioned about Regents Park. And I got my annual invitation from the Ebony Rose Society for women who once lived in Mt. Pleasant, my childhood neighborhood in Ohio.

I see smoke connects my life and work; in my narrative my heroine wants to talk to the police but is afraid. But it's not smoke. She thinks someone is going to kill her.

My ex-writing student's mother called from Albany. She is upset that her daughter has been out of school for three years and is writing obscure plays and poems and doesn't have a job. Since her daughter received an A in my class and I've written letters of recommendation for her, her mother wonders if I have an opinion about what direction T—— should take. She is alarmed (she knows her daughter is brilliant). She doesn't want her coming back home penniless.

We discuss graduate schools, another degree in English or a degree in Creative Writing, perhaps one in Theatre.

"An energetic person can write and teach," I say. I suggest a graduate degree in English and a future post teaching.

"I'm going to talk to her," T——'s mother says. "I'm going to think about what you've said carefully and talk to her. She wants to go away and live in Ireland and work for a theater company for no money. I'm going to talk to her tonight."

T—— called in less than a month. She's going to get her doctorate at Harvard in American Studies (they offer her tuition and an allowance). She will try to teach and write instead of going to live in Ireland working for nothing for a theatre company in Dublin. (She writes about being Irish and Black.)

When I was in Cambridge T—— typed a few letters for me. And we talked. At twenty-three she still longs to be penniless in Ireland writing masterpieces walking by the sea. Graduate school with its codes, hierarchy and killing workload is very difficult.

"I never solved this," I said, sitting in the Courtyard at Adams House, "I taught as much as I could and I wrote as much as I could. But I never really solved the balance between writing and teaching. I'd like to live by the sea too."

"Do you think I could have a child while I'm teaching and researching my book?" a Brown professor asked me when she came to interview me for a literary magazine. She's thirty-seven and wants to have a child. Her husband is a painter and often they're living only on her income.

"I love my children more than anything," I say.

"But where did you get the time for both?" she asked.

"I don't know."

I read *2000*.

7

I continued to work on my *2000* narrative but was secretly stymied as to how I would go on living. Would I make it through winter? I'd had these moods before. I couldn't seem to finish the play for the Public Theater.

"We're happy," —— said again. "The advice you gave us three years ago was perfect."

The phone rang. It was my student Maria from Cambridge. She wants me to work with her this semester (as a tutorial) to complete a long play.

"What should I read?" she asked.

We decided she would reread two of her favorite novels, *Villete* and *Jane Eyre,* criticism by Roger Fry, *Beethoven* by Sullivan and Van Gogh's *Letters to Theo.*

Maria is writing about her family's Irish servant who came from Prince Edward Island. She was Maria's nurse before she died. Maria wants to trace Hilda's life from Prince Edward Island to Boston and then to Apthorp House at Harvard. We discuss the best scenes in the one act play she's just completed, the struggle of Hilda's parents, their poverty in Prince Edward Island. Hilda's flight to Boston, her loneliness (which Maria conveyed in letters), her struggle to learn to become a servant, her diabetes and final amputation of a leg.

"Thank you for your help," she said.

That same day I got a letter from Eliot, another student. He wondered if he should put his parents' separation in his play (on a Christmas trip to Cairo, his father announced his relationship to an Egyptian woman).

Although he is only twenty his play illuminates the pressures his parents were under to be a perfect married couple, and their unhappiness. And how they were haunted by their younger, happier spirits called *Dandelion Fairies.*

We discussed an essay he had written on Kate Chopin that might become a part of his play, as will his writing about a trip to the pyramids. These two pieces might enrich his play.

I called Hettie to tell her my students at Harvard liked the excerpts from her book *How I Became Hettie Jones,* and that three people had written term papers on Baraka and specifically on the years he and Hettie were a young couple in Greenwich Village in the 50's. She said she'd been asked many times to talk about the Beats, Jack Kerouac, Gregory Corso, but she'd never focused on only herself and Amiri Baraka. She said there was interest in making a musical from her book. We discussed the problems in letting another person write the book for the musical. The material has love and passionate perceptions of that Greenwich Village world of the 50's.

"I need your advice," she said.

I encouraged her to write the book to the musical herself. Although she'd already agreed to let another writer work on the screenplay of her material. "The students were drawn to you and Baraka and the culture of the Village and the reflection in his play *Slave* of your marriage. They were very drawn to the catastrophic ending of your marriage... the Jewish girl from —— and the young Black aspiring writer.

"People were drawn to us in those days," she said.

I read the list of a calendar/diary I often carried:

The spring garden, flowers for cutting, the wild garden, the walled garden, the water garden, the Italian garden, the arbour, the lawn, the orchard, flowers for drying, the greenhouse.

And on the border I had written, eleven years ago,

"To love to live to lose with good grace and just play the melody."
—Jackie Gleason.

Then I re-read passages from my early unpublished novels, written sitting near the vase of daffodils from Broadway on our kitchen table and always rhododendron. "She" read Emerson's *Self Reliance.* I again reach for Ollie's play. I see the Adrienne of 1955 sitting under the Monet print of poppies, dreaming of capturing life on paper.

8

I reread a passage.

"You almost gassed yourself," my former husband Joe said.

I again explained how gas had been leaking and I thought the odor was my asthma medicine.

Again, "You have to keep going," he says when I say I feel so exhausted.

And again when Adam calls he asks where the imagery in my play *A Rat's Mass* comes from. He wants to submit a script to the *X Files* and has been pondering the source of imagery. I go down the list of images, most of which come from my childhood Italian immigrant neighborhood in Cleveland and coming of adolescence in World War II. I tell him about my Italian classmates, their communion dresses, Catechism, their love of the Virgin Mary, the beginning of World War II and a loss of safety, fear, and the Nazis.

My mother says the trees at Adam's house in Virginia look as if they would fall if there were a storm. In fact one "great big tree" fell the day before she went for a visit at Thanksgiving.

I don't want to live a long life I think. I don't have the courage. I'm not as brave as my mother is. Maybe it's because she grew up alone in a boarding school. But I can't endure as she does.

I order two Amaryllises.

Often I think of Ollie. He is my student who took me to dinner. What an enchanting evening. He wants to bring Peter Sellars back to Harvard. I got Sellars' address from my publisher. Ollie says I can be on their committee. I give him a copy of a book Peter Sellars gave me at the L.A. Festival. It's by Bothius. Peter said I was like Bothius, I wouldn't be famous until I died.

I love Ollie's play *Libertyville*.

My mother called to say she doesn't have any milk and will have to pay the girl on the front desk in her apartment building to go down the hill to the store. Also the middle of her back hurts.

"Is it hibiscus?" my son asks, "the flowers all over Accra?'

"I don't know."

Apple blossoms, daisies, daffodils, are some of the flowers his children on the Explorers project drew.

My mother says she threw up all of her dinner last night. It was the gravy on the chicken.

"I told Mrs. C—— when she made that chicken, not to put any gravy on it. I tried to take it out but it was all over the potatoes and peas. And I had to pay her. That gravy had a lot of black pepper.

"I'm hungry this morning," she says. "I'm just as hungry as I can be but I'm afraid to put anything else into my stomach."

"I thought you had a lot of food in the freezer," I said. "Why did you need to get Mrs. C—— to cook something? When I was there Earl and I bought you a lot of food."

"I just felt like a little roast chicken," she said. "I have to go back to the clinic next Tuesday. If I have to take that barium again I'll die."

Barium was a blue medicine that my mother had also thrown up. She weighs ninety pounds.

Tivoli was surrounded by olive groves I think. And *Angelloi* is the name of my student Glenn Nano's play. The poem that begins the play is:

> Angeloi
> The things that are and ere have been
> The things that last or pass each day
> The things that mortals do and say
> 'Tis all these things that we have seen.
>
> Throughout all time and every place
> We watch and share our sacred gift.
> And try with kindness to uplift
> The saddened eyes upon each face.
> We bear this perfect love
> To these who would receive its force.

9

"Is it hibiscus?" Joe asked again, "the flowers at the Achimota Guest House?"

Daisies, daffodils, and dandelions were some of the flowers the children at his school drew.

"Where did you get those roses?" I ask my friend —— who lives on Park Avenue.

"From our garden in the country," she said.

We sat in the great Edwardian drawing room. She asked how do I think I was able to continue writing after having children. Her daughter, a powerful novelist, is having a second child.

"I stayed up until one or two in the morning. I drank coffee very black every hour. I read Proust, drank coffee every hour. Every week Joe and I bought daffodils, rhododendron, and paper whites on Broadway at 121" street. Sometimes I'd sit in Union Theological Seminary and read random religious texts. Sometimes we bought a single hyacinth, and Joe gave me violets we bought at Fifth Avenue and 50th street. I always imitated his work habits . . . long work hours, lack of trivial diversions.

Adam called. He saw Lady Bird Johnson on the CBS Evening News. I remind him I went to Austin and saw the fields of wildflowers where she walked. I saw bluebonnets.

——— called. She wants to know how she could find out how to really talk to her mother, whom I've known since 1943. Her mother is quiet about her feelings.

"She won't talk. The only things I know about her past are the stories you tell me. We never knew she used to speak French and did watercolors."

"Ask her about the orchestra she plays in, about orchestrations, conductors, musical compositions. She loves all those things."

My son Joe Jr. called. He reminded me about the copy of his nature portfolio he'd left in my apartment when we returned from Cambridge. We were only in the apartment a few hours before I had to take the train to Cleveland. My mother was being released from the hospital the next morning.

He reminded me there was also the book from his companion. They had been together a few years and in that time she had "taken" every holiday that I once spent with Joe Jr. She took my birthday (hers was the next day), Mother's Day (she was now a stepmother to my grandson), Easter, random summer weekends and trips to Ohio (she was from Ohio too). And now she'd planned a trip for them to be on the train Christmas morning. For a very long time I had spent a few hours of Christmas Day with my son.

I looked through her book. It was filled with bon mots about happiness. The preface to the book with happiness bon mots my son's companion gave me said:

"Go little book and wish to all flowers in the garden, meat in the hall, a bin of wine, a spice of wit, a house with lawns enclosing it. A living river by the door. A nightingale in the sycamore."

I tried to reread my play. And I saw more than ever my *Narrative 2000* was about succumbing to darkness, hatred and death.

10

I remember far too much when my sons both came to my 48th birthday on West 79th Street. They bought me chocolate cake and a blue flowered tea set.

After talking to —— I think again of 1956–1959 when I drank coffee hourly and worked on my novels. There was a Monet print on the wall, *Wild Poppies.* I looked at it all day. And into the night. How hard I worked. Today they still remain unpublished. But how happy I was working on these novels in our tiny apartment at Columbia University.

Rachel, my friend since we were eleven years old, sent me a book called *Fountain of Youth.* And a green straw basket crowded with three amaryllises.

When I called to thank her she tells me about her lessons, violin, cello, tennis. I think perhaps I should take singing lessons. So I could sing in old Broadway musicals, *Guys and Dolls, Gypsy.*

—— called again.

"Ask your mother about composers and conductors. And the year she studied music in New York. That was very unusual, for a young Black woman to study musical composition. Her teacher lived in Harlem. As I remember your mother knew about Bernstein, Toscanini, and Heifetz. She knew the songs of Broadway musicals. I remember once when we were in high school she explained the difference between Bach and Beethoven.

Tomorrow my friend's daughter will visit. She wants to make a short film about her extraordinary mother and wants me to tell her stories of the 40's and the 50's.

"I'm sure your mother knows all about the interworkings of orchestras," I say. "She's been in an orchestra as long as I can remember."

I work on the Bronte passages.

11

In the winter dawn I called London. My friends Ann and Carlton once produced a play of mine in Rome. And we lived in London at the same

time in the sixties. They still live on Cheyne Walk. Ann reminds me
that hydrangeas were in my yard at 35 Chalcot Crescent. And chestnut
trees are the trees the children and I sat under in Primrose Hill. She reminded me of the umbrella pines of Rome and the plane trees along
the Arno in Florence. She's studied in Florence.

"What do you think the flowers were in the Florence greenhouse?" I
ask.

"Probably Azaleas."

I don't know whether it's Rome or London, but just as I hang up
Ann mentions Linden Trees, Lyme Blossoms and Palms.

Erskine wonders if small bits of meat will help his fatigue after the
years of being a vegetarian.

He's working on a book about Spirituals and teaching at a famous
university. He knows I still eat meat. He's been feeling desperately tired.
We discuss the eating of small bits of liver. We discuss his long hours of
study and teaching over the last twenty years. He was very young when
he got tenure at Berkeley but seldom takes time off. I suggest he try to
take off a month, perhaps in July, every year instead of studying straight
through the summer.

I re-read one of his passages on the Negro Spiritual.

My narrative ending in suicide still plagued me. I heard from Ann
about flowers and trees in London and Rome.

Dear Adrienne

Life got away with me recently and it has crossed my mind to write
you about the plants and I haven't done more than think about
Primrose Hill . . . I did go to see a friend in Camden Town on a very
wet and windy day, and forgot all about gardens and flowers and
Primrose Hill which has plane trees and a few oaks. The flowers in
gardens there are like flowers in Chelsea gardens: impatiens called
"Bizzie Lizzie" adds bright colour and is quite sturdy provided it
gets water. Camelias flower beautifully, and roses are a favourite in
some places. Delphiniums are tall bluish purple flowers that bloom
at the beginning of the summer.

The trees around Rome include plane trees, poplars and some cypress but most characteristic are the umbrella pines, or parasol pines.
Flowers the Italians like include clivia, which has thick spatulate leaves
and bright big trumpet-like flowers. It is in the lily family I think.
There are many geraniums everywhere (Primrose Hill gardens, too)

because they are sturdy and brightly coloured. Cypress and poplar and the same flowers in Florence, and a source of VERY ACCURATE DETAIL which is not to be found in guide books is Henry James' RODERICK HUDSON, an early novel set in Rome.

Smoke connects my winter with *Narrative 2000*. My heroine wants to talk to the police but is afraid. It's not smoke. She thinks someone is going to kill her.

Adam is trying to reconstruct the play we wrote together, *Sleep Deprivation Chamber*. He wants to build the character based on himself and de-emphasize the character based on me. The character Suzanne, based on me, is a character I'd used several times. In his screenplay Adam wants to use less of Suzanne's dreams and more of real events that happened to "his" character. We talk again about Black characters in movies. Are movie producers interested in stories about Blacks? He is filled with doubts but continues working on the material. We're happy *Titanic* won the Oscars but still note there were only five Blacks on the stage when all Oscar winners were introduced in the 70 year tribute.

"It is always early evening or night, twilight or dusk," is a line from Monica's play, "never morning, or summer."

Roses and chestnut trees were what Ann mentioned about Regents Park. And I got my annual invitation from the Ebony Rose Society from women who lived in my early childhood neighborhood in Cleveland.

My niece called. Newly married to her French husband, she is coming to New York to live for a while. She wonders if I have an opinion about how he can do well. He is thirty. And an actor-writer.

"All the actor-writers I know are in a theatre group or they have their own group, they try out for commercials, plays and movies. And most write and direct and teach. They seem to do it all." I tell her about the Ibsen Group. I tell her my students and ex-students like Sam Shepard and David Mamet. I re-read Ollie's play. I'm thrilled by this group of mad people on a train.

The person who smokes appears to have a Spanish maid. When I knocked on the door to discuss the density of smoke, perfumed candles and pot, a voice in broken English said she couldn't open the door because she doesn't speak English.

In real life I never met him but in my *Narrative 2000* my heroine tracks down the policeman who beat her son in Bolinas, California. *Sleep De-*

privation Chamber (Adam's screenplay) covers the Virginia trial and our victory.

"There is someone who can break in on my telephone line," I tell Adam.

"Mom that's not possible."

"It's true. Someone can. Someone calls me with different voices. And very often they break in on my line when I'm talking."

I got Caller I.D. Perhaps, I think, I could put that in my *Narrative.* Even though I have Caller I.D. I can't catch the person.

Maria called from Cambridge. I still tutor her. She doesn't understand what I meant in the note I wrote her about the material she sent me. She continues to write about her family's housekeeper. "The pages veer off into an imaginary life. I think for the first layer you should *document* Hilda's life." She says she could write at length about the progression of diabetes, Hilda's disease, and later she could research what was happening in the world in Cambridge and Prince Edward Island when Hilda was nineteen. She was nineteen when she left her family in Prince Edward Island to come to Boston to learn to be a servant. We decide on this course. In June Maria will go to Ireland and visit the village where Hilda's family came from. We discuss again the books Maria loves: *Villete, Jane Eyre, A Room with a View.*

"Hilda is a kind of Jane Eyre," I remind Maria.

I'm surprised when she tells me that Prince Edward Island is where *Anne of Green Gables* lived. We decide after she amasses material on diabetes, Prince Edward Island in 1910 and the village in Ireland, then her *imagination* can connect the material. We will talk again in three weeks, when she sends the diabetes material.

When I look for Ollie's play in the magazine stand I find a portfolio I had forgotten. *Great Flower Prints.* They are postcards of a Camelia, a Cowhorn Orchid, a Satin Poppy, a Celandine, a Tiger Lily, Turk's Cop Lily, a Bird of Paradise and a Yellow Iris.

I'd had this portfolio for years, yet I had never taken the time to read the introduction. "The finest botanical paintings came out of France, Holland, Germany, Austria and England."

12

Scott's mother sent me a beautiful gardenia brooch. When I called to thank her she asked my opinion as to how her son could succeed at making writing a career. She and her husband wanted to help him.

"Help him through his mid-to-late twenties," I said. "Most people give up around that time."

Scott gave his mother, who loves writers, a souvenir napkin from the Morrison party.

In the past six years my mother has made her health the most important thing in my day. "What can I do?" I asked a childhood friend. "Another person's health cannot continue to dominate my day. She's killing me softly."

Two amaryllis buds are about to bloom and I get a letter from Brett. "Your play is a feat of the imagination," I had written on his critique. I'd loved Brett's piece on the death of his father.

We read it in our class at Sever.

"We're like those guys at MGM sitting around the table analyzing our works," Samuel Baum said. We laughed.

Analyzing symbols, characters, language was a joy to all of us. The class was from 1–3 in the afternoon. As winter came sometimes it got dark before class ended. Each time I arrived at Sever I realized how much I loved my students.

Samuel's play was about the entertainment business in New York.

I remembered how much I loved their letters.

Joe called. "You've got to keep going," he said, when I again mentioned my exhaustion.

"I found a book you gave me when we went to church," I tell my son Joe. "It's called *How Not to Worry.*"

Angelloi is the name of Glenn Nano's play, I remember again.

"I'll save the primary seat for you at my play," Brett Egan wrote to me.

Adam wonders again whether white editors have rejected his political thriller because it is about the 1960's Congo. We talk again about another political thriller he wrote earlier. The hero's name was Alexander Rome. He says perhaps he will keep C.W. as the main character and will add as his son Alexander Rome. We talk about merging material and the joy of characters who appear in later work. We both love Sherlock Holmes.

I'd mentioned Tivoli to Adam as well as Joe Jr. He says he will find out exactly what flowers there were at Tivoli.

"I know Tivoli was surrounded by olive groves," I say.

We discuss all the detectives we like in fiction and film. *Secret Agent,* the television series with Patrick McGoohan; James Bond; Columbo; George Smiley and Holmes.

"Remember when we went to the London Zoo almost every day? The summer of 1967. There was a walk on the side of the Zoo, it was the beginning of Regents Park, where these plane trees shaded the walk. After the zoo we'd go to the Planetarium or Madame Tussaud's and eat at an outdoor café near Baker Street."

Another book of flowers that I read in the winter had Heather, Sunflowers, Yellow Irises, French Roses, Hydrangeas, Hollyhock, Poppy, Anemones, Frangipani and Tiger Lilies.

"Could you send me copies of flower drawings your children made?" I beg Joe Jr. "What did the children do with these drawings of daffodils, daisies, dandelions?"

"We put some on the classroom walls. And I have some drawings in my Close to Nature portfolio. They wrote stories about their flowers."

I had to finish my critiques. I reread my student Jessica Jackson's play. She has a character called January. January returns for a week to her past life.

It's called *After Midnight Standing on the Edge of a Half Bridge.* It has astounding use of language and metaphor. In the end a character called Finn kills herself on the edge of the half bridge, a place where all the characters' "lives" are.

Jessica's play ends with this passage.

"Finn walks to the edge of the bridge, slowly she drops to her knees, then lays down on her stomach and dangles over the edge of bridge. She repositions herself so that more of her body is out over the water. She does this again until she is merely teetering on the edge. Slowly she brings her arms up like an airplane. She stays like this flying, breeze on her face as lights fade."

What joy I experienced sitting on the faded rose colored sofa, reading my student writing.

Sara Newfold wrote about a family whose father left them on Christmas Day. In *Keepers* Steven Turner remembered his brother had a breakdown and was sent away on the day of the young writer's birth:

"I grew up into his pain. I didn't witness it. I wasn't aware of it. But now I know this and I am stunned. It's something I don't want to get close to. I mean how would you feel if you found that your birth pushed him over the edge, added to his delusion. I am stunned."

Then I read Oliver Lewis' play. It ended with the characters (who are on a train) working on a baby's obituary. It was a comedy.

How I loved my students.

I got a note from Scott. It said,

Dear Adrienne,
I want you to know how eternally grateful I am for your inviting me to Toni Morrison's splendid book party. It's an experience I'll never forget and always treasure.
Scott.

And I got a card from my mother. The card was bordered in crimson, yellow, and white roses. It said,

Thank you for sending me the Campbell's soups.
Love, Mother.

I remind Adam to draw into his well of memories to give his material authenticity. He is writing about London where we lived three years when he was a child.

I got the material Maria sent me on her main character's diabetes. I write her.

Maria
I thought you were going to write a factual paper on diabetes as a resource. You have written a fictional diary. How can you know that Hilda's disease progressed along that time line? It might be better to write about Hilda's diabetes as you actually observed it over the years. She was your nanny. When you start your play next fall you should be accurate about her illness.

On the day I left the apartment for four weeks because of the smoke forsythia was in bloom in Central Park.

I came to Virginia. Outside my window are azaleas and white oak trees.

In Williamsburg I bought a group of postcards. One was of a dogwood tree. It said:

The Legend of the Dogwood

"There is a legend that at the time of the Crucifixion dogwood had been the size of oak and other forest trees. It was chosen as the timber of the cross."

I heard from Brett.

"I am beginning to work on a new theater of images, holograms, films, bodies," he said.

I watched a documentary on Conquerors . . . Napoleon planted trees of Liberty.

I called Erskine from Virginia. His line was disconnected. I guess he's writing another book, I thought. So I called his office. The line was disconnected. I had to wait until the switchboard opened. The switchboard operator said, "I have a paper here to read to people who call for him," when I said Dr. Peters.

"He's deceased. He died in mid March," the operator said.

The garden he tended at his house in South Bend will die this summer.

He had collards and petunias. Often when he didn't answer the phone he'd say, "I was out in the garden."

For the rest of my life I will wonder: did Erskine know he was going to die the last time I talked to him?

"I'm anemic" was what he'd said.

"I don't want you to worry about me."

The End

Sisters Etta and Ella
(excerpt from a narrative)

/

Troupe was unable to stop Etta Harrison from leaving messages on his office machine about a coming murder. In July when he went into the office of his brownstone sometimes there were as many as five messages from her in one night.

He'd forgotten about Ella and Etta Harrison in recent years. They weren't prominent anymore in his circle, since the strangling incident and their public fights.

He had been surprised to see that Etta was a member of the Vanishing Literary Club, until he learned she was an old friend of Jerry Loren's and he was making an opera of some of her early writing.

When Troupe had seen Etta on Broadway at the bookstore she'd looked hopeless and her dress careless. Nothing like the dazzling suits she and her sister used to wear to M.L.A. meetings. He remembered especially one Christmas in New York their dress—their suits, the coats and shoes—had been talked about constantly in the elevator of the Sheraton. He remembered them coming down to breakfast together, hair in upsweeps, pearls, high heels, laughing together. Everyone wanted to join them on their excursions, their teas at the Waldorf.

But he did also remember now, after Ella had given a paper on the history of their childhood neighborhood in Ohio, in the elevator she had burst into tears and said:

"My paper didn't have half the impact it should have. In her presentation my sister used parts of an interview I showed her. But I'm the one who spent the winter in Cleveland talking to all those people." And then she laughed.

Troupe was surprised to see in an interview the next day in the *Amsterdam News* that they were both planning separate books on their brother, who had been mute the last years of his life because of an automobile accident. And they *each* had the idea of holding imaginary conversations with him.

One morning Troupe sent his researcher Robert to the library to find an old *Black Scholar* magazine.

"It should be about 1990 Winter," he said. "There was an article Ella wrote about Etta. I want to read it."

The article had part of an interview between the sisters, and was preceded by a short bio of Ella.

"Nine years ago Ella Harrison married the well known writer Henderson Young. Ella Harrison is currently a fellow at the Bunting Institute in Cambridge, Massachusetts. She is writing about her family, which includes a study of the South in the 20s, the Depression, and World War II.

Following is an interview between Harrison and equally well known sister Etta. Etta Harrison is currently teaching in New Haven. She's traveled extensively in Africa with her ex husband—Fanon's biographer.

ELLA: Etta what are you teaching this semester?

ETTA: Creative writing and my play. I have pieces I wrote in Ghana on the savannas and drives in Liberia through the Goodrich plantation. These pieces were experiments with narrative.

ELLA: During the first days in Liberia you used narrative from your first novels, People and Strange Possessions. At least that's what you told me. Why is it you don't write or talk about the murder of your baby daughters by the English professor who was their father.

ETTA: He's free. Somehow he's free.

ELLA: But you know he killed himself that night in 1952.

(Suddenly Etta stood up)

ETTA: Ella I've asked my editor, can I stop you from writing articles about me? He told me to leave you alone. I told him you're making me sick. "I think if you leave her alone she'll stop. I don't want to further upset you Etta. But I saw parts of a manuscript she submitted to Grove on you. Do you want to see it? I took a look at it to see if she's violating your legal rights. I feel this is leading to something terrible between you." And it is."

Etta left the interview. Troupe laughed.

Sometimes Etta'd think about how her sister had copied her upsweep hairstyle. Even now as an apparition, Ella's hair was carefully arranged in the hairstyle Etta was known for.

Troupe called Etta one afternoon in June. He had never called her. He started talking about the late '70s when he had to hire people to take care of Kay and Boulting after their mother died. He'd promised their mother he'd look out for them. And now they wanted to get away from him. They hadn't even wanted him to come to the Vanishing. And he hung up. Kay and Boulting were the children of an English woman Troupe had lived with.

For some reason, Etta thought of what the Vanishing had read the night before:

"A tall candelabra supporting a single lamp burned beside the narrow bed. Its rays fell over the face of his enemy and he was happy to see how his enemy's face had changed. The color was gone. The life of his enemy's blood and soul were gone. He spoke: 'I come to you in the dead of the night.' As the steed starts from the path of the tiger, —— sprang up. . . ."

Troupe was determined to discover more of what led to Ella's strangling.

He sent Robert once more to the 42nd Street Library. Robert brought back another *Black Scholar* with a longer piece by Ella, a longer version of the 1992 piece. He remembered Ella had written a play about her sister's devastating college years and her play had received considerable attention in the Ohio Press and she'd sold it to television. The Press ignored Etta's version of her own life (which had been performed earlier at the same theatre) and considered it an inferior piece. This happened the spring before Yale. It was no doubt Ella cherished and coveted her sister's college tragedy.

At the end was a story Ella wrote when she was twenty.

Sitting in his crate filled room Troupe laughed again.

Troupe had never realized how much the sisters had written together. And how in their separate stories they had used the same names for their characters. And fought over the name Suzanne. And over the years it was impossible to distinguish their experiences.

No wonder, he thought, their minds were in such turmoil. This jealousy, he now heard from Robert, extended into every phase of their lives.

In their collected work each claimed material from their Ohio childhood, Ohio State, their years in New York, their trips to Africa.

Robert said he heard they first stopped speaking to each other over stories of their relatives and both claimed an early story about their cousin. Finally they both signed it. And from what he'd heard Robert said he doubted seriously that Ella was living peacefully in the Oakland

Hills. From what he'd heard of her she probably had a new plan and would certainly retaliate from the musical Etta and Jerry Loren were working on about their family.

"I remember seeing the sisters once walking in the eucalyptus trees at Berkeley. They had on pink dresses and held hands," Robert said.

"I didn't know they both loved the same people, their cousins, the photographs of their grandparents, their parents. I didn't know that even then there was a dispute over the division of the family scrapbooks."

Robert said they'd gotten into a bad argument at N.Y.U. at a public lecture in the Tisch School of the Arts onstage.

Ella contended that Etta had never paid any attention whatsoever to their cousin, and laughed when she heard he ran away. And she'd laughed when she saw him with Sylvia Klein.

"There was no such person as Sylvia Klein," Etta said tensely right in front of the writing students, "we made her up." And she kept laughing tensely. Then they couldn't agree on what sections of the story to read aloud.

For the first time Troupe felt he understood their violent preoccupations. He knew they had been superb teachers but he saw how he'd never understood how unstable they were under their upsweep hairdos and corsages on 1940's black dresses.

One Sunday the Vanishing watched *Breakfast at Tiffany's* and went for a walk across the Brooklyn Bridge. At Brooklyn Academy of Music they saw a play by Wole Soyinka called *Swampdwellers.*

Etta called the Precinct all day on Saturday, July 1 and got the answering machine.

She told them she wanted them to know there would be a coming murder. And while she had them on the phone she wondered did they know what happened to the Thalia and the New Yorker (her favorite movie theaters on the Upper West Side). Why had they torn them down? And had anyone claimed responsibility for the bombing at 72nd and Broadway?

All summer Troupe worked on an essay on Professor Thomas Dorsey. Although Dorsey and "Lead Me On Precious Lord" were subjects he'd written about thirty years ago he'd promised a young filmmaker he'd narrate a new essay about Dorsey and the lyrics to "Precious Lord."

"Precious Lord

Take my hand, lead me on, let me stand. I am tired. I am weak. I am worn.

Through the storm, through the night, lead me on to the light.
Take my hand
Precious Lord. Lead me on."

Troupe thought of Etta and Ella.

Etta dreamed she saw Harold Troupe upon the shores of a noonday
sea in a dark mood, a jealous mood.

She dreamed she passed through a grove. Before her was a priest and
another man in earnest conversation. She was struck by the loudness of
their voices. They seemed drunk or mad. Suddenly one of them raised a
knife. She darted forward too late to arrest the blow. The man had stabbed
the priest. In anger she struck the murderer to the ground. He fell
without a struggle which surprised her. He said, "I've recently recovered
from a severe illness."

Etta realized when she woke that she had made a mistake in confid-
ing in Troupe. She remembered all the scathing articles he'd written
about his contemporaries. And the lawsuits he'd been involved in. She
so hoped when her eyes improved that she could make a comeback . . . a
high academic post. Perhaps a presidency. It would be a mistake to seek
Troupe's help. Still, she went on helplessly leaving him messages.

When the Vanishing met, Troupe insisted on showing Etta a small
bedroom she could have most of the winter. He would be on a lecture
tour. Etta went upstairs and opened a door. She found herself within a
tiny bedroom. She felt a daybed, a desk. She knew Troupe had never
totally renovated the second and third floors. There were alcoves behind
walls, stairwells that led to rooms behind the old kitchen, and a sealed
up dining room. An entire back staircase still existed. When Etta opened
another door she was in a closet where this staircase began.

"Does Troupe hope to trap me here?" she thought. "And why?"

That night she dreamed she asked her old student from Prague could
she see Etta's fate. "The night is the sole time we can decipher the de-
crees of fate," the student said.

"If you want precise answers your questions can be answered in an
infant's voice but I have no speaking stone."

The next day Robert, Troupe's researcher, called Etta. He said, "Professor Troupe's concerned about your confusion, your eyes. He was upset you got lost on the closed stairwell last night. He again wants you to
know you're welcome to stay here this winter."

Etta wrote that night:

"The living are ghosts to me. Am I going to be murdered in Troupe's stairwell? Is my sister's apparition ever going to leave me?"

The Vanishing literary club met at the carousel in Central Park.

Troupe worked on the outline of one of his lectures: a talk on Derek Walcott. He wrote down the themes:

1. search for spiritual history
2. seeing History differently from what one was taught
3. the enslaved mind
4. race
5. class
6. money
7. self worth
8. longing for a spiritual path
9. survival through language

"From Frederick Douglass to Derek Walcott these writers are preoccupied with these themes," he wrote.

On August second Ella's apparition visited Etta. She carried a single lamp and sat beside her bed. Its rays fell over Etta's face.

Ella was happy to see how her sister's countenance had changed over the summer. Her color was gone, the lips pallid, fierce was her struggle between reason and madness.

Her strength was ebbing. Ella sat quietly, Etta unconscious of her presence.

After a pause Ella spoke.

"We have been enemies. I come to you alone in the dead of the night."

Etta sprang up breathless . . . the apparition of her foe.

"Am I dreaming?"

"No, you are awake. You tried to kill me. I can prove you were bereft of sense. But you must confess your crime. Sign this paper acknowledging your hand in my attempted death."

"What reverse is this? It seems that but a day ago I walked amid roses healthy, loved. Ella, I confess to having hurt you that I loved so. I want to perish. I could not help myself when I tried to strangle you under the underpass in New Haven. You had no right to take my life and make a play."

A deserted wing of Yeshiva School faced Riverside Drive where abandoned children hid. Shattered steps led to a yard of stones and weeds. Etta sat on the steps and wrote:

"I think I know who the murdered will be."

That Sunday she tried to follow one of the members of the Vanishing to warn him. She stood on the other side of the street opposite the Strand Bookstore and watched Boulting come out. She started to cross the street but her eyes hurt violently. She went home on the number five bus. Why, she thought do I follow Boulting? My only friend.

Sometimes in the night Etta walked up the closed stairwell that led to the walled up original dining room of the brownstone. The floor of the stairs was covered with sand from sand blasting on the street years ago. She thought she heard a prolonged laugh. But by now she knew it was her sister's apparition. She tried to look through a slit in the door into the vanished dining room but she could see nothing. When Etta came back into her room there was a key on the floor underneath the lamp. She picked it up.

And decided to try it everywhere she went in Troupe's house. She discovered finally the key was to the tiny shed at the end of the garden. The shed had several sets of garden implements, shining. They looked unused.

Boulting told Kay that he'd heard from their cousin who lived near Elizabeth in London and had seen her on the King's Road that Elizabeth was planning to seek legal custody of their daughter Rose.

That night Kay dreamed James and his daughter Rose were sailing on a fatal river.

He called back to her: "Let us sit down my sister. I am wearied with the heat of the sun." They sat beneath a plane tree, an arbutus clustering around them. James read Kay a song, "Regrets for Childhood":
"It is not that our earlier Heaven, escapes its April showers, or that childhood's hearts is given no snake amidst the flowers. Ah twined with grief each brightest leaf, that wreath'd us by the hours. Young though we be, the Past may sting, the present feed its sorrow. But hope shines bright on everything that waits us with the morrow. Like sunlit glades, the dimmest shades some rosy beam can borrow."

When Boulting came to see Kay the next day he asked her to walk with him to Columbus Avenue to buy some paper dolls of Victorian royalty that he'd seen for Rose.

Kay suggested they stop at Chemical Bank. She wanted to give James money. He wouldn't take it.

"That's our mother's money," he said. "I'm going to get money of my own."

As they walked down Columbus Avenue, James told Kay about a story he was writing:

"It's about a severed head," he said. "It takes place in Yorkshire where I walked this spring. Two men are going to fetch horses from the fields. They find a man's head.

A Mr. Michaels whose field it is declares that a month previous a Mr. Hamilton brought the head to his house in Yorkshire, saying it was the head of an arch traitor who was slain by his company. Hamilton brought the head into England from Ireland and was paid head money, and he could bestow the head wherever he wished. He offered to leave it with Michaels who refused to let the head suffer and offered to bury it in the garden. Michaels gave it to his servant to bury but the servant set it upon a tree."

My poor brother, Kay thought.

She again tried to get him to move in with her. His building was broken into every day.

Even though she was exhausted Etta read Boulting's Zen poems and tried to help him organize his tapes of the "Sounds of Streams." He was the only member of the Vanishing that she let into her humid book filled rooms. He was concerned about the noise of the sandblasting in the street and the sand filled air. He brought her a potassium drink and stargazers.

"You can stay with me, Etta, until the sandblasting on the next apartment is over," he said. "I can clear out a room I have now that Elizabeth and Rose are gone."

He took her to the Village in a taxi. He said he wanted her to see one of his favorite movies, the 1960's *Ipcress File*. Afterwards James insisted on going to East 2nd Street and showing Etta the room of dolls, a baby carriage, a cradle, flowered wall paper, miniature Dover books he'd read to his daughter Rose. It was the only decorated room in the apartment.

He took Etta back home, but before he left he read to her from a book on Beethoven he'd had since college. Boulting was the only person Etta had shown her pages of *She Talks to Beethoven* to.

"I hope I finish by autumn," she said, "and by Christmas I hope to have it performed somewhere."

"I'll get someone to put it on for you," he said. "I'll be Beethoven."

Etta had impatiently awaited the arrival of Ella. She was prepared for her sister for the first time this summer. She had a bowl of the coldest purest water placed on the back table.

"Do you have the pure water?" Her sister's apparition asked.

"Yes," Etta trembled.

"And you have left the garden gate partly open?"

"Yes."

"And placed beautiful fruit nearby?"

"Yes, I walked to Broadway this afternoon for the fruit."

"That's good. And the gate is open so that the demon may pass through. Now Etta open your door and give me a lamp. I will breathe my spell over its ray. You now must follow me. I will lead you to the answers." Etta followed her sister's apparition through the door down the stairs past the crate filled living room down to the garden.

"I want to take my garden shears," Etta said. "They protect me."

"Of course."

They set off toward Riverside Drive and, as always when Etta was accompanied by her sister's apparition, her vision was vivid.

On the night Ella's apparition led Etta to the Drive in the moonlight a water main broke in the street. They passed rows of torches and barricades. It was just as the Vanishing had read their very first night:

"By the light of these torches, parties of fugitives from previous bombings encountered each other, some hurrying towards the sea, others fleeing the sea back to the land, for the ocean had retreated from the shore."

It seemed to Etta that utter darkness suddenly lay over the street.

"I can't go any further," she said to Ella. But Ella held her arm. Then they passed firemen bearing more torches heading toward the burst water mains.

But Ella forced her down a remote stone staircase toward the Hudson shore. Etta couldn't escape.

On that murder night Etta's eyes hurt violently but against her will her sister pulled her out of Troupe's brownstone and along Riverside Drive, all the way to 79th Street. And down to the gully: the apparition consumed Etta. Ella's apparition fell into the grass, when Etta tried to stab her...

"There's someone here recording the sounds of the Hudson." Ella laughed.

"Someone you must see."

Ella's apparition had led her to Boulting. Etta kept stabbing. Her only friend.

Grendel and Grendel's Mother

When my son Adam was in High School at Riverdale he owned a red paperback book of *Beowulf.* Adam told me he didn't understand this assignment and would I please look at the book and help him with a paper. When I was in college at Ohio State we had read a section of this savage story. But I had never read the entire text. Yet I'd always remembered Grendel and Grendel's mother.

I sat down on the edge of the bed to look at the first pages. A passage in the introduction set the stage.

> "They could see the water crawling with snakes,
> Fantastic serpents swimming in the boiling
> Lake and sea beasts lying on the rocks
> the kind that infest the
> ocean in the early
> Dawn often ending some ship's
> Journey with their wild jaws."

In the preface the scholar added "the poet had never seen anything like this lake of monsters." That morning I ended up reading half the book. In the next days I finished this poem of triumph over darkness. That was twenty-one years ago.

In those twenty-one years I spent a lot of time trying to make *Beowulf* into a play. But failed. I'd read and re-read the early sections.

> "Herot . . . that towering place, gabled and huge
> Stood waiting for time to pass for war
> to begin . . .

A powerful monster living down in the darkness, growled in
    pain
impatient...
Hrothgar's men lived happy in his hall
Till the monster stirred,
that demon, that fiend
Grendel, who haunted the
moors, the wild marshes,
and made his home in a hell"

               *   *   *

"Then, when darkness had dropped, Grendel
Went up to Herot, wondering what the warriors
Would do in that hall when their drinking was done.
He found them sprawled in sleep, suspecting
Nothing, their dreams undisturbed. The monster's
Thoughts were as quick as his greed or his claws:
He slipped through the door and there in the silence
Snatched up thirty men, smashed them
Unknowing in their beds and ran out with their bodies,
The blood dripping behind him, back
To his lair, delighted with his night's slaughter.
    At daybreak, with the sun's first light, they saw
How well he had worked, and in that gray morning
Broke their long feast with tears and laments
For the dead. Hrothgar, their lord, sat joyless
In Herot, a mighty prince mourning
The fate of his lost friends and companions,
Knowing by its tracks that some demon had torn
His followers apart. He wept, fearing
The beginning might not be the end. And that night
Grendel came again, so set
On murder that no crime could ever be enough,
No savage assault quench his lust
For evil. Then each warrior tried
To escape him, searched for rest in different
Beds, as far from Herot as they could find,
Seeing how Grendel hunted when they slept.
Distance was safety; the only survivors
Were those who fled him. Hate had triumphed."

               *   *   *

I'd try to see these scenes onstage. Often I reread the section where Grendel was killed.

"Out from the marsh
from the foot of misty
hills and bogs hearing God's hatred
Grendel came, hoping to kill
anyone he could trap on the trip
to high Herot.
He moved quickly through the cloudy night
up from his swamp land, sliding silently."

    *   *   *

Always I was transfixed by Grendel's mother and reread the sections over hundreds of times during those twenty-one years. Beowulf the character interested me less. But during that time I bought many copies of the book, snatched out sections pasted them in empty notebooks and tried to create a play. In the twenty-one years of course a great deal had happened to my son. He was now married and lived in Virginia. At first I'd tried to love his wife as a daughter. But failed. Then I'd tried as a solace to write about this white woman. Ever since I'd been an undergraduate at Ohio State there were few white women that I didn't dislike. At Ohio State there had occurred cruel encounters with white women students. Even earlier than college my mother's stepmother who was white had shown such racial hatred toward my mother and to me as a child. White women, I felt since the days of American slavery were instigators of racial cruelties and evil. In my play *Ohio State Murders* I chronicled these cruelties.

Now both my sons were with white women. I'd searched for a way to rid myself of the conflicting torment I felt at seeing my sons with these women. I tried to write about this torment in my essay *Letter to Flowers,* then I started a murder novel in which both women were found dead in a garden in Virginia. But what could I tell my sons I thought if I wrote such a novel? I tried more material called *The Paper Doll Disasters* in which these two white women were headless paper dolls. And were drowned in a storm after being left on a lawn by sweet children.

I had written:

"There was a stabbing in two separate rooms the headless victims were rolled down a long lawn into a lake. Nearby children played.

As the headless victims floated in Lake Aurora. Before they sank it was revealed the dead were two women. There was a burial at sea."

I wrote and rewrote variations. Then I'd cry. Months passed.

Then one September evening I had just arrived in Cambridge to teach and prepare for my course *Black Playwrights of the World*. I started to reread Philip Fisher's essay, *Thinking about Killing: Hamlet and the Paths Among the Passions*, on sleep and death while sleeping. The following evening I found myself rereading *Beowulf*. I'd forgotten that the soldiers were always asleep when Grendel came and killed them. I read the description of how Grendel's mother killed:

> "So she reached Herot...
> where the Danes slept...
> her rest ended their
> good fortune, reversed
> the bright vane of their
> luck...
>
> She moved still faster,
> Took a single victim and fled from the hall,
> Running to the moors, discovered, but her super
> Assured, sheltered in her dripping claws.
> She'd taken Hrothgar's closest friend,
> The man he most loved of all men on earth;
> She'd killed a glorious soldier, cut
> A noble life short. No Geat could have stopped her"

Grendel, Grendel's mother, the white students, my mother's white stepmother, burial in a Virginia garden, drowned paper dolls in a rainstorm... I wasn't able to concentrate in preparing my course. It was Monday and on Sunday I always had to talk to these white women when I talked to my sons. That night I read birthday cards from them:

> Happy Birthday
> Mom wishing
> you happiness
> Happy Birthday
> Mom wishing
> you happiness

During the next nights of brooding and anguish I saw that in my heart, these two white women, for me, were inevitably Grendel and Grendel's mother, monsters living down in the darkness. I reread a passage on Grendel:

> A powerful monster, living down
> In the darkness, growled in pain, impatient
> As day after day the music rang
> Loud in that hall, the harp's rejoicing
> Call and the poet's clear songs, sung
> Of the ancient beginnings of us all, recalling
> The Almighty making the earth, shaping
> These beautiful plains marked off by oceans,
> Then proudly setting the sun and moon
> To glow across the land and light it;
> The corners of the earth were made lovely with trees
> And leaves, made quick with life, with each
> Of the nations who now move on its face. And then
> As now warriors sang of their pleasure:
> So Hrothgar's men lived happy in his hall
> Till the monster stirred, that demon, that fiend,
> Grendel, who haunted the moors, the wild
> Marshes, and made his home in a hell

I began to cry as I'd cried for more than a year.

"Beowulf" I cried out. Although Beowulf had never interested me as much as Grendel and Grendel's mother I needed his strength now. I cried for him to arrive. And I reread the passage where he arrived to kill Grendel and Grendel's mother.

> "You know (if we've heard
> The truth, and been told honestly) that your country
> Is cursed with some strange, vicious creature
> That hunts only at night and that no one
> Has seen. It's said, watchman, that he has slaughtered"
> And how Beowulf killed Grendel.

> "The monster's hatred rose higher,
> But his power had gone. He twisted in pain,
> And the bleeding sinews deep in his shoulder

> Snapped, muscle and bone split
> And broke. The battle was over, Beowulf
> Had been granted new glory: Grendel escaped,
> But wounded as he was could flee to his den,

His miserable hole at the bottom of the marsh,
Only to die, to wait for the end
Of all of his days, And after that bloody
Combat the Danes laughed with delight.
He who had come to them from across the sea,
Bold and strong-minded, had driven affliction off"

And Grendel's mother.

"Then he saw, hanging on the wall, a heavy
Sword, hammered by giants, strong
And blessed with their magic, the best of all
       weapons
But so massive that no ordinary man could lift
Its carved and decorated length. He drew it
From its scabbard, broke the chain on its hilt,
And then, savage, now, angry
And desperate, lifted it high over his head
And struck with all the strength he had left,
Caught her in the neck and cut it through,
Broke bones and all. Her body fell
To the floor, lifeless, the sword was wet
With her blood, and Beowulf rejoiced at the sight."

I felt I was at one with Beowulf. And that after much anguish I had
killed Grendel and Grendel's mother. And after twenty-one years I had
finally made a play of *Beowulf.*

Copyright and
Original Publication Information

Adrienne Kennedy, award-winning playwright and author, was born in Pittsburgh in 1931 and attended Ohio State University. She is the recipient of the Obie Award for her plays *Funnyhouse of a Negro, June and Jean in Concert,* and *Sleep Deprivation Chamber,* which she wrote with her son Adam. She has been a visiting lecturer at Yale University, New York University, Harvard University, and the University of California at Berkeley, and she has been commissioned to write plays for Jerome Robbins, The Public Theater, Mark Taper Forum, Juilliard School, and the Royal Court in England. She has lived in Africa, Italy, London, and the United States.

Werner Sollors is professor of English literature and Afro-American studies at Harvard University.